Exordium

And let me speak to th' yet unknowing world
How these things came about. So shall you hear
Of carnal, bloody, and unnatural acts,
Of accidental judgments, casual slaughters,
Of deaths put on by cunning and forced cause,
And, in this upshot, purposes mistook. . . .

But let this same be presently performed,
Even while men's minds are wild, lest more
mischance,
On plots and errors happen.

William Shakespeare,
the final scene of *Hamlet*

NIGHTMARE IN WICHITA

THE HUNT FOR THE BTK STRANGLER

NIGHTMARE IN WICHITA

THE HUNT FOR THE BTK STRANGLER

Robert Beattie

NEW AMERICAN LIBRARY

New American Library
Published by New American Library, a division of
Penguin Group (USA) Inc., 375 Hudson Street,
New York, New York 10014, USA
Penguin Group (Canada), 10 Alcorn Avenue, Toronto,
Ontario M4V 3B2, Canada (a division of Pearson Penguin Canada Inc.)
Penguin Books Ltd., 80 Strand, London WC2R 0RL, England
Penguin Ireland, 25 St. Stephen's Green, Dublin 2,
Ireland (a division of Penguin Books Ltd.)
Penguin Group (Australia), 250 Camberwell Road, Camberwell, Victoria 3124,
Australia (a division of Pearson Australia Group Pty. Ltd.)
Penguin Books India Pvt. Ltd., 11 Community Centre, Panchsheel Park,
New Delhi – 110 017, India
Penguin Group (NZ), cnr Airborne and Rosedale Roads, Albany,
Auckland 1310, New Zealand (a division of Pearson New Zealand Ltd.)
Penguin Books (South Africa) (Pty.) Ltd., 24 Sturdee Avenue,
Rosebank, Johannesburg 2196, South Africa

Penguin Books Ltd., Registered Offices:
80 Strand, London WC2R 0RL, England

First published by New American Library,
a division of Penguin Group (USA) Inc.

First Printing, March 2005
10 9 8 7 6 5 4 3 2 1

Cover photo of Nancy Fox courtesy of the Fox family.

Design by Leonard Telesca

Printed in the United States of America

For the families and friends of the victims,
in memory of whom and what they've lost

For the forgotten grievers,
including those who investigated
and reported on these crimes

and

For Kirby and Pandora,
I'm sorry that I wasn't more sensitive

Contents

PART THREE: The Ghostbusters—1982–1986

PART FOUR: The Hunted Emerges from Hiding—January 1999–March 2004

Introduction

An American Mystery

For over thirty years, from 1974 to 2004, the serial killer self-named BTK (for "Bind, Torture, Kill") has telephoned and written to police and press advising that he is still stalking victims, still waiting in the dark, and preparing to kill again. He murdered at least ten people and attempted to murder at least six more. And he has always done what he threatened to do.

BTK is unique. He may be the only criminal that meets the federal criteria to be defined all at once as a mass murderer, a serial killer, and a domestic terrorist. He is the only killer to communicate with police and press for more than thirty years and remain unidentified. Other infamous killers, including Zodiac, the Green River Killer, Ted Bundy, and Jack the Ripper, either stopped communicating or were identified after no more than twenty years. BTK is now in his fourth decade of committing state and federal crimes, including making death threats. He has been suspected of committing murders outside of Kansas. At one time police concluded that he murdered a New York resident in New Orleans, Louisiana, but they kept that secret.

BTK phoned the police to report one of his murders. He wrote to law enforcement and the media offering details of the crime scenes. In 1974 and 2004 he left packages in the main branch of the Wichita Public Library. He's sent messages via a television station, a newspaper, a library, a UPS box, the police department, and victims. He taunted that he enjoyed seeing the terror in women's eyes. Victims were attacked in the security of their own home, and most were strangled in the safety of their own beds. The killer called them "home-icides."

Some tough cops coped with this horror by muttering, "Well, there's no place like home," turning the famous Kansas phrase from *The Wizard of Oz* into macabre black humor. In 2003 one detective told me that, in his retirement, he has not been able to enjoy fishing in his boat on the lake without imagining he sees BTK crime scene evidence. He was waiting for the day when BTK was identified and he would be able to go fishing and just fish.

BTK attacked both in the daylight and at night, both when the family was at home and when the victim was alone. Wichitans became suspicious of people they knew, the people they worked with, strangers—every male in town.

Frustrated police investigated a wide swath of possible suspects, anyone who might have been given voluntary access to the victims, including utility workers, plumbers, and reporters. Eventually, many cops' DNA was tested to see if it matched that of the strangler. So were former Wichita State University students, postal employees, Coleman employees, and any male reported to the Wichita police's anonymous BTK hotline. As of the time of this writing, about five thousand men have been tested.

During BTK panics in and around Wichita, where I live, wild suspicions festered in our souls at night when we just knew that he was hiding somewhere in the darkness. We know that at least twice at night he had hidden in a woman's bedroom closet and waited for her to return, with Nancy Jo Fox and Anna Williams. There was no relief from fear in the daytime, because we knew that he could appear at the front door and use a ruse to gain entry, as he did with Shirley Vian.

The book you are reading started as a chapter for a classroom exercise. When I wanted my students to learn about this aspect of Wichita history I looked for a book about the BTK case. To my surprise and disappointment I learned that not only was there no book, but that the story was largely unknown, forgotten, misunderstood, or mistaken.

Early in my career I worked in the emergency room at Wesley Medical Center with the Emergency Medical Service ambulance, and then as a firefighter-medic. I met many officers and detectives who worked on the BTK investigation, and they told me many facts about the investigation. Many years later as I started to write about this case, I learned it was going to be difficult to accurately chronicle. Like an unpleasant death in the family, BTK conversation was taboo. Many who knew the facts were reluctant to be forthcoming. I have conducted interviews with more than 130 people, but perhaps an equal number declined to talk. Even those I interviewed were often circumspect with what they revealed.

I had no idea of my project's consequences. Many detectives tell me they believe the first edition of my book caused BTK to begin making contact again in 2004, that without my book being written he might not have came out of hiding.

I interviewed many Wichita women who told me that for the past thirty years they have lived only in second floor or higher bedrooms because they knew that BTK had broken into the homes of women who had first-floor and basement bedrooms. Dozens of men and women told me that on returning home their habit was still to check their phone for a dial tone because BTK was known to cut telephone lines. Before entering their residences many women used a cell phone to call home and verify that their answering machine was working, indicating that their home phone line had not been cut. Some slept beside their cell phones—and their guns.

Cops who had worked on the case told me that when new detectives started working on the case, they were told not to talk to the old detectives who had preceded them, so as not to be "contaminated" by them. The reasoning was that since the previous detectives had not solved the case, they must have made errors. Each time I talked to a retired detective I was surprised to hear the same litany: No investigator from the police department had asked them a question about the BTK case since the day their assignment to it ended. I obtained more cross-generational knowledge of the police investigation than most of detectives on the case.

After the investigation began anew in March 2004, I learned that because they had never talked with the old investigators, the current investigators were at times operating with mistaken information. On at least one occasion the young cops thought what I communicated to them was wrong and they checked with the old cops. The old cops told the young cops that my version of the facts was correct. The young cops, the current investigators, still thought that the old cops and I were wrong—until they found an old report verifying that what I was writing was right.

I am keeping my pledges to withhold certain information and I've changed the names of some individuals who wish to maintain their privacy, but, in my view, this is a story that deserves to be told about people who deserve to be remembered: the victims, their friends and families, the cops who have investigated this case year after year and have endured almost pathological frustration, the press who have suffered crises in their lives and their institutions, the psychologists who helped those who had to cope with this tragedy, and the community that never knew when the terrorist would next appear.

PART ONE

THE SLAUGHTER BEGINS 1974–1976

History is lived forwards but it is written in retrospect. We know the end before we consider the beginning and we can never wholly recapture what it was to know the beginning only.

—C. V. Wedgewood,
William the Silent

Chapter 1

The Day Wichita Changed

On Tuesday, January 15, 1974, fifteen-year-old Charlie Otero walked home from Wichita High School Southeast. The afternoon sunshine had melted some of the snow into slush. Charlie was thinking about the girl he was to meet with that evening to study. Because of his two moves in one school semester—from Panama to Oaklawn, Kansas, then to Wichita, Kansas—he felt behind in his studies. As he arrived home at about 3:40 p.m. he heard his fourteen-year-old brother, Danny, and thirteen-year-old sister, Carmen June. They had just entered the home a minute or so earlier. They were in their parents' bedroom, wailing in grief.

When Charlie entered, Danny tearfully cried out, "Mom and Dad are playing a bad joke on us." Danny was cradling their father, thirty-eight-year-old Joseph Otero. Carmen June was cradling their mother, thirty-four-year-old Julie. Joseph and Julie were tied up, and bags covered their heads.

Joseph—a recently retired Air Force pilot and mechanic and native of Puerto Rico—was dead. He had been found with his body facedown on the floor at the foot of the bed, wrists and ankles bound with cord from Venetian blinds. Julie was found lying facedown on the bed, also bound.

Charlie used a kitchen knife to cut the ropes off of his father's neck, then off his mother. He could not rouse them. He tried to use a phone in the kitchen to call for an ambulance but there was no dial tone.

Charlie ran from neighbor's house to neighbor's house, screaming for help. He got the attention of neighbor Dell Johnson of 815 North Edgemoor, who was outside shoveling snow.

"Come quick! My father's dead, I think!" Charlie cried.

Johnson later said, "I went to the house and went through the living room and through a hall. I went into the hall and they [the Oteros] looked motionless to me. I didn't examine them but went immediately to call the police. The child said something about the telephone wires being cut. I told him I was going to my house and I would get help as quick as I could."

Johnson dialed 0 on his rotary phone and spoke with the operator. He asked for an ambulance to be sent to 803 North Edgemoor. In this pre-EMS era, Wichita, like most American cities, had multiple, competing ambulance services. The telephone operator called the nearest service on the list, which was the American Red Cross ambulance. Then the telephone operator called the police dispatcher. There were six separate radio dispatchers for the six different city and county emergency services, each with separate seven-digit telephone numbers. The telephone operator advised the police that a Red Cross ambulance was en route to 803 North Edgemoor. Lieutenant Harold Klein took the call. Unless all units were occupied, it was routine police procedure to dispatch a patrol car to any call for an ambulance. The nearest Wichita Police Department patrol officer was Robert "Bob" Bulla. Bulla had a rookie law enforcement officer just out of the police academy riding with him for that shift only. Klein radioed Bulla to "follow-up an ambulance."

So far, this was a routine afternoon for all the involved emergency services personnel. At this time neither Klein, Bulla, the rookie officer, the telephone operator, or the two-member Red Cross ambulance crew knew that they were becoming involved with a homicide case that would remain unsolved for more than three decades and eventually draw international attention.

In the meantime, Charlie Otero's mind was racing. He was bitterly angry with his father, blaming his father's activities for this carnage. He did not want his beloved youngest siblings, eleven-year-old Josie and nine-year-old Joey, to see this. They would be dismissed from Adams Elementary School at 4:00 p.m. and walk the three quarters of a mile home. Charlie sent Danny and Carmen June out to intercept them.

Officer Bulla arrived moments after the ambulance and he saw Charlie talking with the ambulance crew in the front yard. Charlie was tugging on the members of the ambulance crew's arms, trying to get them to rush into the house. The ambulance crew, hearing Charlie's story, were shaking their heads, saying that the police needed to enter first.

The Otero home was on the northwest corner of Edgemoor and Murdock streets. The house was a white wood frame with fake black shutters. There was a small front porch with two concrete steps leading up to it. Two evergreen trees grew on either side of the house. There were shrubs along the front of the house on either side of the porch steps. A brown throw rug had been tossed over the porch railing.

Bulla stepped out of his patrol car wearing a flat-topped and brimmed police officer's hat and gloves, and tan uniform pants with a dark green stripe up each side. Bulla remembers that he wore Red Wing boots he'd purchased from Champs, a store that catered to many in Wichita who wore uniforms, located not far from the intersection of Lincoln and Hydraulic streets. The manager of that Champs shoe store told the author that she sold many Wichita police officers Red Wing brand boots. But other officers reported that they wore Frye brand motorcycle boots obtained from Heads shoe store located near Douglas and Oliver streets. The type of boot an officer wore—and many other details, including the brand of cigarette smoked—would later become controversies in the investigation.

Bulla entered the house with Charlie, the ambulance crew, and the rookie officer riding with him. Entering the master bedroom, Bulla saw that Joseph and Julie Otero were both bound with rope and already cold from death. The bodies had entered rigor mortis, which indicated they'd been dead for hours. The ambulance crew confirmed Bulla's assessment.

Joseph had been positioned by the children on his back on the floor so that his stockinged feet were resting on his black briefcase. Joseph was wearing white socks and blue pants that were cuffed at the bottom. His ankles had been tied tightly together with cord. On top of Joseph's dresser drawer were eyeglasses, an ashtray, and a variety of personal items. There was a large butcher knife next to Joseph's body, which Charlie Otero had used to cut the ropes from his mother and father's necks. Pieces of intricately tied cord lay on the floor next to

Joseph Otero's arm and the butcher knife. The cord was very white and appeared new. Marks on the wrists showed where they had been bound together. While Joseph's wrists were close to the normal size, his hands were grossly swollen. The bindings had permitted blood and lymph to enter his hands but restricted its exit, causing the swelling. Both Joseph Otero's nose and mouth had bled. There was a plastic bag lying next to his head.

When the police photos were taken, Julie Otero was sprawled on the bed, lying across the middle with her feet stuck off the side. Her face was covered with dried blood that had come from her nose and her mouth. In life she had been beautiful; now her face was swollen and almost unrecognizable. Blood from her nose had dripped down both sides of her face and had gathered in her ears, and her long black hair was loose beneath her. A single slim cord bound her ankles. She was barefoot. Her neck was bruised where the binding had been pressing until Charlie cut the rope away with the butcher knife. Julie's hands were open and rested palms down on her midsection, her neatly trimmed nails unmarred. She was wearing a blue quilt button housecoat and light blue zippered and top-button cotton pants. Her eyes were closed.

Bulla glanced around quickly and saw that the drawers to the Oteros' dressers had all been pulled out and someone had rummaged through their contents.

Bulla ordered the ambulance crew out, put Charlie in the patrol car, and called for a supervisor and homicide squad. The multiple murder alarm was just before 4:00 p.m.

By phone and radio, Lieutenant Klein began making notifications of field commanders, command rank officers, homicide detectives, and the lab men, now called crime scene investigators.

Wichita Police Department sergeant Joseph R. Thomas was drinking iced tea at the Pancake House at Ninth Street and Broadway when he received the dispatcher's call over his portable radio. The WPD sergeants always met there near the beginning of the second shift to confer about that shift's tasks, compare notes, and attend to paperwork. Sergeant Thomas raced to the crime scene, red lights flashing and siren wailing, in his big-engine prowler.

He arrived after Field Lieutenant Jack Watkins. With the rookie officer remaining outside, Officer Bulla reentered the house with Watkins. They found the body of Charlie's nine-year-old brother, Joseph Junior, on the floor of his bedroom near the base of double bunk beds, his feet pointing toward the foot of those beds. Joey was bound with Venetian blinds cord and wearing maroon-colored corduroy pants with white pockets. Those pants had white stripes down on the outsides of the trouser legs and along the inseam. Joey also wore brown socks.

Joey was on his back, leaning slightly to his right side. His hands had been tied behind his back so that he was partially lying on them. There was a rope around Joey's ankles. The rope was very tight around Joey's wrists, and when the ropes were removed, his trauma resembled that of his parents, with normal-sized though bruised wrists and grossly swollen hands. The officers saw a spot of blood next to Joey's body on the brown rug. A Wichita phone book, 1973 edition, was on the floor of Joey's room next to his hooded head.

Officer Bulla took a closer look. A patterned pillowcase had been put over the boy's head. That was covered by two white plastic bags, and then over that was tied a blue T-shirt.

With the exception of the dead body on the floor, it looked like a normal boy's bedroom. There was an Encyclopedia Britannica, a black and white television with a rabbit-ears antenna, and phonograph records. Sitting on the floor was a window unit air conditioner.

After examining the three bodies upstairs, the officers found a partial bloody bootprint on a sheet next to the elder Joseph on the floor of the master bedroom. The print was not complete enough to determine the size of the boot. The police on the scene couldn't help but notice that the partial bootprint came from a Red Wing boot.

Officer Bulla reentered the Oteros' living room, which was furnished with a red velvety sofa and two matching easy chairs. The walls and curtains were white. Dominating the center of the room was a table with a blue-glass vase with tall flowers. Wall shelves held a silver pitcher and several silver drinking goblets.

Bulla saw a heating grate on the living room floor, near the entrance to the kitchen, and next to that grate was a leather woman's purse on its side, its contents spilled out onto the floor. On a billfold with a passport protruding from it, Bulla could read the ID signature: Daniel Otero.

Bulla moved into the kitchen, where a table was surrounded by vinyl chairs. An open lunch box sat on the table, along with a cereal bowl with a spoon in it, a plastic milk or juice container, and an open jar of peanut butter with a knife in it. Someone had been making a peanut butter sandwich when they were interrupted. The knife stopped before completely spreading the peanut butter across the bread. The interruption of spreading the peanut butter on that bread seemed to define the moment the crime started.

Officer Bulla was first to enter the basement. He descended the carpeted stairs, taking care not to leave fingerprints on the wooden railing and using a flashlight so as to not touch or move any light switches. At the bottom of the stairs he saw Josie's Beatle boots, made popular by the Beatles, just to the right of the foot of the stairs. One of the boots stood upright and the other had been tipped over on its side.

The basement consisted of a bedroom area, a living room, and a hobby area where the boys had been assembling model airplanes. A couch and a rocking chair were facing a TV set. At the far end of the basement, around a corner, was a small utility room with a floor freezer, a washer-dryer, and storage. Just inside the door, in the dark, Bulla bumped into something. "I've had nightmares about that moment," he said. He had bumped into the body of Charlie's eleven-year-old sister, Josephine. She was wearing only a sweatshirt and socks; her bra was cut in front and dangling. She was hanging from a sewer pipe by her neck. Her panties were above the cord around her ankles and below the cord around her knees.

Josie had been hung with a hangman's noose made out of Venetian blinds cord. Four knots were tied in the noose. The noose was around her neck, digging deep into her neck. Her hands had been bound behind her back, first tied together and then bound to her buttocks with the rope that encircled her hips.

Because of the low ceiling, her stockinged toes may have barely touched the floor, but her heels were in the air. She wore dark blue socks. A dustpan hung on the wall next to her head.

Josie was gagged with what appeared to be a strip of towel, but her now brownish tongue had swollen and protruded in a ghastly fashion, pushing the gag out. Her long black hair spilled down over her shoulders. Almost twelve, the young victim had entered puberty. There was a substance that would prove to be semen on her leg and on the pipe directly behind her.

Josie had died with her eyes closed. Her lips had puffed out and turned purple. Autopsy photos would reveal deep compression indentations in Josie's neck along a diagonal. The indentations remained after the ropes were removed. Her body was like stone with rigor mortis. Even when placed on the ambulance cot her head slumped to the right exactly as it hung in the basement.

Bulla reported what he found to Lieutenant Watkins inside and then to Sergeant Thomas outside. After conferring with Thomas, Bulla helped put up the rope to keep a growing crowd away from the crime scene, then walked the Otero property perimeter.

Circling the house, carefully he noted everything he saw. The backyard was surrounded by a short white picket fence, and when Bulla got closer, he saw a German shepherd mongrel, the family dog Lucky, back there, barking.

The phone line ran up the wall close to the south end of the house, not far from the picket fence. It had been cut about three feet off the ground. Bulla saw no signs of life, except the dog, and he circled back around the garage and returned to the front of the house.

In the photos and video of the Otero crime scene repeatedly published and broadcast by the press, Officer Bob Bulla is seen frequently. He is the tall, lanky uniformed officer. He was the first uniformed officer on the scene that afternoon and he was the last uniformed officer to leave around 2:45 a.m. on Wednesday morning, January 16.

According to those who tell me that they were there, others who were in the house during the crime scene processing were Chief Floyd Hannon, coroner Robert Daniels, forensic pathologist Dr. William Eckert, District Attorney Keith Sanborn, Assistant District Attorney Ted Peters, police chaplain Reverend Jack Middleton, Deputy Chief Clyde Bevis, who was the head of the WPD laboratory and chief crime scene investigator, and crime scene investigators.

The partial bloody Red Wing bootprint found at the crime scene was troubling. Because the coroner concluded that the Oteros were murdered in the morning, any blood should have dried hours before any officers walked into the home.

In 2004, Lieutenant Watkins recalled the Otero case: "It was the most baffling case I've ever worked," he said. About young Joey Otero, Watkins remembered: "The way he was killed. I thought, what in the world did this little boy do to anyone?"

Detectives Bernie Drowatzky and Gary Caldwell were also called to the crime scene. Detective Caldwell said, "It was one of the most bloodcurdling scenes I ever worked, and I worked a lot of murders in Wichita."

When Detective Bernie Drowatzky arrived on the scene, he learned that there had been five Otero children. The three surviving children—Charlie, Danny, and Carmen June—were taken to the police station, where they were interviewed by Otero case lead detective Ray Floyd.

Drowatzky learned that Joseph was last seen that morning at 8:00 a.m. driving his older kids to school. According to Charlie, his father had an appointment and was not expected to return home. Drowatzky thought that Mr. Otero must have gone home just after dropping off the older kids, otherwise, the younger kids would have been at school. They were interrupted while their school lunches were being prepared.

Canvassing the Oteros' neighborhood, police found a witness who saw a short man of "Middle-Eastern" appearance drive away in the family four-door station wagon at around 10:30 a.m. The killer or killers, it was theorized, must have stayed around for nearly two hours after the family was dead.

Another witness came forward and explained that he was driving east on Murdock Street and had to brake hard when the Oteros' station wagon backed onto the street in front of him. He was certain the time was about 10:30 a.m., because he was on his way to pick up his mother to take her to a doctor's appointment. The police contacted the doctor's office and verified the time of the appointment, and verified that the woman did appear on time and that she was brought by her son. The son said he stared at the driver, who appeared to have dark hair and a swarthy appearance.

The Oteros' station wagon—a beige 1966 Oldsmobile Vista Cruiser with a luggage rack on the roof—was found around 7:00 p.m. about a half mile away from their home in the parking lot of a Dillons grocery store at the southeast corner of Central and Oliver. Twenty-three fingerprints were found on the car. Six of them belonged to Joseph Otero. Most of the rest belonged to Julie. None were thought to belong to the killer.

The front seat had been pulled all the way forward, as if a short person had been driving it. The car keys were found on the roof of the grocery store, but the key chain was missing.

A woman in the parking lot saw the man who had parked the Oteros' station wagon. Even after trying hypnotic memory refreshing techniques by psychologist Dr. Donald Schrag, Idell Goldsteen could not recall details of the driver's appearance, but she always reported his demeanor as the same: When he exited the station wagon he was trembling and shaking. That was why she noticed him, and it made her fearful. She averted her eyes and she hoped to avoid him. She did not see what he did next or where he went.

That evening lead detective Ray Floyd separately interviewed the surviving children, Charlie, Danny, and Carmen June. Charlie was devastated to learn that Josie and Joey had also been found strangled in the home. He had sent Danny and Carmen June to intercept Josie and Joey because he thought they would be walking home from Adams Elementary School.

During his interview, Charlie told of a strange incident the previous Sunday night. He said that the power went off in their home. His father reacted to the power failure by grabbing two butcher knives from the kitchen. He handed one to Charlie and herded everyone else into a closet. He whispered to Charlie to crawl to a window and see whether the power was off in the entire neighborhood or just their home.

Carrying the butcher knife, Charlie scrambled to a window and saw that the power was out in the neighborhood, not just their home. About that time the electric power was restored and the lights came back on.

In 2004 Charlie told me that he thinks that his father knew something was seriously wrong and that there was danger afoot. Charlie did not know what the problem was, but he believed it had something to do with his father's covert operations for the government while he was in the U.S. Air Force. Charlie said that his dad told him he had flown a lot of missions with the CIA in Central America and South America.

Until 2004 police thought there was a strong possibility the killer was known by the Otero family. There was no forced entry, no evidence of robbery.

In 1974 Police Chief Floyd Hannon said, "I've worked homicides in this city for some twenty years, but this is the most bizarre case I've ever seen. If [Joseph] Otero was not at home at the time the man entered the house, it would seem there would only be one person involved. However, if he was at home, it would indicate there was more than one."

Asked to categorize the murders, Chief Hannon was unable to. "The killings don't fit into the nomenclature of what we usually work."

The Oteros had a vicious dog they kept in the house, brought back with them from Panama. As a rule the Oteros put the dog in the backyard when they had company. The dog was found in the backyard, indicating either that it had already been put there before the killer arrived or that the family was comfortable enough with the killer to want to protect him from the dog. In a 2004 interview, Charlie Otero told me that no one could really control that dog, and occasionally the dog would even snap at family.

One theory is that when the killer went to the side of the house to cut the phone wires, the dog created such a ruckus inside the house that he was let out—at which point the killer entered through the front door.

Adding to Charlie's grief, Lucky the dog, which he loved, was put down by the authorities the day that his family was murdered.

The morning paper was found on the front divan. Joseph Otero's watch was missing. Joey's radio was missing. It was possible that other things were taken.

Because the Oteros kept a vicious dog in the house and were all trained in the martial arts, this would not have been the easiest family to control. They would not have been a likely target. This puzzled everyone.

* * *

Before 7:00 p.m. and before the Oteros' car was found, Deputy Chief Lieutenant Colonel Ken Duckworth received a telephone call from a friend who was a pharmacist at Hawk's Pharmacy, near the Otero residence. He told Duckworth of a man who lived near the Oteros, had a history of violence, was a known addict to codeine, and was believed to engage in bondage. This man had gone around that day to every nearby pharmacy and tried to obtain Chericol, a cough medicine that contained codeine. Chericol did not require a prescription but one had to sign for it. This man was behaving bizarrely. He had spent two years in the state mental hospital in Larned, Kansas, after nearly beating his parents to death. The pharmacist thought he should report him as a possible suspect in the Otero murders.

The police were grateful for the call. The reported man quickly became the prime suspect in the Otero murders. Over time, not only did this man remain a suspect in the Otero murders, but he became a suspect in another of the murders attributed to BTK. In 1977 his sister lived near Nancy Jo Fox when Nancy was murdered.

I am calling this man Suspect Barbara.

Detectives Bernie Drowatzky and Gary Caldwell spent the night of January 15 in the Otero home looking out the windows, hoping that the murderer would return to the scene of the crime. The home was staked out for a week. Over the next several weeks homicide captain Charlie Stewart would intermittently have detectives stay in the house. This is consistent with current police practices. In his 2001 book *Dark Dreams: A Legendary FBI Profiler Examines Homicide and the Criminal Mind*, retired FBI profiler Roy Hazelwood cites studies proving what these experienced cops intuitively knew in 1974: more than a quarter of the time, the killer returns to the scene of the crime. Investigators would later learn that serial killer Ted Bundy, for example, would revel in returning to the scene of his crimes. Additionally, the FBI reports show that it is common for the killer to try to insert himself into the investigation, or pose as a law enforcement officer or security or special officer. On occasion, the killer may be a law enforcement officer. Detective Drowatzky looked all night for someone to pass by or try to enter the home.

That night the detectives listened to what was practically a traffic jam outside on the normally quiet street. Unfortunately, the crime was so sensational that a virtual parade of cars passed by all evening and night. It was then a common custom for Wichita teenagers to drive back and forth, east and west, on Douglas Street, just five blocks south of the Otero home. It was an accepted way to meet one's friends and meet new friends. The commercial success of several burger-and-malt shops depended on the practice, which was called "dragging Douglas." That night many who were "dragging Douglas" continued their cruise to North Edgemoor Street.

"It was like Grand Central Station," Drowatzky recalled.

While Drowatzky watched those passing by the Oteros' home, District Attorney Keith Sanborn watched the Oteros' bodies being autopsied.

While the police stayed in their home, that night the surviving children were staying with a friend who had become acquainted with Joseph Otero while serving with him in the Air Force in the Panama Canal Zone.

Lab investigators remained in the house for twelve hours taking samples and looking for clues. No evidence of alcohol, or guns were found in the house.

Later, it was found that a prosecutor had left his fingerprints at the scene on one of the bags that had been wrapped around the head of young Joey.

At first police declined to comment on what the killer might have been doing during the time between the murders and when he left the scene. Years later a reporter wrote that retired "Ghostbuster" Detective Paul Dotson of the WPD said that semen was found throughout the house, including next to Julie's body and on Josie's leg. However, the only reports of semen I have read in official reports or heard from people who were in the Otero house were on and around Josie Otero. One of the most persistent rumors in Wichita is that there was semen near all the victims, but the evidence made available to me does not support that claim.

Another persistent Wichita rumor is that there were "eggs" found throughout the house. No eggs are seen in any of the crime scene photos. No eggs are mentioned in the crime scene reports. And no eyewitnesses who spoke with me remember any eggs. This crime scene legend apparently was born and persisted because a disturbed man, who worked delivering eggs, later falsely claimed to be the murderer.

An early police theory was that the killer had been an opportunistic window-peeper, but this theory was quickly discarded. Police found that the killer brought the Venetian blind cord with him to the house. The Oteros did not have Venetian blinds on their windows, and no cord like that used was found elsewhere in the Otero house. It was thought that a voyeur would not have brought the cord with him to bind the victims. Bringing enough cord to bind the entire family appeared to be premeditated.

Another early theory was that the murders had been a case of mistaken identity—that perhaps the killer was after the married couple who had lived in that house before the Oteros. Before moving out three months before the killings, the previous occupants had lived in the house for eleven and a half years. The man of the house was a cousin of one of Wichita's most notorious crime figures. The woman's first name began with the letter "B." The man's first name began with the letter "T." Their last name began with the letter "C" but it was pronounced with a hard "K" sound. Police could find no evidence that the previous occupants of the house were targeted for the death or retribution because of anything their well-known and colorful underworld cousin had done.

Police found a partial fingerprint that to this day they cannot attribute. The print was on a chair facing Joey's body. From the marks on his legs many police believed it was possible that Joseph was brought to that chair to watch his son Joey be strangled. This is the only print at the crime scene that could not be accounted for.

Newsmen were not initially allowed in the house—but investigators told the press that the knots used to bind the victims appeared to be tied by someone expert with knots, such as an Eagle Scout or train worker.

The ropes on Joseph Otero were tied in a sophisticated and insidious manner. If Joseph struggled by pulling on both ropes, he would tighten the ropes around his own neck, but if only one rope was pulled, as if by the killer, that rope could be tightened and loosened, as if to control the hostage.

After careful study and practice, which he demonstrated by tying the knots for me, Deputy Chief Jack Bruce concluded that unlike the other victims, Joseph Otero could have tied his knots himself. He may have been tied by someone else but he may have been directed to tie himself in this fashion. Or, he may have tied himself for reasons unknown.

The detectives spent weeks trying to track down information concerning, and learning about, Venetian blind cord. Police found that the Venetian blind cords used to tie the victims was of a "cheap grade." The rope was a cotton-braided cord with a cotton core. Unfortunately for the sake of the investigation, the cord was of a type that could be purchased from suppliers all over the country. It came in 1,000-yard spools. Detectives spent time at Schammerhorn Blind, a busy Venetian blind business in Wichita near the intersection of Seneca and Douglas, learning about the blind business.

Chapter 2

A Citywide Manhunt

The victims were taken by ambulance to St. Francis Medical Center. The autopsies were all performed in that facility's morgue by District Coroner Dr. Daniels and his deputy, forensic pathologist Dr. William Eckert.

Of the Otero murders, Dr. Daniels said, "All murders are unpleasant—but this is the worst I've seen."

Dr. Eckert was a well-known and well-liked man with a barrel chest and a jovial personality. Like many coroners, Dr. Eckert kept himself sane around a world of death with a dark humor. He disassociated himself with the tragic elements of his work and reduced his job to abstract intellectual puzzles that needed solving. But it was difficult even for Dr. Eckert to disassociate himself from the tragedy of the four dead Oteros.

"I don't like to do kids," he later admitted.

On this night, he went about his task grimly, with a lit cigar in his mouth. Dr. Eckert had seen all kinds of tragedies. He had been working over dead bodies since he was a child, tagging along with his father, a police surgeon in Union City, New Jersey, but he had never seen anything like this before.

Dr. Eckert finished the four back-to-back autopsies by 2:30 a.m. It was confirmed that Josie had semen on her leg, apparently from the excited killer. She had been wearing a white bra, which had been cut at the front.

Dr. Eckert believed that the family was dead by 8:45 a.m. He noted that none of the victims' neck hyoid bones were broken, which is very unusual in a strangling. He theorized that the killer *knew how* to strangle a human being.

On the morning of January 16 Eckert told the press, "I was called into the case yesterday to assist the coroner and as consultant to the police to get an idea of the medical side of the evidence for the police report and subsequent investigation. Strangulation, as in the case of the Oteros, occurs when there is an obstruction of the airway through external pressure causing asphyxia.

"Another point is that the arterial blood supply to the head continues when ligature is applied, but the venal blood cannot escape. Hence there is an engorgement of blood in the head. When the pressure gets high enough you have the appearance of small petechiae—tiny hemorrhages. Those will appear in the white of the eyes and the inner eyelids, the bridge of the nose, and face. When you see those, you know that pressure has been applied. Autopsy dissection also would disclose injuries to the neck aside from bruises. A manifestation of strangulation is the shredding of muscles and tissue, fracture of the larynx itself, hemorrhages in the cartilage of mucosal surfaces. Evidence of manual strangulation [use of the hands to strangle the victim] is found in fracture of the hyoid bone, a small C-shaped bone just under the jaw line. A noose or other ligature ordinarily will not affect it, but manual pressure applied under the throat in most cases breaks the hyoid.

"We also take blood so that we can have the blood groups of the victims. If there has been any bleeding at the scene, we have evidence of type in case the suspect's effects are found to have blood on them. If somebody is hanging, the blood in the body goes to dependent parts. If suspended the blood will take gravity and go to the legs and there will be swelling there," Dr. Eckert concluded.

Joseph Otero Sr., age thirty-eight

The father's autopsy reported: "Final Anatomic Diagnosis: Asphyxia due to compression of larynx secondary to ligature."

Excerpts from the autopsy's verbatim description: "The body measures 5'4" in length and weighs 150 lbs. The face has a very dusky hue.

"Examination of the dura and basal portion of the skull show no fractures.

"The gastrointestinal tract is examined in its entirety. The stomach contains approximately 150 cc. of whitish milky material with some small material identified as fragments of pears.

"The toxicology analysis was performed by Richard J. Taylor, M.D., Director of the Department of Laboratories at St. Francis Hospital. Analysis revealed less than 20 mgs. alcohol, zero barbiturates, zero salicylates."

Julie Otero, age thirty-four

Relevant description from Julie's autopsy reads: "Final Anatomic Diagnosis: Asphyxia due to compression of larynx by ligature; abrasion to base of right index finger, dorsal aspect; contusion of scalp, left temporal region.

"The body measures 5'3" and weights 120 pounds. It is clothed in blue cotton denim trousers and a blue cotton bathrobe.

"Examination of the hands fails to reveal any evidence of recent injury on the right hand and the left hand.

"No fractures are noted. There is an area of hemorrhage noted in the scalp on the left side of the temporal region.

"The gastrointestinal tract is examined. The stomach contains approximately 100 cc. of undigested food of which small orange fragments of vegetable-like structures are seen."

Josie Otero, age eleven

Relevant parts of Josie Otero's autopsy report reads: "Final Anatomic Diagnosis: Asphyxia due to hanging by ligature with obstruction of airway.

"The body measures 5'4" in length and weighs 115 lbs. There is heavy dependent lividity involving the lower extremities up to the buttocks. The body is clothed in a blue T-shirt and there is a white brassiere noted that has been cut in the front, that is found under the blue T-shirt. There are pants noted about the ankles and these are a cotton pants which show multicolored pattern.

"The hands and nails are free from injury. The breasts are of normal size for the age. Examination of the external genitalia reveal pubic hair in normal distribution. There is no evidence of any foreign material in this area. Combing is done by the laboratory investigator, Detective Kiser of the Wichita Police Department. Examination of the labia and external portion of the vagina fail to reveal any evidence of hemorrhage, no ulceration or definite injury can be demonstrated. The hymen is intact. The vaginal cavity is empty.

"Examination of the inner aspect of both legs fails to reveal any evidence of injury and there are whitish, somewhat glossy streaks of dried material on the inner aspect of the left thigh. There are two distinct areas of streaking. They are 10 cm. in length, and 1 cm. in width. They run from a point just lateral to the pubic area on the anterior aspect of the left thigh down for approximately 10 cm. This material is smeared and was found to be positive for acid phosphatase and individual spermatozoa was seen in the smears by Dr. Eckert. (Acid phosphatase is produced by the male prostate gland and is ejaculated along with sperm in semen.)

"SPECIMENS: Specimens taken include blood, samples of liver, kidneys, brain, stomach and stomach contents, fingernail scrapings, smears from oral, anal and vaginal sources.

"Approximately 1.0 ml saline suspension of dried semen scrapings from leg was also submitted. Secretion studies were performed using the Inhibition of Agglutination Technique. The specimen was insufficient for evaluation.

"The toxicology analysis was performed by Richard J. Taylor, M.D., Director of the Department of Laboratories at St. Francis Hospital. It revealed the following:

Acid phosphatase (vaginal) negative
Acid phosphatase (anus) negative
Acid phosphatase (mouth) negative
Acid phosphatase (leg) positive
Microscopic examination of specimen "D" (leg) positive [for acid phosphatase].

Blood: barbiturate, negative; salicylate, negative."

Joseph Otero Jr. (Joey), age nine

Joey's autopsy report reads in part: "Final Anatomic Diagnosis: Asphyxia due to compression of larynx by ligature.

"The body is that of a white male measuring 49½ inches in length and weighs approximately 65 lbs.

"Examination of the neck on the left lateral aspect, there is a line of reddened change in the skin with very small blister-like areas present in this area. These blisters contain clear fluid. There are no evidences of injuries to the fingernails or any damage to the skin of the hands or ear anteriorly or posteriorly.

"The toxicology analysis was performed by Richard J. Taylor, M.D., Director of the Department of Laboratories at St. Francis Hospital. Analysis revealed zero barbiturates, zero salicylates."

Although for more than thirty years there has been a rumor in Wichita that after the murders "semen was found all over the Otero house," semen is mentioned in the autopsy reports as being found only on Josie Otero's inner thigh. Police officers who were at the crime scene tell me that there was also semen on the pipe immediately behind Josie.

These results somewhat puzzled the experienced homicide detectives. Josie had not been raped, but after she was dead her killer rubbed his penis between her thighs and ejaculated. Chief Hannon, who had a long career as a detective and was experienced in investigating sex crimes and rapes and murders, thought that hanging the girl must have sexually excited the killer. He did not think that the purpose of the murders was to terrorize and then hang the girl for the purpose of ejaculating on her hanging corpse. He thought that the Oteros were murdered for some other purpose.

The Wichita Eagle would publish a photo of Dr. Eckert displaying a larynx from one of the Oteros. Dr. Robert Daniels said all four victims had been tortured and strangled with Venetian blind cord. According to the autopsies, all four had died of asphyxia due to the compression of the larynx by ligature, causing pulmonary edema and congestion of the viscera. In other words, they were strangled, slowly.

The other scientific aspect of the investigation is called CSI—Crime Scene Investigation—but was referred to by the Wichita Police in 1974 as the "laboratory men." The crime scene investigators were led by Lieutenant Colonel Clyde Bevis (Deputy Chief), a former U.S. Marine who was often seen in his pork-pie hat and almost never seen without his cigar. Clyde Bevis recalled that the other Otero case investigators were Lieutenant Wheeler, Sergeant Jordon Jones, Everett Miller, and Jim Maloney—described by everyone as a "top man."

Colonel Bevis remembered retrieving lots of fingerprints and a lot of trace evidence, including tiny traces of plants and fibers probably from carpets and clothing. One of the clearest pieces of evidence came from the cut telephone line. Colonel Bevis said that the striation pattern on the cut phone line could be matched to the wire cutters used to clip the line. It was well-known to the laboratory men that the pattern of a cutting implement was as unique as the rifling and ejector marks used in firearm identification. Beginning on January 15, 1974, each time the Wichita police have looked at a suspect, they looked for wire cutters, pliers, or anything that might have been used to cut the Oteros' phone line. If they could match that cutting implement to the Oteros' phone line, and link that cutting implement to its owner, then they would have a good lead to the suspect.

If anyone could catch the killer, they could. The Wichita Police Department had a steady turnover of police officers not from officer dissatisfaction, but because Wichita officers were acknowledged to be well-trained and competent and were highly sought after by other departments.

Wichita's former police chief Orlando W. Wilson, is a renowned figure in America's police administration and sociology. Many of the basic ideas put forth in his 1950 book *Police Administration* have become standard practice across the country. He modernized and professionalized Wichita's department until it became a nationwide model. He was often consulted around the world on police issues. In 1960 Mayor Richard Daley appointed Wilson to head his commission investigating Chicago police.

Wichita continued to benefit from the practices started under O. W. Wilson, and the WPD Police Academy was recognized as the best police academy in the region. The department's reputation was so good that simply being a former Wichita police officer opened doors. Quite a number of Wichita officers went on to become FBI agents, and former Wichita WPD officer Theo Hall became the Chief of Public Safety (police chief) for the occupation forces in Germany after World War II. In 1945 Wichita received the Grand Award from the National Safety Council naming Wichita as the safest city in America.

Wichita politics interfered with police practices in the late 1940s and early 1950s, but in 1957 Wichita returned to its preeminent position with the hiring of Chief Eugene Pond. In 1958, 1959, and 1960 Wichita again received the Safest City in America award.

* * *

Wichita police were acutely aware of a proven fact: Most murders are solved in the first forty-eight hours. If they aren't, it becomes a question as to whether they will ever be solved.

In the days following the murders, police officers stopped cars passing near the Oteros on the off chance that someone who regularly traveled the nearby streets might have witnessed something unusual.

During the investigation's first ten days, seventy-five police officers worked eighteen-hour days. Five hundred law enforcement agencies received bulletins from the WPD. More than 1,500 Wichita residents, mostly those who lived close to the Oteros, were interviewed in the first week after the crimes.

Police put together a composite sketch of the suspect based on information provided by four eyewitnesses. The man was described as in his twenties, between five-two and five-six in height, of slender build, with shoulder-length dark, bushy hair. One witness said that the man had been wearing a crumpled hat. "We're looking for a crumpled floppy hat with a man under it," Chief Hannon said.

In the first reports of the Otero family murders, police referred to the murders as "execution style." Despite this, they couldn't help but notice that the killer or killers had fetishes. Joseph Otero was bound but not gagged. Julie was struck, gagged, and bound. Joey was found bound with three hoods over his head. Josie was hanging by the neck from a rope tied to a sewer pipe in the basement.

The police told the newspapers that they believed the killer was a "person in the community who was suffering from a mental disorder."

Years later Deputy Chief Jack Bruce told me he believed the Otero murders were not the perpetrator's first killings by strangulation. They happened too smoothly, the knots were too complicated and precise and had to be rehearsed. He concluded that the killer may have had previous experience in controlling and murdering humans by ligature strangulation. At the very least, before murdering the Oteros, the killer had rehearsed by strangling animals.

The gory scene was eerily similar to that of the most famous Kansas crime, committed by Richard Hickock and Perry Smith, the subject of Truman Capote's *In Cold Blood*. On November 15, 1959, in Holcomb, Kansas, four members of the Clutter family were murdered on their farm. Three of them were murdered in their beds with

Herbert being murdered in the basement. Herbert, age forty-eight, his wife Bonnie, his daughter Nancy, age sixteen, and his fifteen-year-old son Kenyon were each found tied and shot with a shotgun. Herbert Clutter also had his throat slashed. The murders initially mystified authorities, until Richard Hickock's former cellmate informed on Hickock in exchange for the reward money.

Hickock's cellmate was a former employee of Herbert Clutter. The cellmate lied to Hickock, claiming that Herbert Clutter had a safe in his home office where he kept $10,000 in cash. Hickock told his cellmate that he would steal that money and leave no witnesses.

After they were released from prison, Hickock and a different former cellmate, Perry Smith, went to the Clutters rural farmhouse with the intent to rob and murder them. They did rob and murder them, but there was no safe, no large amount of cash, and they obtained only a little money and stole a few items of little value, including Kenyon's radio.

Just as, in 1974, Joey Otero's radio would be stolen.

In the meantime, the press joined in the hunt. Wichita had two daily newspapers, two weekly newspapers, and several intermittent alternative, specialty, and underground newspapers, as well as three commercial television stations and one public television station.

The two daily newspapers were *The Wichita Eagle* in the morning and *Wichita Beacon* in the afternoon. The two weekly newspapers were the *Independent* and *The Wichita Sun*. What proved to be a one-issue underground newspaper was Wichita's *Central Standard Times*. I obtained one of the few existing copies of this issue and found that many of the pivotal reporters in the BTK story were involved with this paper, including Randy Brown, Cathy Henkel, and Dan Rouser.

The murders sent a wave of panic through Wichita and this was reflected in the stories reported by radio, television, and print press. *Wichita Eagle* columnist Don Granger reported that at a Rotary Club meeting a man described his wife taking their teenage son's baseball bat from his closet and putting it near the door. His wife wanted to be ready to bash any stranger trying to enter the front door. Many at that meeting had similar stories. All across Wichita wives were panicked, as were single women. Most reasoned that anyone capable of strangling a family for no apparent reason could just as easily decide to strangle a single woman.

In a front-page story, the *Eagle* asked readers to call or write the *Eagle-Beacon*'s Don Granger if they had any Otero murder information. This was the Secret Witness Program. Callers were told that they did not have to give their name, but they were asked to give a six-digit number as a personal identification number so that they could be located later in case reward money needed to be issued. In the days following the murders the reward was $5,000. But by the first week in February, the reward was raised to $7,500.

The article mentioned the installation of a new device, a telephone answering machine. If there was no one there to answer the phone, a taped message would play and then a tape recorder would automatically be turned on in record mode. Messages could be left on tape even when Granger was out.

The Wichita police applauded this initiative by *The Wichita Eagle*, but decades later serial killer consultant Dr. Bob Keppel identified this type of press initiative as one of the worst things that reporters could do. Keppel also criticized John Walsh, the host of the television show *America's Most Wanted*, for inviting the Beltway Snipers to call him.

Robert Ressler wrote in his book *Whoever Fights Monsters* that columnist Jimmy Breslin's invitation to Son of Sam to contact him "irresponsibly contributed to the continuation of his [Son-of-Sam's] murders."

No one that I have personally spoken with agreed with Bob Keppel and Robert Ressler that these press actions hurt the respective investigations, encouraged new murders, or delayed capture, but Robert Ressler and Bob Keppel have had tremendous influence on serial killer investigators. Keppel's published works—including his 2003 textbook *The Psychology of Serial Killer Investigations*—may have had a great deal of influence on the 2004 BTK investigation.

Don Granger's January 1974 article attracted responses from crackpots and from the hysterical. One of the first calls to the Secret Witness Program was from a woman who reported a man in a grocery store buying what she thought was a large quantity of broccoli. "Why did he need so much broccoli? I wondered," she said. "I thought it suspicious."

This was not the last time that the anxiety caused by a murderer on the loose would make people in Wichita behave irrationally. Because rumors were running wild in Wichita that the Otero bodies had been sexually assaulted and then mutilated, selected members of the press were invited to look at photos of the crime scenes. Though those images were disturbing, on January 20 reporters from the city's major media outlets were able to report that the bodies were not posed with legs open or mutilated.

Yet the question remained: Where was the killer?

Chapter 3

The Investigation Leads Abroad

Only days after the murders an arrest was made. On Saturday, January 19, a twenty-year-old man named Fred Allen Handy, of Pearce, Arizona, was arrested on suspicion of murder. Handy was thought to have matched the description given by an Otero neighbor of a stranger in front of the Otero house on the morning of the murders.

Kansas City police received a phone call on Saturday morning from a clerk at the YMCA in Kansas City, saying that a man matching the description was in the hotel lobby asleep on the bench.

Handy was picked up by Kansas City police. Major William Cornwell of the WPD then drove to Kansas City to check out the lead. He brought Handy back to Wichita with him for interrogation. By Saturday afternoon, however, Wichita police were convinced that Handy was not the killer.

Handy told the police that his home was in Michigan and that he was on his way to Arizona to visit his foster parents. He had stopped in Kansas City to make some money for the rest of the trip.

He was "definitely cleared" and released. Handy was fed and bathed on Saturday night and given a bus ticket back to Kansas City, where he had a job at a car wash.

Because a majority of witnesses—both before and after hypnosis—described a short man of "Middle-Eastern" appearance as having been seen around the Oteros' home, or as the driver of the Oteros' station wagon, police assigned an undercover detective, Pat Taylor, to infiltrate Arab organizations and a Palestinian Student Organization at Wichita State University. Nothing useful was developed from several months of undercover investigation.

The problem lay in the vague descriptions. Neighbors reported a "suspicious looking man" in front of the Otero home at 8:45 a.m. that morning, and gave police a description: Five feet, ten inches, to six feet tall, dark shaggy hair cut below his ears, dark topcoat or trenchcoat. He had a slender build and a dark complexion, and was believed to be of "foreign extraction." Yet Joseph Otero, who was Hispanic and fairly short, could have himself been the Middle-Eastern man seen around the Otero home.

One witness to the getaway was a man on his way to take his mother to a doctor's appointment who stopped to let what he thought was a white station wagon back out of the driveway of the Otero house at about 10:30 in the morning. Only later, after he had heard what happened there, did he try to come up with a description of the driver of the car, a man he had only briefly glimpsed.

He said the man driving the car had a dark complexion and a rumpled hat. Later formal social science studies by Dr. Elizabeth Loftus, Dr. Stephen Penrod, Dr. Brian Cutler, and Dr. Gary Wells conclude that eyewitness descriptions are notoriously inaccurate, especially when they are asked to remember something that they had no reason to remember in the first place.

The police released a composite drawing which appeared to be based on a photograph of Julie Otero's coworker. Julie had been a worker on an assembly line at the Coleman Company, in Wichita, from the middle of December 1973 until January 3, 1974. Her employment there ended only twelve days before her death. Julie was laid off because of a reduction in the labor force and not fired because of misconduct. She had been recommended for rehire.

The Coleman Company was a major Wichita employer with thousands of people on the payroll. Coleman primarily made camping gear, both for casual campers and for the military. They often had huge government contracts.

Three days before the Otero murders, at 9:00 p.m. on Saturday night, January 12, 1974, twenty-six-year-old Michael L. Williams, who also worked at Coleman, was shot in the abdomen at his home in Bel Aire,

Kansas, a Wichita suburb. Two men knocked at the door and when Michael answered the door he saw that they had guns.

Michael said, "What's going on here?"

He tried to slam the door on them, but one of them shot, striking Michael. One report says that the intruders took a rifle and a radio, but other reports say that the attackers fled after firing the shots. When laboratory investigators arrived at the scene, they were unable to obtain fingerprints because Williams had touched the surface the burglar had touched.

Michael had been a supervisor over Julie's shop when she worked at Coleman. Williams' father said that Michael and Julie had worked on different shifts, and although they knew one another, they were not close friends.

Michael would not be the only possible BTK victim named Williams.

Joseph worked primarily at Cook Airfield, near Rose Hill, Kansas, south of Wichita. He was employed full-time as an aircraft mechanic and flight instructor. He also worked part-time at the AeroClub on McConnell Air Force Base property. He had just applied for a teaching job at East High's Vocational-Technical School.

Joseph Otero joined the U.S. Air Force in New York City on May 29, 1952, and stayed in the Air Force until he retired as a master sergeant on August 31, 1973. During that time he was stationed in the Panama Canal Zone, though he had at one time been stationed in Wichita with the 384th flying wing.

Reportedly, for a time Joseph Otero was the aircraft mechanic for General Omar Torrijos, then the defacto leader of Panama. It is possible that Otero was known to Torrijos' chief of military intelligence, Manuel Noriega. Noriega is currently listed as a prisoner-of-war in an American prison, having been convicted of smuggling drugs by airplane into the United States. Some police thought the excessive violence at the Oteros' house and the sexual display of Josie were symptoms of a drug kill, revenge for a deal gone bad, and a signal to others not to repeat Joseph Otero's mistake.

Joseph had a pilot's license and had been a flight instructor. As far as his friends and family remember, during his time in Wichita he had only flown for pleasure and had not worked as an instructor.

The Oteros moved to the Wichita area from Panama because Joseph had two friends here who worked respectively at Cessna and Cook Airfield. Joseph hoped for a job working at Cessna. He stayed with my classmate Kirby Ortega's family for two months until the rest of his family joined him.

Because Wichita was the "Air Capital of the World," Joseph Otero agreed with his friends that Wichita was the most likely place to find employment using his aircraft-mechanic and flight-instructor skills. Joseph also expressed interest in enrolling in an aeronautical engineering program at Wichita State University (WSU).

On October 29, 1973, Joseph and Julie Otero took out a thirty-year $16,850 mortgage from Fidelity Investment Company. Days later, at the beginning of November, Joseph Otero purchased the home at 803 North Edgemoor, the one with the white-picket fence.

"The Otero children were good students—no trouble at all," said Adams principal David H. Lawson. "That's one reason I didn't know the parents very well. If the children had been a big problem, as some are, we probably would have had the parents in for a conference. But Joe and Josie were just model youngsters. Josie was a talented little girl. She made placemats for the Christmas party, and they were very attractive."

The bulk of the Oteros' furniture, apparently only then arriving from Panama, was moved into their Edgemoor home on Sunday, January 13, 1974, two days before the murders.

The Oteros' Wichita neighbors had little to offer. The family's former neighbors in Puerto Rico told investigators that they knew of nothing that would indicate that the Oteros were anything other than a "religious, God-fearing" family.

Police found that the Oteros did not have a vast number of friends in Wichita, which wasn't unusual since they had not been in the city for very long. They also found no evidence that the Oteros had associated while in Wichita with undesirables of any kind.

By January 17, police were saying they could find no connection between the murders of the Oteros and the shooting of Julie's coworker, Michael L. Williams.

On January 22, 1974, the Oteros' bodies were flown aboard an Air Force VC 135 to Puerto Rico for burial. A *Wichita Eagle* photograph showed Joseph's flag-draped casket being loaded onto a plane at McConnell Air Force Base. After the funeral Charlie, Danny, and Carmen June moved to Albuquerque, New Mexico. That same day the Mid-Kansas Chapter of the American Red Cross and classmates of the Otero children at Robinson Junior High School began accepting contributions to the Otero Fund.

In December 1974 Joseph and Julie Otero's estate was closed after a short hearing in Sedgwick County Probate Court. The three surviving children would split $630. In addition to the estate money, the children would split $20,000 in insurance money.

According to an Otero family member in Puerto Rico, two unknown men ran Joseph off the road with their car less than two weeks before his murder. Joseph reportedly had broken two ribs on his steering wheel when his car ran into a curb. He said he had no idea why the men had run him off the road.

However, in July 2004 Charlie Otero told me that his father had told him that his rib injuries were the result of his car sliding on the ice into a bridge abutment.

Another possibility was that drugs were involved in the Otero murders. On Monday, January 14, 1974, the day before the Otero murders, an aircraft from Puerto Rico en route to Wichita had crashed in Florida. It carried one-and-a-half tons of marijuana.

Three days later, two days after the murders, police announced that they could find no connection between the plane crashes and the Otero murders. "There is nothing to show that the family was involved in illicit activity of any kind," said Police Chief Floyd Hannon. But privately, they still believed that this was a strong lead.

Floyd B. Hannon had just become a Wichita police officer when he began serving as a U.S. Marine during World War II from 1943 to 1946. Brighter than most, Hannon was among the first Wichita police officers to earn an associate's degree, then a bachelor's degree, then a master's degree in administration of justice from Wichita State University. He also received training at the FBI National Academy. Later he taught police science at Hutchinson Community Junior College, Wichita State University, and, notably, at the FBI Academy. His resume lists having served on the boards of a dozen organizations, including the International Association of Chiefs of Police. Chief Hannon was more than a cop's cop, he lived what most law enforcement officers only dream. Since 1968 he had served first as deputy chief, then chief. In 1974 he was confronted with a mass murder that panicked Wichita.

In February 1974, Hannon and Homicide Chief Bill Cornwell took their investigation to Panama and Puerto Rico. They spent two days in Puerto Rico and six days in Panama. Years later, I learned details of that trip from Cornwell during both a face-to-face and a telephone interview.

Because they had the horrid crime scene photos in their briefcases they were held up in Miami by U.S. Customs until their story could be verified. Customs officials feared that the two men might be hit men who were returning to Puerto Rico with the photos as proof that their hits had been successfully carried out.

In Puerto Rico they were escorted by the FBI.

While on that island Hannon and Cornwell interviewed Joseph Otero's parents and other relatives. Twenty-five persons were interviewed in all, but little of worth was learned. They confirmed that Julie Otero was a martial artist and self-defense instructor, that Joseph Otero was a boxer and a martial artist, and that the Oteros' dog was a trained guard dog. Some of Otero's personal letters and photographs were thought to perhaps contain leads, but nothing hot.

In Panama they were escorted by the U.S. Air Force, but again the purpose of their mission was questioned, this time by the Panamanian "Dennys" (military police). The Panamanian chief had a machine gun on his desk and a carbine in the corner. Once their bona fides were established, the detectives finally began questioning witnesses. A few of the Oteros' former neighbors did not want to talk with the Americans, so the Panamanian military threw them in jail until they changed their minds.

Hannon and Cornwell checked a report that Joseph Otero had a mistress in Panama. That report came from one of Joseph's surviving children. In verifying the report, they learned that, while in Panama, Joseph Otero was a man who led two lives.

In one life he was married with five kids. In the other he lived in an apartment with a girlfriend. Joseph Otero had told Julie and his children that he was an agent for the CIA. Most police speculate that his CIA stories were a cover to get out of the house and see his girlfriend. After talking to the former girlfriend, however, the cops concluded the murders were not due to any love triangle.

The policemen discovered that Joseph Otero had had "monetary conflicts" with five persons in Panama. The conflicts were over business deals involving flying merchandise into Panama from South America. All five were in the United States and were being searched for by the Wichita police. Two of them had already been interviewed, one in Wichita and another in New Mexico. With the new information about the business deals, however, both of those individuals were reinterviewed.

The commander of the investigative branch of the Panamanian National Guard was "very interested in the knots" the killer had used. The commander said that those knots had been tied "by a sailor." Hannon later learned that instruction on how to tie such knots were given in U.S. commando training.

Because the evidence did not develop suspects or good motives, a detective came up with a theory that Joseph Otero had killed his family and then died either by committing suicide or by accident. This came up because of the possibility that he tied his own ropes. A detective thought he may have intended to be found alive, but accidentally strangled himself.

When Hannon returned to Wichita in mid-February he announced that, from that point on, every person arrested in the city would be fingerprinted, and that those fingerprints would be checked against the unidentified prints found on the chair at the Otero crime scene.

Hannon asked that all persons with a Puerto Rican background living in Wichita get in touch with the police, in the hopes that they would be able to provide additional information about the Otero family.

The police had run out of leads. A horrendous crime had been committed by a killer who had left no traces behind him. This fiendish cleverness was only the opening round, though, for a man who soon would be taunting the police to find him.

Chapter 4

The Murder of Kathryn Bright

Although no one realized it at the time, in the 1980s a Wichita police special investigative unit known as "The Ghostbusters" would conclude that the man who killed the Oteros struck again less than eleven weeks later. In the spring of 1974 no one made a connection between the crimes.

On April 4, 1974, a man broke into 3217 East 13th Street North. Inside, he hid and waited for twenty-one-year-old Kathryn Bright to come home.

On this day, however, Kathryn was not alone. She arrived with her nineteen-year-old brother Kevin, who was visiting from Valley Center, a town north of Wichita. Kevin had earlier cosigned for a loan application for his sister. If the killer had previously stalked Kathryn, Kevin's presence would have been a surprise.

When Kathryn and Kevin entered her residence, a man emerged from hiding in a bedroom. He had made a "chair" out of clothing in her bedroom closet and apparently sat and waited there. He was wearing a stocking cap and gloves—and he had a gun.

"He just told us to stop and hold it right there," Kevin Bright said afterward.

The man held a .22-caliber Colt Woodsman automatic pistol on them. The intruder told them he was wanted by police in California and was on his way to New York. He wasn't going to hurt them, but he demanded $100 and Kathryn's car keys. Kathryn, later described by friends as feisty, refused.

"He had me tie up my sister and then he tied me up, in separate bedrooms," Kevin later recalled. The killer left him, and Kevin remembered hearing the man rummaging through the house for several minutes. He then returned to where Kevin was bound.

"He just kept going back and forth from where she was to where I was," Bright said. "He was gentle and he took control. It was like he'd done it before. He wasn't worried about anything that I could tell. He was methodical, is what I'd say. He didn't push me down, didn't slap me around. He laid me down on the bedroom floor, and I remember he put a pillow under my head."

The intruder would soon show his true colors, when he tried to strangle Kevin.

"He came in, leaned down on the floor and had a stocking. He started strangling me . . . He wasn't going to shoot me, he was going to strangle me," says Bright.

Kevin struggled and finally managed to get his hands free. Immediately he grabbed the killer's gun.

"That's when I jumped up and broke loose and got ahold of him, got ahold of the gun. He should have been lying there dead, because I got ahold of the gun and the trigger and pulled it twice, but it didn't go off. He pulled it away from me and that's when he shot me the first time. I just went on the floor. So, he thought I was dead, I guess, and left me alone for a while. I just lay there and he went into the other room."

The intruder had shot Kevin in the forehead. Nevertheless, he quickly regained consciousness and heard his sister say, "What have you done to my brother?"

Kevin looked around the room for something to use as a weapon but found only a coat hanger.

Kevin then heard what he interpreted as the man strangling his sister. Kevin managed to grapple with the man and again took the gun from him. Kevin tried to shoot the intruder, but the gun misfired.

The man wrested the gun from Kevin and shot him in the face, the bullet entering just below his nose. This time Kevin feigned death until he could gather his wits.

The intruder returned to Kathryn.

"So, I thought the best thing to do was maybe get out and look for help. So, I got up and went to the door and opened it and went outside," said Bright.

Kevin rolled over and ran out a side door, almost immediately running into some passersby.

"I've been shot. There's a guy in the house doing a job on my sister," he said.

The passersby took Kevin to Wesley Medical Center, about a mile away. Witnesses at Nail's Automotive across the street phoned the police.

"I figured he probably heard me going and probably left out the back door at the same time," Bright said. "I thought he was sure of himself and he had been in that situation before and he knew how to control people. At one time he just asked me, 'Haven't I seen you at the university?' I had nothing to do with the university, so I said, 'No.' He used a knotted-up stocking, is what he used, to tie me up."

After Kevin's departure, the intruder stabbed Kathryn Bright three times in the abdomen. Kathryn was found bound and semi-nude, with ligature marks on her neck. Unconscious when police arrived, she died five hours later at Wesley Medical Center.

Though Kevin survived, he was hospitalized at Wesley for two weeks. The wounds from the gunshots and the loss of blood reportedly gave him some brain damage.

Over time, Kevin Bright gave inconsistent descriptions of the man. Initially, according to police and press reports, Kevin described the intruder as white, about five-foot-ten, stocky, with dark brown or black hair, a black mustache that reached the corners of his mouth, and wearing some type of uniform. He said the man was about twenty-five years old and wearing a black stocking cap, orange shirt, and orange jacket.

This description later changed, and remained firm: Kevin later insisted his sister's killer was a shorter "Oriental" or "Mexican" man wearing an olive-drab military fatigue jacket.

By 2004, his description had reverted nearer to his original description. Bright described BTK as around twenty-five or thirty years old, about five-foot-ten, and 180 pounds. He says he had a slightly darker complexion and a black mustache. He possibly had dark eyes, although they were hard to see, because he had a black stocking cap almost covering his eyes. He was not wearing an orange shirt and orange jacket.

"A camouflage jacket, that's what I remember," Bright said.

The only other detail Kevin could remember was a watch.

"He was wearing a silver watch," Kevin said. But there was a more sinister detail: "Even though I surprised him when I was with my sister, he was in control from the time it started until I got out of there. He knew what he was doing."

In 2004, former BTK case lead detective Mike McKenna told me that he was standing next to Kevin Bright while Bright lay on a Wesley Medical Center emergency room cot. He said that all of Bright's remarks were audiotaped in the emergency room. He said that Bright's description was not something that they could rely on in court.

At the crime scene the police recovered shell casings from an automatic pistol. Wichita Police identified the make and type of weapon, but did not publicly release that information. Kathryn's keys were stolen. A quantity of drugs was found by police in the Bright home, but details were not disclosed.

The Brights' neighbor found rope and scuff marks under a tarp in the bed of his truck. The police determined the rope was identical to that used to tie up the Brights and realized the perpetrator was probably hiding when the police arrived. Police speculated that the killer must have just exited the crime scene when police entered, and he managed to hide under the tarp. After police entered the house, the killer must have emerged from hiding under the tarp and fled.

Kathryn had lived at that 13th Street address for less than a year. Like Julie Otero, Kathryn was an employee of the Coleman Company. She worked as a metal brazer until March 11, 1974, and as an assembler after that. She worked in the same department, the same assembly line, as Julie and Michael L. Williams, the supervisor who was shot three days before the Oteros.

Kevin Bright had also been a Coleman employee, from March until June 1973, and then again during July and August of that year.

Because of the killer's reported statement that he was wanted in California and was headed to New York, Wichita police did not look for a Wichita resident in connection with Kathryn's murder. They, instead, focused their attention on men who were "just passing through."

According to two reliable sources, Kevin positively identified a suspect in a photo array. He also stood outside of the Coleman Company at shift change and looked for the man who tried to kill him.

It was Suspect Barbara, the same suspect that Ken Duckworth had developed as a suspect in the Otero murders within three hours of the discovery of the Oteros' bodies. However, because of the inconsistencies in Kevin's description, and because of his brain damage, District Attorney Keith Sanborn would not file charges against the man Kevin identified.

In 2004 attorney Jackie Williams, who was Keith Sanborn's deputy district attorney and would serve as U.S. Attorney for the district of Kansas, told me that in practice one could not prosecute a suspect for murder based on the testimony of a lone brain-damaged witness whose story had changed. According to some sources, the refusal of the district attorney's office to prosecute this suspect caused conflict between police and prosecutors under more than one administration.

Once again, the killer slipped under the radar.

Chapter 5

The Letter in the Library

The manhunt continued through the spring and summer until, on October 8, 1974, a young man with known mental problems was picked up by police in connection with the molestation of a five-year-old girl. The young man had been apprehended attempting to have sex with a duck while in a car. The duck protested loudly and the noise caught the attention of patrolling police.

During his interrogation the young man gave "suspiciously accurate" information regarding the Otero murders. He eventually confessed to murdering the Oteros. The confessor implicated two others, one his brother and the other another male relative. The brother, who was in E. B. Allen Hospital, a county hospital for indigents and for many with psychiatric problems, after what appeared to be a suicide attempt on a downtown street, also confessed to killing the Oteros.

The third man implicated, also a relative, was sought.

At that time 780 persons had been interviewed by Wichita Police in connection with the Otero murders, many of them because of past involvement in sex crimes.

The police did not release their names, and Chief Hannon was quick to point out that there was no evidence other than the confessions to connect the men with the Otero murders. "It is not unusual for someone to admit the crime of murder," he said.

The brothers were aged twenty-six and nineteen. Under subsequent separate interrogations they began to give inconsistent accounts of the crimes. The older brother changed his story at least once. The younger brother, the original confessor, was checked into a separate but unnamed hospital for psychiatric examination.

The third relative, who was thirty years old, was listed as "wanted for questioning." He was taken into custody by Wichita Police detectives on Wednesday, October 17. After a brief interrogation, he too was placed in the mental ward of a local hospital.

Police were wary of these being false confessions, but took the men into custody nonetheless. The arrests made the newspaper on October 18, 1974.

Cornwell said, "After we develop as much as we can develop, we're going to start trying to determine if they really did commit the crime. And if so, then we'll try to charge them."

Four days after the capture of the third mentally unstable suspect, on Tuesday, October 22, a phone call was received at the offices of the *Wichita Eagle*. The call, in response to the arrests, was to *Eagle* director of community affairs Don Granger, who managed the Otero murder Secret Witness hotline.

According to press reports, the man on the phone told Granger: "Listen and listen good, because I'm not going to repeat it."

The man on the phone told the columnist that there was a letter from the Oteros' killer in a mechanical engineering textbook in the main Wichita Public Library across the street from the police station. Granger contacted Chief Hannon about the call.

Granger said that the voice on the phone had no accent, just Midwestern United States. "It seemed to be twenty-five to thirty-five [years old], and someone who seemed to be used to giving orders. Not someone who wanted to give orders. Someone who was used to giving orders," Granger said of the voice.

At Hannon's order, Detective Bernie Drowatzky retrieved the letter. The letter, as it turned out, was hidden in a shelf of books on the library's second-floor mezzanine.

The letter was addressed to *The Wichita Eagle and Beacon* Secret Witness Program. It was typed—not a photocopy—and it contained misspelled words and improper grammar.

The first page of the letter read, as it was typed:

OTERO CASE

I write this letter to you for the sake of the tax payer as well as your time. Those three dude *[sic]* you have in custody are just talking to get publicity for the Otero murders. They know nothing at all. I did it by myself and no ones help. There has been no talk either. Let's put it straight. . . . . . .

Joe:

Position: Southwest bedroom, feet tie to the bed. Head pointed in a southerly direction.

Bondage: window blind cord

Garrote: Blind cord, brown belt.

Death: The old bag trick, and strangulation with clothes line rope.

Clothed: white sweat shirt, green pants.

Comments: He threw up at one time. Had rib injury from wreck few week before. Laying on coat.

Julie:

Position: Laying on her back crosswise on the bed pointed ina southwestern direction. Face cover with a pillow.

Bondage: Blind cord.

Garrote: Clothes line cord tie in a clove-hitch.

Death: Strangulation twice.

Clothes: Blue house coat, black slack, white sock.

Comments: Blood on face from too much pressure on the neck, bed unmade.

Josephine:

Position: Haning by the neck in the northwest part o the basement. Dryer or freezer north of her body.

Bondage: Hand tie with blind cord. Feet and lower knees, upper knees and waist with clothes line cord. All one length.

Garrote: Rough hemp rope ¼ dia., noose with four or five turns. New.

Clothes: Dark, bra cut in the middle, sock.
Death: Strangulation once, hung.
Comments: Rest of her clothes t the bottom of the stairs, green pants, and panties. Her glasses in the southwest bedroom.
Joseph:
Position: In the east bedroom laying on his back pointed in eastern direction.
Bondage: Blind cord.
Garrote: Three hoods; white T-shirt, white plastic bag, anther T-shirt. Clothes-line cord with clove-hitch.
Death: Suffocation once, strangulation-suffocation with the old bag trick.
Clothes: Brown pants, yellow-brown stripe T-shirt.
Comments: His radio is missing.

All victims had their hand s tie nehind their backs. Gags of pillow case material. Slip knotts on Joe and Joseph neck to hold bag down or was at one time. Purse contents south of the table. Spilled drink in that area also, kids making lunches. Door shade in red chair in the living room. Otero's watch missing. I needed one so I took it. Runsgood. Themostat turn down. Car was dirty inside, out of gas.

When the writer said, about Julie Otero's position, "Laying on her back," the author had originally typed the word "black" but had put a slash through the L. This is an unlikely typo to make accidentally, since the L is not adjacent on the typewriter keyboard to either the b or the a, the two letters surrounding it in that word. The Oteros were a Hispanic family of dark complexion.

The letter was long and detailed. Included in the letter were "Comments." He noted that the elder Joseph had vomited, that the bed in the master bedroom had not been made, and that the Otero car was dirty inside and was almost out of gas. The letter was determined to be genuine, as it contained details of the Otero killings that only the killer could have known.

The description of the crime scene in the Oteros' master bedroom differs from that shown in police photos. The best guess is that the letter writer's description matches more closely what Charlie, Danny, and Carmen June Otero found when they discovered their parents' bodies, and that the discrepancies are due to their efforts to revive their parents.

"I needed one so I took it," the letter read about the missing watch. "Runsgood."

There would be more death, the note promised.

> I'm sorry this happen to society. They are the ones who suffer the most. It's hard for me to control myself. You probably call me 'psychotic with sexual perversion hang-up.' When this monster enter my brain, I will never know. How does one cure himself? If you ask for help, that you have killed four people they will laugh or hit the panic button and call the cops.
>
> I can't stop it so the monster goes on, and hurt me as well as society. Society can be thankful that there are ways for people like me to relieve myself at time by day dreams of some victims being torture and being mine. It a big compicated game my friend of the monster play putting victims number down, follow them, checking up on them waiting in the dark, waiting, waiting . . . the pressure is great and sometimes he run the game to his liking. Maybe you can stop him. I can't. He has already chosen his next victim or victims. I don't who they are yet. The next day after I read the paper, I will know, but it to late. Good luck hunting.
>
> YOURS, TRULY GUILTILY

According to the rules of the Secret Witness Program, those reporting tips could remain anonymous, but they did have to leave a code name so that multiple tips could be verified as coming from the same source.

In complying with these rules, the killer wrote in a postscript:

> P.S. Since sex criminals do not change their M.O. or by nature cannot do so, I will not change mine. The code words for me will be . . . Bind them, toture *[sic]*

them, kill them, B.T.K., you see he at it again. They will be on the next victim.

BTK's letter referred to recent stories in the newspapers stating that police were close to an arrest. The killer wanted to debunk those stories and make sure everyone knew the police were not close to catching him.

There was no mention in the BTK letter of Kathryn Bright's murder, or Kevin Bright's attempted murder, but there was a promise of future victims.

Not everyone believed the letter was from the Oteros' killer. Because the description of the Otero crime scenes in the letter did not match the crime scene photos, there was strong feeling in the 1974 Wichita Police that the letter was a hoax. The feeling that BTK was a hoax didn't completely dissipate among investigating officers until May 2004. One of the skeptics was Deputy Chief of Police and head of investigations Jack Bruce. A lieutenant colonel, he had worked his way up through the ranks. He was best remembered for having defused a riot during the Coleman strike in the late 1960s. Two groups of Coleman manual laborers, one on strike, one not, were moving toward a confrontation when Jack, alone, faced the aggressors. It was a dramatic moment. In front of a huge crowd, a striker spit in Jack's face. With the crowd ugly, Jack did what none of them expected: with spit dripping down one cheek, he calmly turned his other cheek to the guy. When the man paused, stunned, Jack did not arrest the guy, but wiped the spit off his face and kept himself under control with a look that said, "Brother, do you realize what you are doing?" With his calm but stern and unafraid demeanor, Jack helped quiet what could have been a violent confrontation.

Jack thought that this letter from "BTK" was a prank from someone within the department, and he had good reasons to think so. He went and accused two officers of writing the letter as a prank.

Jack Bruce, Floyd Hannon, and other investigators immediately knew what those outside the inner circle did not know: the letter had errors. Not just typos, but errors of fact. The color of some of the clothing and its description were wrong. BTK writes that Julie Otero was wearing black pants, but her pants were a light blue, lighter than her housecoat, not at all dark. And if the unique pattern on Joey's shirt is difficult to describe, it clearly is not "stripes." It is easy to see why those who knew the facts dismissed the letter as being from a crank.

Still, expert opinions were sought. Over time, up to thirty local psychiatrists and psychologists were asked to read the letter. Police asked that the contents of the BTK letter not be published because they wanted to avoid a flood of false confessors.

There was a difference of opinion among the doctors whether to release the letter to the public. The police didn't want the letter released for several reasons. However, some doctors concluded that if this was an authentic letter from the killer and the killer received no publicity, then he would kill again.

The doctors, according to Chief Hannon, concluded that BTK was "a very sick man . . . who had a fetish for bondage. His reaction sexually is to be bound, to bind other people."

From October 24 to 27, 1974, *The Wichita Eagle and Beacon* published the following personal ad. The ad read:

B.T.K.
Help is available.
Call 684-6321 before 10 p.m.

They received no calls.

On October 31, police asked the *Eagle and Beacon*'s community affairs director, Don Granger, to address a plea to the letter writer in a column in the paper. Granger wrote: "For the past week Wichita police have tried to get in touch with a man who has important information on the Otero murder case—a man who needs help badly. . . . There really is a 'B.T.K.' Police can't say how they know, but they're convinced B.T.K. has information about the murder of Joseph Otero, his wife, and two of his children."

In the column Granger even included his home telephone number, just in case the killer was uncomfortable, for one reason or another, calling the hotline number that the police had set up.

Because the letter stated that only one man had killed the Oteros, police reenacted the crime to determine if this was possible. They decided that it was possible but improbable. "It's rather hard to predict if one could, with a minimal amount of subduing . . . kill all the people," Hannon said.

Still, despite what he would later say about the letter being from a crank, Hannon had to admit that it was written by a very well-informed crank.

On November 6, 1974, Captain Harold Klein made an arrest in the main branch of the Wichita Public Library, where the letter from BTK had been retrieved a couple of weeks earlier. The man had grabbed a twelve-year-old girl and, according to the girl, tried to "play" with her leg. The assailant was quickly identified. He was a five-foot-ten white man wearing a white hard hat, dark blue-green short-sleeve shirt and pants, an olive drab field jacket with .22 caliber ammunition in one pocket and a Sabre pocketknife in another. He had dark hair and mustache and was medium build.

When Captain Klein confronted him, the man was squatting on the floor between book stacks. Captain Klein asked, "What seems to be the problem?" The man replied in a voice as if he was ill and overcome, "It's more than I can handle." The man was told he was under arrest and was read his Miranda rights from a card. Initially the man nodded his head but did not verbally answer. Then Captain Klein handed him the card and instructed him to read it aloud, which he did, though haltingly. The subject remained squatting on the floor throughout this time.

According to Captain Klein's report, at the police station the subject was turned over to Detective Jimmy Langford.

When Captain Klein showed me his report in 2004, he said that to this day he never heard a further word about it and never found any further record of the arrested subject, whose name I am withholding. If the man went to court, then Captain Klein was never called to testify or contacted about the arrest in any way. It is possible that the man was released.

The significance of this incident became apparent only after the 1980s Ghostbusters investigation into the BTK case and with knowledge of how other killers evaded identification even when confronted by the police.

The Ghostbusters would collect a lot of suspicious character calls in

BTK's known target neighborhood that would describe a white man, five foot ten, medium build, dark hair, mustache, wearing a military field jacket. These descriptions precisely match the man Captain Klein arrested.

This was hardly the first time a serial murderer had escaped from the clutches of the law. Jeffrey Dahmer, Edward Kemper, Gary Ridgway, Zodiac, and many other serial killers had, when confronted, talked the police out of holding them responsible for murder and attempted murder.

In Milwaukee, in May 1991, tall, blond, handsome, well-spoken serial killer Jeffrey Dahmer had drugged fourteen-year-old Laotian Konerak Sinthasomphone into unconsciousness. Around 2:00 a.m., Dahmer departed from his apartment to obtain some supplies and left Konerak naked on his living room couch. While Dahmer was gone, Konerak woke, disoriented and confused, and walked naked into the street. Two women saw him and called 911. Before the police arrived Dahmer returned and tried to force the struggling Konerak back into his apartment.

When police arrived the two women, Sandra Smith and Nicole Childress, told them what they had seen. Dahmer was calm and explained to the police that Konerak was his nineteen-year-old gay lover, who was drunk. He was sorry to be a bother, and if the police would help him bring Konerak back to his apartment, they wouldn't cause any more trouble. The two women told the police that they did not believe Dahmer's story.

The police believed Dahmer, and accompanied Konerak back to Dahmer's apartment. They noted that it smelled bad, but they did not want to deal any further with this gay couple's argument.

When the police left, Dahmer immediately strangled Konerak. He then had sex with Konerek's corpse and later dismembered the body, keeping the skull as another trophy.

A murder victim had escaped, but the murderer was so calm and smooth that the police themselves helped the killer take the victim back to the room where the victim would be strangled.

Jeffrey Dahmer would later be sentenced to fifteen consecutive life terms.

California serial killer Edward Kemper murdered at least ten people. He committed his first two murders when he was age fifteen and was sent to a mental hospital. He was released at age twenty-one on the condition he regularly meet with a psychiatrist. After he again started committing murders, he once drove to a meeting with his psychiatrist while he had a victim's head in the trunk of his car. At that meeting the psychiatrist concluded that Kemper was no danger to society.

Although Kemper was frequently seen on the University of California college campus, where young women were disappearing, he was never a suspect. When he called the police to confess, they did not initially believe him. Edward Kemper was sentenced to life in prison.

Gary Ridgway, the Green River Killer, who murdered at least forty-eight women, eluded police for more than twenty years. Yet in 1980, when a woman accused him of attempting to strangle her, the police let him go. The woman had escaped from Ridgway as he was attempting to murder her. In her struggle for her life, she bit him and fled. The police believed Ridgway's characterization of events, which was that he was the victim of a prostitute who had bit him. Later, a polygraph examiner concluded that Ridgway was not being deceptive when he answered questions about crimes he was suspected of committing, yet Ridgway, on all pertinent points, was being deceptive. Like serial killers Dahmer and Kemper, Ridgway remained calm when questioned, and the authorities believed his denials.

California's Zodiac serial killer of the 1960s and 1970s was stopped by the police only blocks from a murder Zodiac had just committed. San Francisco police were looking for the killer of a taxicab driver. Zodiac remained calm and the police concluded he was not the man they were looking for and let him go. Zodiac later wrote that he was the man police released.

One of the things common to serial killers who successfully elude capture is that they are able to deceive police and other authorities. Did the man whom Captain Klein arrested talk his way out of prosecution? Was he the BTK Strangler?

Chapter 6

The Murder of Sherry D. Baker

Days after Captain Klein's arrest of the man at the Wichita Public Library, another murder shocked Wichita. At about nine o'clock in the morning of Tuesday, November 13, Sherry D. Baker's mother went to Sherry's home at 603 North New York Street in north Wichita. When Kathryn Bright's killer said he was going to New York, was this the New York he meant?

The mother had not heard from her daughter and was visiting to see if something was wrong. The doors were locked and Sherry did not respond to knocking. Her mother began looking in the windows and soon saw her daughter motionless. Twenty-three-year-old Sherry was dead, wearing only a negligee and panties, lying facedown on the living room floor.

A pair of scissors was protruding from the back of Sherry's head. Her hands were tied behind her back with her coiled telephone receiver line. She was gagged with part of a torn towel. Another part of the towel was tied around her neck. She had been stabbed more than seventy times. Her throat had been slashed. A bloody six-inch-long butcher knife lay at her side. The entire house was "in shambles." Police said the south window in the living room appeared to be "tampered with." One investigating officer said, "The window screen had been torn and the metal frame storm window may have been pried open."

According to Detective Major Bill Cornwell, Sherry's blood had splattered against the south wall of the living room, where the victim was apparently killed. Bloodstains were found on the living room floor and couch, and on a bedroom windowsill and in the bathroom. The blood in the bathroom had apparently come from the killer washing his hands.

Later on Tuesday, district coroner Dr. Robert Daniels determined that Sherry, a WSU student, had been murdered sometime late on Sunday, November 11, or early on Monday, November 12. Sherry died of multiple stab wounds to the head and neck. Dr. Daniels said the most serious wound was to the jugular. The stab wounds to Sherry's head had been done with the scissors, and one of the scissor blades had snapped off in Sherry's skull.

Daniels told reporters that Sherry's hands were bound together with the telephone's coiled receiver cord and that the receiver was placed back on the phone carriage. The cord was not severed.

Sherry's personal life was troubled. She had a child, but it "lived with relatives." When police learned that Sherry had twice reported her boyfriend, Jason Miller, for assault, they thought they had the case solved. Police also learned that Sherry had been hospitalized because of being beaten up, but she refused to name the man who had done it to her. Police hauled Miller in for "routine" questioning on Tuesday, but he was released on Wednesday.

Later in the week police would say that they wanted to question another boyfriend of Sherry's, one who didn't live in Wichita.

Funeral services were held for Sherry at 2:00 p.m. on Thursday, November 15, in Wichita's New Zion Baptist Church.

603 North New York Street is only a block away from the Coleman Human Resources Department. This was the office—separate from the factory where Julie Otero and Kathryn Bright worked—where Michael Williams' father was head of personnel at Coleman.

Sherry would tie into the BTK case through the psychiatric evaluation of an anonymous drawing sent in at this time.

Chief Hannon wanted a mental health practitioner to evaluate the BTK letter and thought no one better qualified than Wichita's mayor, Dr. Garry Porter. Dr. Porter thought the respected psychologist in the next office, who had also been a homicide detective, Dr. Samuel Harrell, should be consulted.

Starting as a military policeman, Harrell so impressed his superiors that they promoted him to OSI, the Office of Special Investigations. He became a detective and received assignments around the world, in such places as Morocco and the Belgian Congo in Africa and Germany. He quickly became an experienced homicide detective.

As his four-year tour of duty was ending, he happened to be assigned to a U.S. Air Force base called Forbes Field near Topeka, Kansas. Sam obtained a job as a psychiatric assistant at Menninger psychiatric hospital and attended college at Washburn University in Topeka. Menninger's psychiatrists encouraged Sam to become a psychologist, and Sam eventually earned his Ph.D. and licensure as a clinical psychologist. He and his girlfriend married and moved to Wichita, where Sam worked in a building with psychiatrist Garry Porter, M.D.

Dr. Harrell was provided access to all the police reports, autopsy reports, crime scene photos, autopsy photos, and the letter from BTK. Additionally, Dr. Harrell was shown a drawing that arrived in a separate envelope. Dr. Harrell did not know details of how the police came to receive this drawing. In it a woman was shown with one end of a pair of scissors embedded in her skull. Dr. Harrell told me that it was a good black-and-white pen ink drawing.

After evaluation and thought, Dr. Samuel Harrell was ready to present his findings and recommendations to Chief Hannon.

Harvey Glatman.

That was the name that came to the mind of Dr. Harrell and some of the doctors on what later became called the psychology task force. Harvey Murray Glatman was the California bondage killer of the late 1950s who lured his victims into a trap, photographed them, then strangled them.

Glatman was an expert with ropes and bondage. He learned his craft experimenting on himself during the 1940s. As a teenager, he choked himself to the point of blacking out, hanging himself in the attic of his home, as a method of enhancing masturbation.

When Glatman graduated to murder in 1957, he lived in Los Angeles and found his victims through "Model for Hire" and "Lonely

Hearts" want ads. He was initially known as the "Lonely Hearts" murderer.

Glatman posed as a photographer for detective magazines as a ruse to get his victims to allow him to tie them. He photographed his victims while they were bound but before raping and killing them. Then he took photos after they were dead. He typically pulled a gun on them. Glatman murdered three women before a botched abduction led to his arrest in 1958 and subsequent execution.

Several influential law enforcement officers, including Los Angeles's famed Pierce Brooks and the FBI's Roy Hazelwood, mention Harvey Murray Glatman as the man who changed their views on criminals. British crime author Colin Wilson said, "To understand Harvey Glatman is to understand the basic psychology of the serial killer."

Dr. Harrell concluded that whoever sent the drawing with the sharp scissors embedded in a bound woman's head—apparently a drawing of the murder of Sherry D. Baker—knew the victim. This drawing showed an intimacy between the victim and perpetrator.

But the Otero murders were different. As a psychologist, Dr. Harrell was convinced that BTK must have participated in bondage for some time prior to the murder of the Otero family. He believed that these murders were not the first murders committed by this killer. He believed it possible, if not likely, that there were two people involved in the murders. One, Dr. Harrell believed, would be the dominant personality, the other the dominated personality, but they both would participate in bondage and domination of others. It is likely that one of the killers had military experience and was probably a Vietnam combat veteran.

From Dr. Harrell's experience as a homicide detective, he thought it unlikely that someone who had gotten away with mass murder would send a letter claiming responsibility for the murders unless the letter contained crucial elements of deception. Because the letter's author so insisted that he committed the crimes by himself, perhaps he had not.

Dr. Harrell recommended:

(1) The authorities advise prostitutes that reward money and legal consideration would be given to those providing truthful infor-

mation about any clients who in the past or future wanted to engage in bondage

(2) The authorities should pay for subscriptions to bondage periodicals that circulated in Wichita

(3) Then the authorities should place advertisements in these bondage periodicals in an effort try to lure BTK into revealing himself.

During Dr. Harrell's presentation Floyd Hannon grew tight-lipped. While Floyd Hannon was not thinking of Harvey Glatman, as the psychologist was, Floyd Hannon was thinking about the errors in the "BTK" letter and his own conclusion that the letter was a hoax. Now this headshrinker wanted him to spend the taxpayers' money on perversion magazines and let prostitutes ply their trade in exchange for turning in weirdos. This was making him angry. The room grew still and quiet. Slowly at first, then explosively, and quite distinctly, Wichita police chief Floyd B. Hannon Jr. replied: "Ain't nooooo ci-ty mon-ey being spent *on no per-vert*!!!"

That would be the end of Dr. Harrell's consultation with the police.

Chief Hannon said he does not remember that. But he did tell me that at least thirty doctors had seen the BTK letter and apparently many had copies of it. After a long interview with Dr. Harrell in August 2004, I came to understand that so many doctors were consulted in part because most doctors legitimately wanted to consult for colleagues, but also because the police rejected their recommendations. Most police who were intimately familiar with the case thought the letter was a hoax. They wanted a psychologist to agree.

After enough doctors were consulted, some of them agreed with every possibility. Some doctors thought the letter was a hoax, some thought it was not. Some thought the letter should be made public, some did not. There was no unanimity of opinion about the letter and what should be done about it.

In December 1974, someone decided to act on his own initiative.

Cathy Henkel always knew that she wanted to work in journalism. She started as a journalist for *The Wichita Eagle* as a teenager writing obituaries. She earned her bachelor's degree while working full-time and at the *Eagle* earned other assignments, including reporting on higher education, youth culture, and crime. She tried to improve conditions at *The Wichita Eagle* by helping to organize a union, which led to her leaving the *Eagle* and earning a master's degree in counseling. In 1974 she started working at a Wichita weekly paper, *The Wichita Sun*, and her work as an investigative reporter began.

Only two months into the *Sun*'s existence, one of Cathy's contacts began asking her about the Otero murders. After some preliminaries, Cathy was told the astonishing story and was provided a copy of the letter from BTK.

Along with the letter, the small newspaper also learned of the conclusion of one or more of the behavioral scientists that unless BTK received publicity, he would kill again. They knew they had a bombshell.

Under reporter Cathy Henkel's byline the *Sun* ran a front-page story about the letter and BTK, the first of two articles, beginning on December 9, 1974. The story began:

> A man who identifies himself as BTK has written police, claiming that he murdered four members of the Joseph Otero family here last January, and is planning to kill again, the *Sun* has learned.
>
> Those code letters are not the person's initials, but are instead derived from the letterwriter's characterization of his method of operation.

The series included a mention of Michael L. Williams, Julie Otero's work supervisor, who had been shot three days before the Oteros were murdered in an apparent robbery attempt.

It also mentioned Kathryn Bright, who had been stabbed to death on April 4, and who had at one time worked on the same assembly line at the Coleman Company with Julie Otero. The police called the fact that Williams, Otero, and Bright had all worked at Coleman "coincidental."

In the days following the leak, Chief Hannon was furious. "Chief Hannon was so angry," Cathy later told me, "so red-faced, that the temple on the side of his forehead was visibly pounding." She kept her distance, afraid he might strike her.

The *Sun* article did talk about the crashed aircraft that was carrying marijuana, but quoted Cornwell on the subject. "We feel the drug-related motive to be doubtful," said Cornwell.

There was also a mention of the five men who had had money problems with the elder Joseph Otero. "Yes, we found that he [Joseph] had financial problems, but we have not been able to connect them with the case," Cornwell said.

Years later, Henkel told Fred Mann of *The Wichita Eagle* that she had spent several days working on the story. She and the paper felt good about publishing it because they had been told by psychologists that the printing of the letter might have a soothing effect on the killer and prevent him from killing more people.

"The advice I got was that the killer needed that kind of exposure or he would kill again," Henkel said. "That seemed to fit with logic and everything else."

The day after portions of the letter appeared in the *Sun*, the paper held a news conference. They confirmed that the letter existed and said that it was very likely that the author of the letter was the man who killed the Oteros. The only other possibility was that the person who wrote the letter was familiar with the killer, or had been told about the Otero crime scene in great depth. At the press conference it was revealed that the letter revealed details of the Otero killings that even the police had not known.

The *Sun* article reported that Wichita police had been in touch with psychiatrists and psychologists about the BTK letter, but Chief Hannon refused to verify that.

The *Sun* stated, "Police maintain that other suspects connected with the case have not been ruled out, despite the existence of the letter. The most prominent suspect is a nineteen-year-old who confessed to the crime and then implicated his twenty-six-year-old brother and another man, age thirty. All three are under psychiatric care in separate hospitals."

About those three suspects, Chief Hannon commented, "The nineteen-year-old gave us details of the murder but none that he couldn't have read in the newspaper. That's one of the problems in the case—too much publicity."

Perhaps the young man had correctly guessed that there was semen on a body. The press had inferred perverseness without sexual abuse. Anyone with the mind-set of the man under interrogation would easily fill in those parameters and decide the killer masturbated on a corpse.

When asked if those three men were still under suspicion, detective Major Bill Cornwell told the *Sun*: "At this time, we have insufficient evidence. We're not saying they are and we're not saying they aren't."

A week after publishing a portion of the letter, the *Sun* published a follow-up story, which discussed the small number of tips that had been phoned into the police hotline.

Chief Hannon was not shy when discussing how highly critical he was of the BTK letter release: "I think we've taken one hell of a risk," he said. "He might have to go out and commit the offense again to prove he committed this offense." The chief added, "I want to solve this thing, but the longer it takes the harder it gets. This isn't a game of marbles or checkers—it's a murder investigation."

Speaking through the *Eagle and Beacon* newspaper, Hannon asked the letter writer to contact police or some other agency. "He is a sick man who needs help," Hannon said. "He should surrender to authorities. The man will not be harmed in any way. No way are we going to harm this man or allow anyone else to harm him. All doctors basically felt we're dealing with a very sick man. The man is mentally disturbed and has a great problem. We are looking for a man who had a fetish for bondage. His reaction sexually is to be bound or bind other people."

Police management had wanted to keep the letter's contents secret, but their need for outside advice regarding the letter led to copies of it being distributed among a lot of people. "When the department started approaching other people for analysis on the letter, we started losing our closed-door policy," Hannon said. Regarding who leaked the letter, he said, "We fairly well know, but we do not intend to make an issue of it."

Hannon did single out, as a man to be commended, Don Granger, the man who had manned the Secret Witness hotline. "Don had a scoop here but did not demand to see the letter, and it was through Secret Witness that we were able to see the letter," Hannon said.

As for why the *Sun* published news of the letter, the newspaper said, "The responsibilities of a free press and those of the police sometimes clash, but the public good is the usual result. . . . [The *Sun*] feels that, after some two months under wraps, this letter should be made public for two separate but equally important reasons: the community's right to know and the possibility that the *Sun*'s comprehensive circulation and the letter's contents could bring forth information on the case."

The paper noted that it had left the meaning of the initials BTK undefined, and had not revealed any of the details regarding the Otero crime scene in the letter, so the police could make use of that information as a test for any future confessor.

When the news that a man with a bondage-fetish and the initials BTK had claimed to be the Otero killer in a letter, the police received so many phone calls on the subject that they set up a special Otero phone line to answer questions and give out information. The phone line was manned twenty-four hours a day. Police quickly discovered that most calls were from people who were concerned about their personal safety.

Why was BTK contacting the police? Former FBI profiler John Douglas answered that question in his book *The Cases That Haunt Us*. "One thing that motivates many serial offenders is the desire to create and sustain their own mythology. The press is often a willing collaborator, giving them such names as the Freeway Phantom, the Hillside Strangler, and the Green River Killer. When the media is not so cooperative, they often insist upon their own designations, such as the Son of Sam or the BTK Strangler. The reasons they feel a need to do this are obvious to those of us in criminal investigative analysis. These are insignificant nobodies whose only 'accomplishment' in life, the only time they feel in control and fulfilled, is when they are causing suffering or fear in others."

Chapter 7

The Momentum Is Lost

In January 1975, on the anniversary of the Otero murders, Colonel Jack Bruce of the WPD's investigations division said, "Hardly a day goes by that we don't discuss the Otero case. And I know for myself that sooner or later we will find the killer."

At that point, police had questioned more than eight hundred people regarding the murders, and the Otero file at police headquarters was two feet thick. Every person arrested in Wichita for a sex offense was questioned about the Oteros.

Police did not throw out any files, even those involving subjects who had been apparently cleared. There was always the chance that detectives had interviewed the killer without knowing it. Bruce said he thought that was a "distinct possibility."

Police made a list of things they believed they knew, and acknowledged things they didn't know. From an analysis of the crime scene, they were fairly certain that the Oteros were not alarmed at the first sight of the killer. The knife that was being used to make sandwiches in the kitchen when the killer arrived had been set down neatly. The person using the knife could see the front door.

The fingerprint found on the chair near young Joseph's body remained the best clue. It did not belong to any member of the Otero family, their friends or acquaintances. It also did not belong to any of the suspects who had been questioned either in Wichita or in other cities where "similar murders had occurred."

This fingerprint, actually a partial print but with enough print visible to make a positive identification, had a controversial history as a piece of seemingly solid forensic evidence. The WPD and the FBI disagreed as to how the print should be classified.

Descriptions by eyewitnesses who saw a suspicious man out in front of the Otero home on the morning of the murders, as well as those who saw a man driving the Otero car away from the house later that morning, had been all but discounted by the police. They no longer had any faith in those descriptions or the composite drawing they spawned. No longer were subjects being considered suspicious or being cleared of suspicion based on the similarity of their appearance to the eyewitness descriptions.

Police were certain that the crimes were not spontaneous. The facts that the telephone line was cut and that he brought his own ropes for binding the victims were adequate evidence of premeditation.

Police could not determine where the killer purchased the plastic bag that had been tied over young Joseph's head. Police had been unable to locate a manufacturer that made that type of bag "anywhere in the world."

The Venetian blind cords used by the killer, on the other hand, were very common, and could have been purchased anywhere. They were not, however, taken from the Venetian blinds that the Oteros had stored in their garage.

Police were certain that the murders were not the work of professional killers because pros lean toward efficiency. These crimes appeared to have been done for fun, with the killer lingering unnecessarily at the crime scene to savor the moment.

Police had also come to believe:

- Josie was the last to die.
- Rope marks indicated that the elder Joseph may have been tied, untied, and then tied again. Police believe the father might have been moved so that he could be forced to watch his son die.
- The killer was not only a bondage fetishist, but a necrophiliac as well, sexually aroused by corpses.

In 1975 and 1976 Chief Hannon organized two special meetings with law enforcement, forensic, and psychological experts from around the country. He called these meetings the Western Conference. A slide show called "The Otereo [sic] File" was created and shown at these conferences. Opinions and advice were solicited. But without new breakthroughs the Otero case slowly receded from public memory.

Floyd Hannon retired so respected a lawmen that he was invited to guest lecture at the FBI Academy. His son Floyd III became an FBI agent and his daughter Mary Ann became a KBI agent.

In November 1976 a new detective was placed in charge of the Otero case, Darrell Oakley. He had been one of the original detectives to arrive at the crime scene, and thus felt a personal connection to the case.

When interviewed after three months of being at the BTK helm, he was still reading reports and taking notes—and he still had not yet read many of the reports. Although Detective Oakley had other cases he was working on, he tried to find time every day to read Otero reports. He tried various mental approaches to looking at the facts, hoping to come up with insights.

"You pursue one angle too many times and you step over good information," Oakley said.

By this time more than ten thousand fingerprints had been compared to the unknown print found at the Otero crime scene, with no matches.

Oakley said that he did not believe that the age of the case diminished the chances that it would be solved: "It only makes it a little more difficult to check out leads—people forget dates, exact circumstances. There's no statute of limitations on homicide. So what's time?

"The only thing that hurts you time-wise is that the killer might *hurt someone else*. The only way the case will not be eventually solved is if the perpetrator is killed or dies before we can tie him to it."

And as 1976 closed the killer *was* about to hurt someone else.

PART TWO

THE HOT DOG SQUAD 1977–1981

A connected matter is the examination of the virtue of a good man in comparison with that of a good citizen. A citizen is somewhat like a sailor, one among a number of partners on a ship, each with different tasks and functions. Although each has a specific virtue according to his capacity and duty on the ship, there is also a general virtue similar to them all, which is the preservation of the ship. In a similar way, the virtue of the citizen is with a view to the regime. It is possible, therefore, for a person to be an excellent citizen yet not an excellent man. Will the virtue of the citizen ever be the same as the virtue of a human being?

—Aristotle, *Politics*

Chapter 8

Shirley Vian Is Strangled

At 11:45 a.m., Thursday morning, March 17, 1977, at 1311 South Hydraulic (near Lincoln and Hydraulic streets, close to a Dillons grocery at 1227 South Hydraulic) a man approached a five-year-old boy (he was almost six) named Stephen Relford. Steve was on the sidewalk walking home the short distance from Dillons. He had just purchased two money orders.

A retired detective told me that the man said to Steve, "Excuse me, boy, but I've lost my dog. Have you seen a lost dog?" The boy had not.

"Is your mother at home?"

"Yes."

"Let's ask her. Maybe she can help me find my lost dog," the man said. The boy then brought the man into the house. According to a detective and a contemporary article published in *The Wichita Eagle*, the man was carrying a "bowling bag" or small suitcase.

However, that is not the story that Steve Relford told me in January 2005.

Steve told me that the man, who was dressed in a business suit and was carrying a briefcase, showed him a photograph. The photograph was of a woman holding a baby.

Steve, his mentally handicapped brother and sister, and his mother, Shirley, were living in a small house with her boyfriend Rick Vian. Rick went to work that morning but Shirley was ill and had not felt up to preparing her children for school, so they were home. The children frequently stayed home from school.

Stephen, known as Steve, had been sent to the grocery store twice that morning by his mother. The second trip had been to purchase two money orders, total value: $40. It may seem unlikely now that a small child could get a money order drawn, but the staff at the Dillons grocery knew the children and such an occurrence was not contrary to local custom. Wichita was still in transition from local Mom and Pop neighborhood groceries to corporate chain groceries and most of the people who worked in Dillons had recently worked in small neighborhood groceries. It was upon returning from the second trip that the small boy encountered the man with the photograph.

Steve said that the man asked if he knew the people in the photograph. Steve said no. The man asked, "Are you sure?" Steve said, "Yes." The man said, "Look again." Steve said, "Sir, I don't know who this is." The man said, "Okay" and let him pass. The man went to the Relfords' neighbor north of their house.

Ten minutes later there was a knock on the Relfords' door. Steve and his brother Bud were watching television but raced each other to the door. Their sister Stephanie was also home. Steve pulled the door open and it was the man who had stopped him on the street. Steve asked, "May I help you?" The man asked, "Is your parents at home?" Steve said, "Mom is but she is sick." At that time the man forced his way in.

Retired detectives had told me that the Relford boy brought the man in the house in response to the "lost pet" question at which point the man produced the gun, but Steve is adamant that version is wrong. Former detective and press reports also left an ambiguity as to whether Shirley may have known the man, but Steve said that is wrong.

Steve said that after he forced his way in the man immediately stepped over and turned the television off. Then he reached over and pulled down the window blinds. Then he reached under his jacket and removed a pistol from his shoulder holster. The man was right handed and the gun was under his left shoulder. He said, "Where is your mother?" The children all replied "In there," pointing at their mother's bedroom.

Shirley appeared at the bedroom door at that time and shouted, "What the hell are you doing? Who the hell are you?"

The man said, "Shut up and get in here."

At that moment the telephone rang. Steve asked his mother, "Do you want me to get that?"

The man said, "Leave it alone."

The man told Shirley to put some toys and a blanket in the bathroom. She did. There were two doors to the bathroom, on its sides, each door going into a bedroom. The doors opened outward from the bathroom.

The man then tied a rope around the doorknob and tied that to the drain under the sink. He then put the children in the bathroom, closed the remaining door, which led to Shirley's bedroom, and pushed the bed up against it. The children were trapped in the bathroom. Steve, angry and defiant, said, "I am going to untie the rope." The man yelled, "You better not or I'll blow her fucking head off!" Steve said, "My mother begged me not to untie the rope." Steve did not untie the rope.

According to Stephanie Relford, the killer then turned to her and said, "You can't hide from me. I can smell you wherever you go." Stephanie believed the man so much that in 2005 she was still terrified and did not want her location revealed.

Shortly thereafter Steve told me that he heard a sound from his mother's bedroom that he took to be adhesive tape being pulled and torn off. He stood on something in the bathroom, probably the bathtub, and looked out a small transom window into his mother's bedroom. He saw the man had his mother naked and facedown on her bed, her hands taped behind her, a plastic bag over her head, and a rope around her neck.

Stephanie said that she also looked and saw the same thing, but also saw that the man's face had been scratched, so her mother must have fought back.

Bud climbed up on the sink and tried to reach the room's one tiny window. He wanted to get out the window and he broke it, but he cut his hand and was badly bleeding. Bud stood and hollered and screamed for help out the broken window, as did his sister from the floor.

Steve summoned all his strength and busted through the door panel on the door that was tied shut. He ran through the other bedroom and to his mother's bedroom. He was ready to fight but the killer was gone. His mother was not moving. He ran outside hollering for help. He ran to a neighbor's south of their house. He pounded so hard on the neighbor's door that its window broke. By the time the neighbor opened the door Steve said he stood momentarily shocked, mute, unable to speak. Then he shouted, "Call the fucking cops, my mom is dead."

The adults in the neighbor's home called the police and they went over to Steve's house. Steve's brother and sister were with their mom, Shirley, in the bedroom. Steve said they were "tripping out."

The children were interviewed by Detective Don Goseland and, according to him, later by psychologist Dr. Donald Schrag. The children were quickly taken to southeast Oklahoma where their mother was buried. They lived with their grandparents, their mother's parents. Rick Vian asked for but did not receive custody.

Steve was so traumatized he said almost nothing for the next two years. He has since spent nearly half of his adult life in jail. As of 2005 he was married and doing well.

Based on the children's reports and the evidence of how she was found, once naked, Shirley was bound at the wrists and ankles with white Venetian blind cord (the same as that used at the Otero crime scene), Shirley's own panty-hose, and black electrical tape. Shirley's nude body was tied to the bed in the same manner Joseph Otero had been tied.

She was then suffocated to death. A plastic bag had been placed over her head, just as a bag had been placed over young Joe Otero's head. There was no sexual assault. There were no defensive wounds on her hands. After she was dead, the killer ejaculated into Shirley's blue panties and placed them beside the body.

One theory was that she had allowed herself to be bound because the killer had promised that, if she did so, he would not harm her children.

The killer himself later wrote that he was scared off from the crime scene by the kids' crying and by the phone ringing. In that same letter he said that he had planned to kill the children, by putting bags over the heads of Bud and Steven and by hanging Stephanie as he had hung Josephine Otero.

Later, removing the bag, police found cord wrapped tightly around her neck. According to FBI profiler John Douglas, "When [the bag] was removed at the crime scene, her face was almost completely blackish red from cyanosis and hemorrhaging, and bloody vomit had dried around her nose and mouth." Douglas later wrote that he found the crime scene photos of Shirley Vian to be even more horrific than the photos of the Oteros.

Emergency personnel arrived at 1:00 p.m. and made an unsuccessful attempt to revive Shirley.

As with the Otero murders, this attack started with an apparent front-door entry during the morning.

The killer also took the two money orders totaling $40 that were drawn that morning at the nearby Dillons.

According to the *Eagle*, Richard Vian, Shirley's common-law husband, returned from his job at a local construction company around 4:30 p.m. and learned of the murder.

Neighbor's described Shirley Vian as a friendly person who "did not have things together." Two days before her murder, Shirley had visited a neighbor complaining that she had no money, no food, and no car. The neighbor gave her money for food.

The boys were supposed to be attending Linwood Elementary School, 1340 South Pattie, that morning. They were absent from school that day, as they frequently were. They were reportedly very poor students. One detective told me he thought that they may have been retarded.

Shirley's body was removed from the scene by Cochran Mortuary. The autopsy was performed by Deputy District Coroner William Eckert. In addition to showing no signs of defensive wounds, Dr. Eckert also found no evidence of sexual assault.

Days later Shirley was buried in lot 39AA, Muse Cemetery, LeFlore County, Oklahoma. After the service her children stayed with their grandparents in Poteau, Oklahoma.

Police initially considered the possibility that, because the two money orders had been stolen, robbery was a motive for the murder. Even then, however, the theory was considered "thin."

It was acknowledged that this was a sex crime, but most police believed it to be unrelated to any other murders. Only Detective Bob Cocking believed, right off the bat, that this was a BTK crime.

Dr. Bob Keppel in his book *The Psychology of Serial Killer Investigations* reports that police departments are slow to recognize and reluctant to acknowledge that they have a serial killer in their jurisdiction. Detective Cocking experienced that firsthand. He was still irked in 2004 when he told me what happened. He said that he was standing next to Shirley Vian's body, recognized that she was bound and strangled in a manner very similar to Joseph Otero, and said, "This looks like BTK" (meaning that this looks like BTK's work). He was immediately scorned and told to "Knock off that shit," so he said no more.

According to a contemporary newspaper report, the children said the man had dark hair, was in his late thirties or early forties, with a heavy build and a "paunch." Detective Don Goseland interviewed the children. When other detectives read the report, they observed that the children's description also described Goseland. Did the children misunderstand what Goseland was asking, maybe thinking that he was asking them to describe him.

He reportedly asked the children, "Give me a description."

Perhaps they thought it was a test of their ability to describe.

Doctors at Kansas' Menninger Foundation Psychiatric Center in Topeka, Kansas, offered to carefully interview the children and try to obtain a description. The Menninger's staff were experienced in these interviews, but for unknown reasons, the interviews were never conducted.

During the initial investigation into Shirley's murder, police interrogated forty-eight people, including Shirley's ex-husband and common-law husband.

In 2005, Steve Relford told me that the man who killed his mother was trim, with a slim to medium build. His suit fit well. He was very clean cut, very neat. Dark hair. He was in his thirties to age forty. He carried a briefcase, or satchel.

Steve also showed me a copy of the photo he believes the man showed him. His grandmother had a copy. She said it was a photo of baby Steve with his mother and that only four copies existed. Steve is convinced that the killer had obtained a copy of that photo.

Steve also emphasized to me that his mother's name was never Vian but was always Relford. He asked that I correctly have her name in this book as "Shirley Relford, which is the name on her grave's headstone."

The investigation into Shirley's murder had barely grown cold when a killer struck again. On May 15, 1977, nineteen-year-old Wichita State University student Julie Ladd was found murdered in a storage room in the basement of her dormitory, Brennan Hall. Julie taught Sunday school for five-year-olds for a Christian fellowship group at WSU.

The day before she was found, a Saturday, Julie had put in a shift at the shoe store where she worked. Julie then went shopping with her boyfriend for an engagement ring. After shopping, they returned to her dorm, made a pizza, and shared it with friends.

Because it was the end of the spring semester, the dorm was mostly empty. Many of the girls had already moved out for the summer.

It was the end of Julie's first semester living in Brennan Hall. She had reportedly graduated from a Wichita high school in 1976 and spent her first semester at WSU commuting from home.

On the night of her death, her boyfriend left at about 10:30 p.m.

Earlier in the day WSU security had received reports of a "flasher in the area." Between 12:30 and 1:30 a.m. residents of Brennan Hall heard screams coming from the basement.

A security guard did visit the dorm at 12:50, but left at 1:05 a.m. without checking the basement. Security at the dorm was very lax. It was routine for the alarm system to be disconnected—as it was at the time of the murder—and an outside door was frequently left ajar so that residents could get in without having to use their key.

The following morning, a girl went to the basement to do her laundry and discovered the horrifying bloody scene. Julie's body was in the storage room. She had been stabbed in the neck and slit open, reminiscent of the murder technique of Jack the Ripper. The knife wound went from the top to the bottom of her abdomen.

An FBI blood-splatter expert, Herbert McDonnell, said he had never seen that amount of blood and spatter from a single victim. McDonnell was in Wichita at the time for a conference and took a look at the scene because his friend, coroner Dr. William Eckert, asked him.

The *Eagle* reported: "Although an autopsy revealed Ladd died of stab wounds to the heart . . . the assault left her with a 'gaping wound' to her abdomen and chest."

She was wearing only a T-shirt, and that had been pulled up over her face. Her reading glasses were still on her face. There were no signs of a sexual assault.

Upstairs, in Julie's dorm room, a radio was left playing, and a light was on. Her Bible was left open and her Sunday school lesson plans were laid out. According to the *Eagle*, during her last Sunday school class, which she taught on May 8, Julie said, "I know for certain, if I die, I will be ready to go with the Lord."

Throughout May 15, Wichita Police processed the crime scene and interviewed residents of Brennan Hall. Residents provided information for a police sketch and several suspects were questioned.

This case was considered a possible BTK crime until 1979, when it was solved by Bernie Drowatzky. There was an arrest and, following a plea bargain, the suspect, named Bell, pleaded guilty at the trial.

Two people charged with a drug violation had entered into a plea bargain and accused a man named Bell. They said he bragged about killing "that WSU chick."

The man was already in a Colorado prison for murdering a Colorado woman, and a person fitting Bell's description was seen near Brennan Hall on the night of Julie's murder. Bell confessed to Julie's murder.

Although the connection to the BTK Strangler was ruled out in the Ladd case, the identity of the killer in another murder that year was not as certain. Denise Rathbun was living at 5332 East Pine, one block from the Oteros' home, when she turned up missing on November 27, 1977.

Pushing a baby carriage full of clothes, she had left her home and gone to a Laundromat just around the corner. She never returned. She had made it to the laundry and dried one load of clothes when she was either abducted or accepted a ride with someone.

The twenty-six-year-old married mother of two was found by a hunter in a frozen creek around 4:00 p.m. on Sunday, December 11. She had been missing for fifteen days.

The baby carriage she had used to carry her laundry was found nearby. She was wearing the same clothes she had on at the laundry.

Denise was reported missing by her husband, Kenneth, a medical technician at McConnell Air Force Base. (Joseph Otero had worked part-time at the AeroClub at McConnell Air Force Base.) Kenneth told police that he last saw his wife at about 8:00 p.m. on November 26, when she was on her way to the laundry. This caused an initial time discrepancy, since several witnesses told police they had seen Denise at the laundry as early as 4:30 that afternoon. Other witnesses concurred with the husband, saying they saw Denise in the laundry between 8:00 and 9:00 p.m.

Denise's body was found in a creek seventeen miles away, partially beneath a bridge, on 133rd Street North. After learning of the discovery of Rathbun's body, a man contacted police saying that he had found a coin purse along Hydraulic Street, about two miles from the 133rd Street Bridge. The man showed police where he had found the coin purse and, near that location, Denise's larger purse. A hundred dollars she had been carrying in her purse was missing.

Dr. William G. Eckert performed the autopsy on Denise and determined that her lungs were filled with water. This indicated that she was alive when she entered the creek. Dr. Eckert's conclusion might have led him to believe that Denise had accidentally fallen in the creek and drowned, except for one thing.

"It's pretty obvious that it's got to be a homicide," Wichita Police lieutenant colonel Bill Cornwell said. "I can't believe she pushed that baby carriage all the way out there."

Denise had not been stabbed or strangled but there were bruises on one side of her face, and Dr. Eckert determined that she had been struck several hours before her death.

The victim's hands showed no defense wounds or any signs that she had struggled with her attacker. Her skin had a pink color, which indicated that exposure had been a factor in her death. Dr. Eckert determined that it was unlikely that Denise had lived more than five minutes after she went into the creek.

Investigators learned that Denise and her husband, Kenneth, had been planning to leave Wichita in December 1977, that same month. Kenneth was to begin a ten-month tour of duty in Italy and Denise had been planning to take the children—Bryan, three, and Kerri, one—to Miami to live with her mother while Kenneth was overseas.

Like Julie Otero and Shirley Vian, Denise Rathbun was a mother with young children. That she was abducted only a few houses from where the Oteros lived and that her body was dumped on the same street where Shirley Vian lived seemed to be a chilling coincidence.

Wichita was hardly a likely location for a spate of murders involving young women. Yet because the methods of death were different, the police were not connecting them. This serial killer was not following a pattern—at least not until the next murder, two days before Denise Rathbun was found.

Chapter 9

Nancy Jo Fox—Strangled

Christmas was only seventeen days away and Wichita had their yuletide decorations up. Christmas tree lights could be seen through living room windows. In the department stores, Christmas songs serenaded the hordes of shoppers.

Shortly after 9:00 p.m. on Thursday, December 8, 1977, twenty-five-year-old Nancy Jo Fox walked to her car in the Wichita Mall parking lot. Nancy worked at Helzberg's Jewelry Store, Wichita's most upscale jewelry store.

With Nancy was Candy Dufrene, Helzberg's assistant manager. When Candy walked out to the parking lot that night, she had no idea that her life was about to be forever changed for the worse.

They said good night, and according to Candy, it was a perfectly normal night at work. Nancy then drove through Wendy's and purchased a hamburger, which, based on the wrapper and bag later found, she apparently consumed while driving home.

Nancy's home was a pink duplex at 843 South Pershing. It had no back door and the other half of the duplex was unoccupied. She had lived there for about two years. According to her father, Dale Fox, Nancy had lived alone in her apartment for more than a year and living alone did not bother her.

Nancy entered and hung her heavy sweater on a rack near the door. Then she went into the kitchen sink and filled a glass of water. She needed a cigarette. Nancy was rarely seen without a cigarette. When Nancy's mother gave me photos for this book, she wanted a photo of Nancy holding a cigarette to be used. Nancy sat at the kitchen table, drank some water, and lit a cigarette. The burned cigarette and partly consumed glass of water would still be on the kitchen table when detectives arrived the next morning.

Nancy then went to the bathroom. Afterward, she entered her bedroom and began to undress. She hung her skirt neatly on a wooden stand.

A potted plant near the back window was knocked over, and the room was hot. The thermostat had been turned up to ninety degrees Fahrenheit, its maximum. The thermostat might have been elevated to help cover up the cold from the broken back bedroom window.

The killer emerged from her bedroom closet. As had been the case in Kathryn Bright's home, the intruder had made a "chair" out of clothing in the closet to sit there and wait for her.

No neighbors reported hearing anything unusual.

Police learned about the crime when the killer himself called the police dispatcher to report it. Nancy was found bound and strangled in her apartment.

Around 8:18 on Friday morning, December 9, 1977, beat officer Lowell Hollingshead was patrolling the area near the intersection of Lincoln and Oliver when he received a call from the police dispatcher to make a call on a landline. At this time, except for a few radio channels that were "scrambled" and required a coded device to descramble them, all Wichita police radio transmissions could be heard by the public. It was a very common pastime for many Wichita citizens to listen to the police calls. One never knew when one was going to hear of a crime in progress, a police chase, or another intriguing event.

Dispatchers told officers to make calls on landlines when they did not want the public to hear the message. Generally the messages were of a personal nature, such as to call home because son Johnny was in trouble at school. Other times, the police did not want the public to know about a reported crime. This was one of those times. The dispatcher did not tell Officer Lowell Hollingshead about the report of a homicide; the dispatcher told Officer Hollingshead to "check the residence at 843

South Pershing." Officer John DiPetra was similarly dispatched. They parked their patrol cars on the narrow street and approached Nancy's duplex.

First, they walked around the building. At the back of the house, they stopped when they saw the broken window and the cut telephone line. Then they looked at each other. They both had the same thought, though John DiPetra spoke first. "You know what we're going to find in here? There's a body in here." The men became grim.

Although the police department was split over whether BTK existed, DiPetra and Hollingshead were two of the officers who believed that Wichita had an active serial killer calling himself BTK.

With both officers ready to draw their firearms, in case BTK was still in the house, Hollingshead knocked on the front door. There was no answer, and when Hollingshead tested the knob, he found the door unlocked. They pushed the door open and hollered, "Is anyone home? Is there anyone in there?" There was no answer.

After entering, they quickly located Nancy. She was prone on her bed, her face to the side, her own panty hose tied tightly around her neck. She wore a long-sleeved pink sweater. She had been dead for several hours.

Nancy's panties had been pulled down. A second pair of her panty hose had been used to bind her wrists behind her back. Panty hose of various colors had been used to gag her. Her ankles had been tied together with her own sweater.

Blood spilled from her mouth and nose. Her body was a reddish hue from petechial bleeding. There were no defensive wounds.

There is a strong suspicion that BTK photographed Nancy perhaps before but certainly after her murder. BTK later drew a detailed rendition of this crime scene.

Nancy had not been sexually assaulted, although the killer had left his semen on one of Nancy's negligees and laid the soiled lingerie by her head.

A necklace of Nancy's has never been found, and it is possible that the killer took one of her many tiny collectable jewelry boxes. Also, Nancy's driver's license was missing, and it was assumed that the killer took it as a souvenir—just as he had taken Joseph Otero's watch.

The contents of her purse were dumped on a coffee table.

In this case, the killer did not take his victim's automobile for a ride after the murder, for it was still parked in front of her duplex the morning after her death. The killer did take her key chain.

The killer took a key chain from each of his crime scenes.

The killer himself called in the crime, using the special emergency hotline the police had set up. From a pay phone on the outside wall of Organ's Market, 527 East Central, the killer called the operator about 8:18 a.m. on December 9, asking for the police dispatcher.

"Dispatcher," she answered.

"Yes. You have a home-icide at 843 South Pershing, Nancy Fox," the killer said calmly. The dispatcher was trained to keep the caller on the line. Because the number and location appeared on her screen, she was simultaneously trying to dispatch a patrol car to the pay phone at Central and St. Francis Streets even as she said: "I am sorry, sir. I can't understand you. What is the address?" She wanted to keep this caller on the line as long as possible so that he would still be there when police arrived.

However, the killer had called the operator and asked to be connected to the police. The operator was still on the line. The telephone company operator was trained to be helpful and include information and get callers off the phone as soon as possible. She injected herself into the conversation.

Telephone operator: "He said 843 South Pershing."

The killer said, "That is correct."

Then, leaving the phone dangling, he walked away.

As it happens, City of Wichita fire department captain Wayne Davis intended to use the same pay phone, saw it in use, went inside a store to get change. When he emerged he saw the phone dangling by its cord. He picked up the phone fifty-nine seconds after the call reporting the homicide. He initially told authorities that he wasn't really paying attention, but he thought that the man who was using the phone when he pulled up was a six-foot-tall, blond-haired man dressed in a blue-gray industrial uniform and possibly a hat with ear flaps. According to police, the man in the phone booth might have been driving a "late-model van, probably not over two or three years old, which may have had some type of writing, possibly advertising, on the side of it." The van had no windows.

The description, just like all of the others police had received, was not considered certain enough to make any arrests. "I wouldn't put two cents into what [the fireman] said," Detective Bernie Drowatzky later said. "He pulled up, was going to use the telephone, comes back from the store, the phone's dangling, and he just glances down the street to see who it was? I just never could feel comfortable putting any stock into his description."

The phone booth was only two short blocks from the Coleman Company, where victims Michael L. Williams, Julie Otero, and Kathryn Bright had all worked.

The voice of the killer reporting his own crime was taped on a new automatic system that had been instituted. The tape was sent to the FBI laboratory in Washington, D.C. The tape, the lab said, was too short, and there was too much background noise, for making a voiceprint suitable for comparison with the voices of known criminals.

After ranking personnel arrived they remembered that a crime scene expert might still be in Wichita. The previous day this expert had delivered a presentation in Wichita. Everyone, including Bernie Drowatzky and Richard Cole, remembered that the expert was Dr. Thomas Noguchi, the famous Los Angeles medical examiner. A patrol car was dispatched, red light flashing and siren blaring, to the Wichita Airport to bring this crime scene expert to 843 South Pershing.

The crime scene was examined in a more sophisticated fashion than ordinary. A tent was erected around Nancy's body, and the tent was "fumed" with chemicals designed to bring out fingerprints or palm prints. A black light was used, which several officers said they had never before seen used at a crime seen. A partial palm print and partial fingerprints were obtained.

Semen was sent to the KBI lab in Topeka, where it was determined to be that of a PGM-1 nonsecretor. The three facts the authorities could determine from the semen was ABO blood type, secretor status, and phosophoglucomutase type. Because the semen was from a nonsecretor, they could not determine blood type. Knowing that the killer was a PGM-1 nonsecretor was not much help because 63 percent of the population had this tissue type.

According to Major Cole, Nancy's body was removed by 11:00 a.m.

On the six o'clock news that evening, Captain Al Thimmesch was interviewed by a TV reporter while standing out in front of the taped-off crime scene. He confirmed that it was a "home-icide," and he pronounced the word in just that way. Thimmesch would have heard the audiotape before he did that interview, so he may have been deliberately parroting the tape.

After the autopsy, district coroner Dr. Robert Daniels confirmed that Nancy died of strangulation.

Gloria Patterson was one of Nancy Fox's closest friends. At the time of Nancy's murder, Gloria was a young bride enjoying the fullness of life. At 9:45 a.m. on Friday morning, December 9, 1977, while working as a secretary at Pizza Hut World Headquarters, Gloria received a telephone call from her sister-in-law that changed her life forever.

Her sister-in-law called and asked where Cue Quilty might be at this time. Gloria said that he would be found attending an English class at Wichita State University.

Then, after answering a series of questions about Nancy, Gloria demanded to know why she was being asked these questions. Her sister-in-law said, "Please just answer the questions."

Gloria refused. "I'm not answering any more questions until you tell me why you are asking."

A police officer came on the phone and said that he was sorry to tell her that Nancy was dead.

Gloria became hysterical.

When she calmed down enough, a coworker took Gloria to Watkins Incorporated, where she asked to see Verna, another of Nancy's closest friends. They went to a break room, where Gloria told Verna of Nancy's death.

After a long cry, the young women composed themselves and went to the police station together. Soon Nancy's family and other friends joined them at the police station.

The police questioned them for ideas about possible suspects and played the audiotape of the killer reporting Nancy's "home-icide." Neither Gloria nor anyone else recognized the voice.

It was determined that Gloria and Verna were perhaps the last living persons to be in Nancy's home—except for Nancy's killer. In the afternoon police took Gloria and Verna to the house to see if they could tell if anything was disturbed or missing.

Gloria, seeing that Nancy had the 1977–1978 bowling team picture in a frame on her bureau, started crying again. Nancy's dates and boyfriends came and went, but her girlfriends were constant. Gloria still had the 1976–1977 bowling team picture.

Gloria and Verna at first found nothing out of the ordinary in Nancy's apartment until they got to the bedroom, where they couldn't help but notice the empty six-pack of beer. Nancy didn't drink beer.

That night Verna was too shaken to stay at her home alone, so she slept at Gloria and her husband Larry's home, which was cluttered with half-filled cardboard boxes because they were preparing to move.

That night as she went to bed—numbed by the day's events, grief-stricken, shaken—Gloria reflected that she was no longer the same person who had answered that telephone that morning.

Eventually, in her husband's arms, Gloria dropped off into a fitful, surreal sleep that was unlike any she had ever known.

Nancy's boyfriend up until a few weeks before her murder had been Ron Dunigan. Nancy met Ron when she briefly worked as a cashier at a car wash. Dunigan, a patron who often washed his car, started flirting with the pretty cashier. They dated for several years. Ron worked as the doorman at Scene Seventies, and that is why Nancy and her friends started going to that club. Nancy spent time in bars only because that's where her friends went, but she did not drink.

On occasion, when the bar suddenly was overflowing, Nancy would volunteer to help out as a waitress. She was not paid; she was just trying to help. However, one of her father's friends happened to see Nancy carrying a tray of beer to patrons, and told Nancy's father that Nancy was working as a barmaid.

Dale Fox became infuriated when he learned his daughter was serving alcohol and associating with the type of men who frequented such places. Sadly, Nancy and her father had harsh words about the incident and were estranged at the time of Nancy's murder.

Nancy's was a life of routine. She worked during the day as a clerk at the Law Company. She had a desk in a cubicle near the photocopy machine. She worked Tuesday and Thursday evenings at Helzberg's Jewelers.

Her friends say if you knew what time it was and what day of the week it was, you could always find Nancy. She was that predictable. She could have been followed without knowing it.

Yet at the time of her murder, her normally staid life had been thrown into emotional upheaval. She had stopped speaking with her father and mother. She had switched boyfriends within a matter of days and then broken up with her new boyfriend, Cue Quilty.

Cue was a coworker at the jewelry store and, unbeknownst to anyone else, Cue was also dating one of Nancy's other coworkers. Cue Quilty was deceiving everyone by dating both Nancy and Candy Dufrene, despite strict rules at Helzberg's prohibiting employees from dating each other. The company was very strict regarding this policy and had recently fired a couple who had been caught. Police found Quilty to be an odd duck and considered him a suspect. Nancy never knew that Cue was dating Candy, and Candy learned that Cue dated Nancy only in 2004 during the course of an interview for this book.

On Wednesday evening, the night before her murder, Nancy had bowled in the women's bowling league at Seneca Lanes. Nancy bowled for the Kwiky Burger team in the Even Dozen League. Nancy and her teammates wore yellow shirts that read "MMM-MM. JUST HAD A KWIKY BURGER." She was not a bowling fan but enjoyed the company of her friends and the convivial times they had.

Nancy's father was working at Cessna Aircraft Company when police discovered the body. Police took Mr. Fox to St. Joseph Medical Center to identify the body.

When I interviewed Dale Fox the first time, Dale said that he was certain that Nancy's murder came out of her spending time in Scene Seventies.

The victim's younger brother, Kevin, who adored Nancy, was a sophomore in high school. He had cut class that day and was riding around town when he heard of his sister's murder on the car radio.

Nancy Jo Fox's brief obituary notice in the newspaper read:

> Nancy Jo Fox, 25, of 843 S. Pershing, secretary for the Law Co. Inc. and Helzberg's Jewlers employee, died Friday.

> Service 1 p.m. Tuesday, Parkview Southern Baptist Church, 3:30 p.m., Harper (Kan.) Cemetery. Survivors: Father, Dale *[Fox]*, mother, Mrs. Dale Mason *[Nancy's parents had divorced and Nancy's mother married Dale Mason; Nancy's father, Dale Fox, had married Ruth]*, brothers, Fred E., David L., Kevin W., all of Wichita; sister, Mrs. Beverly Place of Roeland Park, Kan. Broadway Mortuary.

During the viewing of Nancy's body at Broadway Mortuary, 1147 South Broadway, Gloria was shocked at Nancy's appearance. Her head was extremely swollen. She was told that Nancy's head looked that way because her head had hung over the side of the bed for a long time. The mortuary staff did what they could.

Gloria had the morticians change the part in Nancy's hair and polish her fingernails. The viewing was tragic for all of Nancy's family and friends.

Recalling the empty six-pack of beer at the crime scene, police believed the killer sat and drank while he watched Nancy's head swell and tongue extrude. Then he masturbated.

Years later, Candy Dufrene said, "I walked out that night with a twenty-five-year-old girl, pretty—lively. What I saw in the casket was a woman that was sixty years old. They told me, that's what fear does. It takes someone, a monster, to do that and I want him caught."

Nancy's funeral procession took her from Broadway Mortuary, to a memorial service at Parkview Southern Baptist Church, where Nancy and her family had long attended services, then to the Harper Cemetery in Harper, Kansas.

At her memorial service stories were told about Nancy. Officiating at the services was Dr. Jim Dyer, pastoral counselor. There was a singer and an organ player, performing "The Old Rugged Cross" and "My God and I." The services at the church began at 1:30 p.m. on December 13, and the ceremony at the cemetery began two hours later.

One of the stories told at her memorial service was of Nancy at age five. Her mother had told Nancy she was going to have to clean her room. Nancy did not want to. She "threw a fit" and said she was going to leave. Little Nancy went to her room, packed her tiny suitcase, marched to the front door, said goodbye to her mother, father, two older brothers, ten-year-old sister, and walked out. She walked about a block and a half before she turned around. But Nancy did not clean her room. Her sister, Beverly, did. Beverly did not want Nancy running away anymore.

The Easter before her murder, Nancy dressed in an Easter bunny costume and hippity-hopped around to the glee of the children at a gathering of the extended family. And for Halloween she took her beloved nephew Tom around to all the neighbors and friends. Nancy loved children and children loved Nancy. Everyone agreed that Nancy was destined to be a great mother.

Nancy was also an extraordinarily talented singer. Everyone agreed that when she let loose, her voice belted out louder than that of anyone else. Nancy sang gospel hymns at the Parkview Baptist Church, and from time to time, as the mood struck, sang along with contemporary music at Scene Seventies.

During the months following her murder, Nancy's friends and family members were paranoid, fearful, and suspicious. They looked upon unknown males with a new suspicion. Behavior and routines were altered. They checked their phone for a dial tone when they got home to make sure the lines had not been cut. They still followed these habits when I interviewed them in 2003 and 2004.

While it is difficult to quantify human "grief," Dr. Jody Gyulay, a grief specialist, says that the worst grief is that of those who grieve for a missing and presumably murdered victim whose body is never found. The second worst is the grief of those who mourn for a murdered victim whose killer is never found.

Gloria Patterson told me that she became irritated with Detective Bernie Drowatzky because he would not refer to Nancy by her name. "Her name is Nancy," Gloria finally said. Bernie replied that he meant no offense but could not allow himself to get emotionally involved with the victims.

The police also couldn't track down the killer. Two weeks after Nancy's death, Captain Al Thimmesch said that the police were "reasonably certain that the man who called to report the homicide was the man who killed Fox. He knew too many things about her."

Thimmesch would not elaborate. After the tape of the phone call was broadcast, it became clear that the only things the killer knew about Nancy was her name, her address, and the fact that she had been murdered in her home.

Sixty-three days after Nancy's murder, the fear her friends and family experienced spread to the entire city. The BTK Strangler wanted to taunt the police once again.

Chapter 10

A Package to KAKE TV

Ron Loewen was at home the morning of Friday, February 10, 1978, when he received a call from reporter Larry Hatteberg. "You'd better come in, Ron," Hatteberg said.

"What's up?" Ron asked.

"You'd better come in," Hatteberg said grimly. Ron asked no more questions but came straight to work at the KAKE TV studios. During the 1970s and 1980s Wichita's activist reporters were working under the direction of Martin Umansky and Ron Loewen. Umansky's weekly newspaper *The Wichita Sun* broke the BTK story in 1974, and Umansky's ABC affiliate KAKE TV-10 was an integral part of this tale as well. Martin Umansky always told news director Ron Loewen to report significant stories. Whenever Martin casually asked Ron, "We haven't done anything significant lately, have we?" an alarmed Ron would meet at once with staff to brainstorm a new investigative report for the community.

That day the woman opening the KAKE incoming mail was shocked at the letter's contents. It was a regular business envelope without a return address. The postmark indicated it was processed in Wichita at 8:00 p.m. on Thursday, February 9, 1978.

The shocking contents included four photocopies. Two pages were of a typed letter. One page was a poem or lyrics, "Oh! Death to Nancy." Although no one at KAKE TV knew how accurate it was, the final page was a drawing of how Nancy Fox's body was found on her bed.

In the letter, the killer claimed to be responsible for seven deaths, and mentioned Vian and Fox by name. Again, BTK promised more murders. The letter read: "Seven down and many more to go."

With spelling and punctuation errors left as they appear, here is an unedited excerpt from the letter:

> I find the newspaper not wirting about the poem on Vain unamusing. A little paragraph would have enough. Iknom it not the news media fault.
>
> The Police Chief he keep things quiet, and doesn't let the public know there a psycho running lose strangling mostly women, there 7 in the ground; who will be next? How many do I have to Kill before I get a name in the paper or some national attention. Do the cop think that all those deaths are not related? Golly -gee, yes the M.O. is different in each, but look a pattern is developing. The victims are tie up-most have been women-phone cut- bring some bondage mater Sadist tendencies—no struggle, outside the death spot-no wintness except the Vain's Kids. They were very lucky; a phone call save them. I was going to /// tape the boys and put plastics bag over there head like I did Joseph, and Shirley . And then hang the girl. God-oh God what a beautiful sexual relief that would been. Josephine, when I hung her really turn me on; her pleading for mercy then the rope took whole, she helpless; staring at me with wide terror fill eyes the rope getting tighter-tighter. You don't understand these things because your not underthe influence of factor)x). The same thing that made, Son of Sam, Jack The Ripper, Harvery Glatman, Boston Strangler, Dr. H.H. Holmes Panty Hose Strangler of Florida, Hillside Strangler, Ted of The West Coast and Many more infamous character kill. Which seem a senseless, but we cannot help it. There is no help, no cure, except death or being caught and put away It a terrible nightmarebut, you see I don't lose any sleep over it. After a thing like Fox I ccome home and go about life like anyone else. And I will be / like that until the

urge hit me again. It not continuous and I don't have a lot of time. It take time to set a kill, one mistake and it all over . Since I about blew it on the phone-handwritting is out-letter guide is to long and type-writer can be traced too,.My short poem of death and maybe a drawing; later on real picture and maybe a tape of the sound will come your way. Before a murder or murders you will receive a copy of the initials B.T.K., you keep that copy the original will show up some day on guess who?

May you not be the unluck one!

P.S. How about some name for me, its time: 7 down and many moreto go. I Like the following. How about you?

"THE B.T.K. STRANGLER", "WICHITA STRANGLER", "POETIC STRANGLER", "THE BONDAGE STRANGLER" OR "PSYCHO", "THE WICHITA HANGMAN", "THE WICHITA EXECUTIONER", "THE GAROTTE PHATHOM", "THE ASPHYXIATER".

BTK is patient. He kept his promise to send a "real picture"—twenty-six years later. The next page read:

#5 You guess motive and victim.

#6 You found one Shirley Vain lying belly down on a unmade bed in northeast bedroom-hand tied behind back with black tape and cord. Feet & ankles with black tape & legs. Ankles tied to west head of the bed with small off white cord, wrap around legs, hands, arm, finally the neck many times. A off white pla stic bag over her head loop on with a pink nitie was barefooted. She was sick use a glass of water and smoke I or Two cizrette-house a total mess-kids took some toys with them to the bathroom-bedagainst east bathroom door. Chose at random with some pre-planning. Motive Factor X.

#7 One Nancy Fox-lying belly down on made bed in southwest bedroom-hands tied behind back with red panty hose-feet together with yellow nitie-semi-nude with pink sweather and bra small necklace-glasses on west dresser-panties below butt-many different color panties hose around neck, one across the mouth-strangled with man belt first then the hosery. She had a smoke and went to the bathroom before the final act-very neat housekeeper& dresser-rifled pursein kiteken-empty paper bag—white coat in livingroom-heat up to about 90 degrees-Christmas tree lights on-cizrette mostly burn down pants in bathroom rifled east top dresser on top- nities and hose around the room-hose bag of orange color it and hosery on bed-driver licence gone-seminal stain on or in blue women wear. Chose at random with little pre-planning. Motive factor "X".

#8 Next victim maybe: You will find her hanging with a wire noose-Hands behind back with black tape or cord-feet with tape or cord-gaged- then cord around the body to the neck-hooded maybe-possible seminal stain in anus-or on body. Will be chosen at random. Some pre-planning-Motive Factor"X".

B.T.K.

The poem was typed on the right hand side of a card. On the opposite side he had typed "B.T.K." four times, each time hand-drawing a small symbol after it, perhaps a hangman's noose.

The poem, as the killer typed it, read:

OH! DEATH TO NANCY

What is this that I can see,
Cold icy hands taking hold of me,
For Death has come, you all can see.
Hell has open it,s gate to trick me.
Oh! Death, Oh! Death, can you spare
Me, over for another year!

I'll stuff your jaws till you can't talk
I'll blind your leg's till you can't walk
I'll tie your hands till you can't make a stand.

And finally, I'll close your eyes so you can't see
I'll bring sexual death unto you for me.

B.T.K.

The drawing correctly showed Nancy Fox as she was found on her bed.

Ron Loewen and Martin Umansky did not consult long before deciding to take the letter to the police. Umansky's call to police chief Richard LaMunyon was immediately taken, and Umansky told LaMunyon a summary of what they had. LaMunyon asked him to bring the letter directly to his office.

On their arrival at City Hall, Umansky and Loewen were ushered right in to meet Chief LaMunyon and Deputy Chief Bill Cornwell. Umansky gave them the letter and told them that they were going to run a story unless they told them that it was a fraud. LaMunyon and Cornwell briefly looked at the letter, then excused themselves for fifteen minutes. When they returned, according to Ron Loewen, LaMunyon was shaken. He said, "Sit down. Here's the story."

Ron Loewen told me that he thought that this may have been the only time that the normally circumspect LaMunyon was totally frank and open. He said that they believed the letter was authentic. LaMunyon understood that Ron Loewen and Martin Umansky now had both the 1974 letter and the 1978 letter, and that they were the press and could publish what they had, but he appreciated their citizenship in not revealing more than they thought necessary. LaMunyon explained that the police had never gone public with the 1974 letter because, although the behavioral scientists they had consulted were not unanimous, their opinion was that if they withheld publicity, this guy would stop killing. That strategy had been proven wrong, so they would go public with a press conference in the afternoon.

LaMunyon said that the killer had chosen to communicate with KAKE, therefore the police would cooperate with KAKE. The police wanted the killer to continue to communicate. However, the men then discussed the wisdom of using the news anchor who might normally be assigned to cover this story, popular reporter Rose Stanley.

She was not the first woman television reporter in Wichita, but she was the first long-term woman television reporter. Because the killer strangled women Rose Stanley's age, they considered the possibility that the killer would think about her more than the communication. Therefore, they unanimously agreed that they did not want her to report the story.

The four men talked for a while about the consequences of what was about to happen. They were men of action and knew how to fulfill their responsibilities, but there was a moment's pause before they ended the meeting and each went out to execute their role in changing Wichita's history.

In BTK's letter he listed a group of real-life serial killers whom he admired and was influenced by. We can get an insight into BTK's mind if we take a closer look at the fiends that he identified.

Son of Sam

Like BTK's murders, the Son of Sam crimes terrorized an entire city, and he sent poems and letters to the police and the press. All the Son of Sam killings were committed with the same .44 Bulldog. All the victims were either pedestrians or sitting in parked cars. Just as BTK seems to have committed all of his murders indoors, Son of Sam did all of his work outdoors. He terrorized New York the way BTK terrorized Wichita.

Whether all the Son of Sam .44 shootings were committed by the same man has been a matter of controversy. The man captured, David Berkowitz, originally confessed to all of the killings but now says he was part of a gang that passed the gun around, with various members getting an opportunity to be the Son of Sam.

He killed Donna Lauria and wounded Jody Valente on July 29, 1976, in the Bronx section of New York. He wounded Rosemary Keenan and Carl Denaro in Queens on October 23, 1976. He wounded Joanne Lomino and Donna DeMasi, November 27, 1976, in Queens.

In January 1977 Son of Sam wrote a letter to police detective Joseph Borelli saying: "I am the Monster—Beelzebub—the chubby behemouth [sic]. I love to hunt. Prowling the streets looking for fair game—tasty meat. The women of Queens are prettyist of all."

Son of Sam killed Christina Freund on January 30, 1977, in Forest Hills, Queens. On March 8, 1977, he killed Virginia Voskerichian, about 100 yards away from where he shot Christina Freund. On April 17, 1977, he killed Alexander Esau and Valentina Suriani in the Bronx and left another note for Borelli at the scene.

On May 30, 1977, Son of Sam wrote a letter to Jimmy Breslin, a columnist for the New York *Daily News*. The letter was published. On June 26, 1977, Son of Sam shot Sal Lupo and Judy Placido in a parked car in the Bayside section of Queens.

On July 31, 1977, Son of Sam shot Stacy Moskowitz and Bobby Violante in a parked car in the Bath Beach section of Brooklyn, killing her and blinding him.

During this shooting, which would turn out to be Son of Sam's last, David Berkowitz parked in front of a fire hydrant and received a parking ticket on his Ford Galaxie, license plate 561 XLB. Eleven days later he was arrested for the Son of Sam killings. Did Son of Sam play a name game? Although the attacks appeared to be random, of eight crime scenes, four had V-name victims: Valente, Violante, Valentina, and Virginia.

Jack the Ripper

Jack the Ripper was the first serial killer to become internationally famous and is arguably the most infamous of them all. Reportedly more books have been written about Jack than about all the U.S. presidents combined.

Between 1888 and 1891 Jack terrorized the east end of London, known as the Whitechapel area, killing and horribly mutilating prostitutes, and then writing letters bragging of his crimes.

Jack the Ripper's known victims were Mary Anne Nichols, Annie Chapman, Elizabeth Stride, Catherine Eddowes, and Mary Jane Kelly. All the victims had their throats cut. All but Stride suffered gross abdominal mutilation. Chapman's uterus was missing. Eddowes' uterus and left kidney were taken, and Kelly's heart had been stolen.

Like BTK, Jack the Ripper gave himself his name. On September

25, 1888, the killer wrote a letter to London's Central News Agency that said, in part: "Dear Boss, I am down on whores and I shant quit ripping them till I do get buckled."

He signed the letter "Jack the Ripper." In a later letter he referred to himself as "Saucy Jacky."

Harvery Glatman

BTK was referring to Harvey Murray Glatman, described earlier in connection with Dr. Samuel Harrell's consultation. Glatman seems to be particularly important to BTK.

Boston Strangler

Boston Strangler was the name given by the Boston press to the man responsible for the deaths of thirteen single women between the ages of nineteen and eighty-five during a span lasting from June 14, 1962, to January 4, 1964.

DNA evidence has since proven that not all thirteen victims were killed by the same man, but the facts have had only marginal impact on the legend of the Boston Strangler, and at the time BTK sent his letter, it was accepted that Albert DeSalvo was the Boston Strangler.

It is possible that the man who confessed to all thirteen murders committed none of them. The Boston cases did have a lot in common. In none of the cases was there any sign of forced entry. All the women were sexually assaulted and all were strangled with items of clothing.

On October 27, 1964, a man entered a young woman's home posing as a detective. He tied his victim to her bed, sexually assaulted her, and suddenly left, saying, "I'm sorry."

The woman's description to the police led to his identification as Albert DeSalvo, and when his photo was published, many women identified him as the man who had assaulted them.

After he was charged with rape, he confessed that he was the Boston Strangler. Asked why so many of his victims were older women, DeSalvo said, "Attractiveness had nothing to do with it. . . . When this certain time comes on me, it's a very immediate thing. When I get this feeling, instead of going to work I make an excuse to my boss. I start driving and I start building this image up, and that's why I find myself not knowing where I'm going."

However, there was no evidence to substantiate his confession. As such, he stood trial for earlier, unrelated crimes of robbery and sexual offenses. He was questioned by the task force that was created to investigate the Boston-area murders, but DeSalvo was never questioned by the police of the respective jurisdictions.

De Salvo was sentenced to life in prison in 1967 and was stabbed to death in 1973, returning him to the newspaper headlines the year before the BTK Strangler killed the Oteros.

According to a newspaper article quoting Wichita psychologist Dr. Donald Schrag, DeSalvo, like BTK, was motivated to kill by a "Factor X," an incident or situation in his life that created a conflict between his conscious and subconscious that could not be resolved. Dr. Schrag believed that DeSalvo felt incestuously lustful feelings toward his crippled daughter when he massaged her legs as part of her therapy.

"Although he subconsciously desired his daughter, DeSalvo consciously knew it was wrong, which set up the conflict between his conscious and subconscious mind. To rid himself of the impulse, he raped and killed thirteen women, and left the victims positioned as DeSalvo's daughter was positioned when her legs were massaged."

Dr. H. H. Holmes

Dr. Henry Howard Holmes (1861–1896) is America's first documented serial killer, just the sort of fellow that would make it into BTK's Serial Killer Hall of Fame.

Holmes, whose given name was Herman Webster Mudgett and who acquired the nickname "The Torture Doctor," worked in Chicago in the late nineteenth century as a chemist in a drugstore. He had graduated from the University of Michigan's medical school in 1884.

He claimed twenty-seven victims, both men and women, killing them by asphyxiation and mutilation. He had no sexual contact with his victims.

Holmes started killing as a way to make money. He figured out an insurance fraud whereby he would insure a fictitious person and then produce a corpse, claiming that the corpse was the insured person. Naturally, Holmes himself was the beneficiary of the insurance policy.

Using his falsely acquired riches, he purchased a large three-story building in the south side of Chicago—which would later become known as the "Murder Castle"—and customized it as a house of torture. There was a dissection lab, gas chambers, trapdoors, a crematory to dispose of unwanted remains, and many torture devices.

In 1893 Chicago hosted a World's Fair known as the Columbian Exposition. Claiming that his home was a hotel, Holmes often had visitors from out of town stay in his house—and because of the fair, there was no shortage of visitors. Like those entering a roach motel, they checked in but they never checked out. By the time the fair ended, Chicago police had figured out that an extraordinary number of people who had come to Chicago to visit the Columbian Exposition had failed to return home, and, in many cases, their trails went cold in the south side of town.

The murderer made extra money by selling skeletons to medical schools. He was finally arrested for killing a confederate and hanged in Philadelphia in 1896.

Hillside Stranglers

When BTK wrote this letter, the Hillside Strangler was still commonly thought to be one man. As it turned out, the Hillside Stranglers were a two-man team: Angelo Buono and Kenny Bianchi, cousins, both originally of Rochester, New York. They prowled Los Angeles in a car and "scammed" girls into thinking they were cops as a method of kidnapping them. Between October and December 1977, the pair killed at least ten women, sometimes dumping the bodies in plain view on the sides of hills.

At first police thought they were looking for one man, but they began to suspect two after one intended victim, the daughter of actor Peter Lorre, managed to flee from an attempted abduction and reported that two men had tried to kidnap her.

The pair split up after their tenth murder, and Bianchi killed two more young women on his own—Diane Wilder and Karen Mandic—in Bellingham, Washington. He was apprehended for these crimes.

Like BTK, Jack the Ripper, Zodiac, and other serial killers, the Hillside Stranglers wrote letters. In this case, the letter was addressed to then Los Angeles mayor Tom Bradley.

The letter said that he, the killer, was a "very sick" man and that he was killing the victims under orders from his dead mother. Police never verified that the letter actually came from Bianchi or Buono, but Mayor Bradley believed it to be genuine.

Ted Bundy

Theodore Robert Bundy was born November 24, 1946, in Burlington, Vermont. The combination of a charming and handsome exterior with a monstrously brutal interior has made Ted Bundy one of history's most notorious killers. He grew up in Tacoma, Washington, where he lived with his mother and stepfather, though he was told that his mother was his sister. When Ted was fourteen, an eight-year-old girl on his paperboy route disappeared in the middle of the night and was never seen again.

Ted graduated from the University of Washington and was accepted at the university's law school. He dated normally, but he was not normal. Between 1974 and 1978 he killed at least twenty-eight girls. He was caught in Colorado in 1977 but escaped to kill again in Florida. He was caught a second time, tried in Florida, and was sentenced to die for the sex killing of twelve-year-old Kimberly Leach.

Bundy was executed on January 24, 1989, in Starke, Florida.

Bundy was such a prolific killer that BTK listed him twice in the letter, both as Ted of the West Coast and as the Panty Hose Strangler of Florida, not knowing that they were the same killer. Ted earned the latter name with the murders of January 14, 1978, only seventeen days before BTK wrote this letter.

As horrific as his role models were, the BTK Strangler was correct in counting himself one of them. Even he couldn't have guessed, however, the consequences of his grisly letter. He set off a wave of terror that gripped an entire city.

Chapter 11

Panic Strikes Wichita

The afternoon of Friday, February 10, Wichita Police Chief Richard LaMunyon and Deputy Chief Bill Cornwell announced to a stunned assembly of reporters that the 1974 murders of four members of the Joseph Otero family and the 1977 murders of Shirley Vian and Nancy Fox were committed by the same man.

LaMunyon announced: "The purpose of this news conference is to advise the public of an extremely serious matter involving a series of murders which have occurred in our city.

"As you know, in January 1974 four members of the Otero family were murdered. In March of 1977 Shirley Vian was killed, and in December 1977 Nancy Fox also was murdered.

"Earlier today KAKE-TV received and immediately brought me a letter wherein the author took credit for the Otero, the Fox, and the Vian murders. In addition, whoever wrote this letter has taken credit for a seventh victim. Frankly, although we have not yet identified the specific homicide, we believe him. We are checking now in our unsolved murder file.

"Based upon information which we have gathered in the past and from the contents of the letter delivered to Channel 10 [KAKE-TV], we are convinced without a doubt that the person who claims to have killed the Oteros, Miss Fox, and Miss Vian is in fact the same person.

"I want to restate that there is no question in our minds but that the person who wrote the letter killed these people.

"This person has consistently identified himself with the initials BTK and wishes to be known as 'The BTK Strangler.'

"Because we are sure this man is responsible for seven murders, we wish to enlist the assistance of each citizen of this community.

"Our police department has already begun special efforts which are as follows:

"1. Additional uniformed officers already on the street.

"2. A special detective task force involving the major case squad has been established.

"3. A special telephone number for citizens to call has been established—316-268-4177. This phone will be staffed twenty-four hours a day.

"4. We have solicited the assistance of the district attorney, the sheriff and of professionals in the field of human behavior and would welcome assistance from any person, regardless of their expertise.

"I would like to emphasize this is a very serious matter of which all citizens must be aware and I am asking all citizens to remain alert.

"I know it is difficult to ask people to remain calm, but we are asking exactly this.

"When a person of this type is at large in our community it requires special precautions and special awareness by everyone.

"Specifically we are requesting that people call us about any suspicious persons or activities, however insignificant they may seem.

"Thank you."

Police said that the other victim might be Denise Rathbun, who had lived within sight of the Oteros, or Kathryn Bright. All of the known BTK murders had occurred within a one-mile radius.

BTK was suspected of committing other crimes, including attempted murders and rapes. Most chilling to Wichita's female population, women were warned to check their telephones for a dial tone, because BTK had cut the home telephone line before strangling women in their own beds.

Within days of the press conference, police were leaning toward Kathryn Bright as BTK's seventh victim. It was the unsolved murder that most resembled BTK's M.O. Although the killer had used a gun on Kevin Bright, it had been suspected since the Otero murders that BTK carried a gun with which to control his victims. Plus, it was assumed that after Kevin escaped, the killer used a knife on Kathryn not because that was his method of choice but because he was suddenly in a hurry to get the job done and escape.

FBI profiler John Douglas later wrote: "We know from his own words that he is closely monitoring the media and craves the recognition they offer. What we would also expect for a police buff of this type is that he would somehow attempt to inject himself into the investigation, such as by frequenting police hangouts where he could ingratiate himself with the cops and/or overhear conversations. This will make him feel like 'one of them,' which is what he wants to be, and at the same time make him feel superior, which he needs to so as to assuage his own inadequacy, since he has been able to outwit law enforcement and create a high level of fear in the community."

On January 31, 1978, the BTK killer sent a postcard in an envelope to *The Wichita Eagle*. The letter was mistakenly routed to the newspaper's advertising department and went unnoticed for days. The letter was in verse, written on a three-by-five-inch index card, printed with a child's rubber-stamping set.

The poem began: "SHIRLEYLOCKS SHIRLEYLOCKS WILT THOU BE MINE."

The card was postmarked January 31, but it wasn't seen as what it was until February 10, when the killer's follow-up letter made reference to it. Since the card had not been addressed to any specific department at the newspaper, it was left up to a clerk in the mail room where to direct it. That person gave the card a quick glance and decided it was a Valentine personal ad for the paper's annual Valentine's Day issue. The advertising department did not see the card as suspicious. Many personal ads have little or no meaning to anyone except those to whom they are directed, and many involve initials. The ad department received the card but, because it contained no money for the ad, did nothing with it. They put it on hold in case there was a later payment. Only after BTK's follow-up letter to KAKE-TV referred to the card did an advertising employee find the card and turn it over to police.

Deputy Police Chief Bill Cornwell said the poem "describes his feeling of the killing" of Shirley Vian.

At the bottom of the poem, the killer wrote, "A POEM FOR FOX IS NEXT." The card was signed "BTK."

According to Cornwell the poem was only seven lines long, and each line rhymed. The poem was later learned to have been patterned after a nursery rhyme called "Curley Locks."

The original went like this:

Curley Locks, Curley Locks,
Wilt thou be mine?
Thou shalt not wash dishes,
Nor yet feed the swine,
But sit on a cushion
And sew a fine seam,
And feed upon strawberries,
Sugar and cream

In the early evening of Friday, February 10, 1978, having not had a radio or television on, I had heard nothing about BTK when my first wife, Pandora, returned from work at about 6:00 p.m. She had just walked in the door, wearing her then fashionable checkerboard coat and carrying folders in her arms from the accounting firm where she worked. Standing near the door, she looked at me expectantly and said, "Well?"

I was reclining on the living room sofa, leisurely reading a book. But when I heard her I looked back at her with the panic of a husband in trouble with his wife, though clueless about why he was in trouble.

She frowned and said, "BTK."

This meant absolutely nothing to me. I was even more perplexed. I was wondering if BTK was a new perfume or brand name. I knew of the Oteros' murders but did not associate it with BTK. In December 1974 the news about the letter from BTK was short-lived, and at that time I was preparing to go to junior college.

Pandora said that she and all the other women at the accounting office had heard about the BTK serial killer on the radio. She said it was the only thing anyone was talking about at work and everywhere else in town. When she summarized the story, though, I laughed.

"That's ridiculous! That's so fantastic I don't think they'd even make a TV movie about it," I said. My wife frowned at me and walked away.

The next morning the first seven pages of the newspaper reported the BTK story. I apologized to Pandora, but it was chilly in my home for a while.

For some time thereafter, Pandora had me check the phone for a dial tone and thoroughly check the house before giving her an okay to enter. On one occasion, after returning from a late movie, I walked into the house and immediately went to bed and fell asleep. I did not return to tell her it was okay to enter. She waited in the car, and when I failed to return she almost drove away and called the police but decided that most likely I had fallen asleep. When she came to bed, she turned on the light and left it on all night to annoy me.

After the blockbuster press conference, the BTK Strangler was a national story.

Wichita was seized by panic.

For several years afterward husbands and boyfriends all over town were the escorts and protectors of their wives and girlfriends. Women were afraid to close their closet doors for fear that when they opened them, BTK would be there. Women became angry if children or husbands closed the closet doors. Women wanted to live in homes that had second-floor bedrooms. Thousands of backyard windows and doors were nailed shut or boarded over. Even a drug dealer I interviewed in connection with the case told me that he nailed his rear windows shut for fear of BTK.

In the days after the press conference, sales of home security systems went through the roof.

The people of Wichita made it a habit to check that their phone lines had not been cut before entering their homes.

Gun sales skyrocketed. Gunshops were selling out of smaller-caliber weapons, sold to men seeking a gun that their wife could use. Captain Earl Wathan said that during the first week and a half after the BTK press conference, police received a huge increase in the number of calls inquiring about whether citizens can legally use guns to protect themselves.

Wathan said the calls had "come in pretty evenly from both men and women. The men predominantly are seeking security for their families, and the women for themselves. And there also have been a good many calls from people who live alone."

Wathan wanted Wichitans to know that it was foolhardy to keep a gun if you didn't know how to use it. "Many people who call say, 'I've had a weapon around here for five or six years and I don't know how to fire it,' " he said. "Using a gun in a situation like that could be extremely dangerous."

According to Deputy Police Chief Bill Cornwell, another key factor in gun safety was to make sure guns were kept in good condition. Older guns often have loose cylinders that can come apart when a gun is fired. "If you're not using the right ammunition or the gun's barrel is dirty," he said, "the gun can explode in your hands."

Another issue in home gun safety was snap judgments. Citizens were warned not to shoot until they were absolutely positive that they knew whom they were shooting at and were in life-threatening danger. "There have been cases in other parts of the country where a family member came home late and was shot because he startled another member of his family," Cornwell explained.

Police also advised everyone to register their guns with the police department so that the weapons could be identified if they were stolen, then recovered. Wichitans were not required by law to register their guns, but they were strongly advised to do so as a favor to law enforcement.

Merchants in Wichita were required, however, to keep records of all firearms sales. And Wichita's city ordinances were explicit that carrying a concealed or loaded gun was illegal.

Suspicious character and check-home calls soared to about three times the number that was considered normal. Deputy Police Chief Bill Cornwell said that the police had received a "flood of calls" about suspicious strangers. Cornwell said: "In other parts of the country, when something comes up, people have been known to panic. There have been cases of people accidentally shooting relatives or friends because they were afraid. We urge people with guns to use extreme caution before using them."

According to a Wichita psychiatrist who preferred his name not be used, it was the apparent lack of relationship between the killer and his victims that made the crimes so terrifying.

"What makes this person seem so terrifying, so frightening to people, is that they fear they could be the next person chosen. They don't know whether they are next—it's this fear of the unknown that makes the terror so personal and so powerful. BTK has gained an almost instant notoriety far beyond the immediate area. Because of our modern communication techniques, this man can multiply his [terrorizing] effect a thousand times."

Chief LaMunyon agreed that the letters were amplifying the fear far beyond the rational. "All this guy has to do is write a letter and he becomes headline news," LaMunyon said. The police chief added that fear did no good, but that it was wise for everyone to be "cautious and alert. If you go out, check your home when you come back—and if you are disturbed about something, call us."

According to former *Wichita Eagle* reporter Casey Scott, "The whole town was talking about it, every barbershop and every beauty shop, gossiping about it for years." He added, "People talked about it endlessly, speculating, wondering whether the cops had bungled the first investigation on the Oteros, wondering if they'd done a good job. It was the source of endless debate."

In 2004, *Wichita Eagle* columnist L. Kelly wrote: "The year Shirley Vian and Nancy Jo Fox were killed, my best friend at high school sat awake night after endless night, too scared to sleep because she had figured out her home's roofline would make it easy for BTK to enter her second-floor bedroom window. On the weekends, she'd have me over so we could stay up in shifts, like soldiers on patrol."

Wichita, like any other town, had its share of youngsters who enjoyed making crank phone calls. Now the favorite thing to do was call up a stranger and say, "This is BTK. You're next."

L. Kelly's mother received such a call: "She dialed the BTK hotline to report it—and as the detective began speaking, the phone line went dead. Back then everybody knew that BTK cut the phone lines of his victim's homes.

"In a blind panic, she ran back and forth between the front and back doors, unsure which exit to take for fear of running directly into her worst nightmare. Finally, in desperation, she grabbed the phone again. There was a dial tone. Shaking, she redialed the hotline number. The detective apologized for fumbling with the phone and cutting her off. Oh. Now, even though she knew it was a hoax call, and even though she knew the phone problem was a total fluke, it hit her as hard as if she really had heard from the killer. It was years before she could walk into the house alone again."

The fear was particularly acute in the neighborhoods where the victims had died. Along South Hydraulic, where Shirley Vian was murdered, one forty-year-old woman who lived in the neighborhood told a reporter: "I can tell you this neighborhood is concerned. In the year since [Shirley Vian's murder] we have had several suspicious things happen. Strangers knock on doors and ask to use the phone."

The residents, she explained, have all refused to allow the strangers in their home but have offered to place a call for them. When the residents went to the phone, the stranger disappeared. "I'm a lot more alert to things like that now," the woman said.

City plumbing inspectors noted that in the past they had been allowed to come inside people's home and check the plumbing without a problem. Since the news that there was a serial killer in town had hit, things were different. "I always have to show my identification now," said one inspector.

Men sometimes teased women about the fact that many women were afraid to be home alone and were sleeping with the lights on. Some homes had extra locks and peepholes installed on the doors.

Many had noticed that all the victims had the numeral "3" in their addresses, and Wichita residents with 3s in their addresses feared that they might be chosen as BTK's next target.

In 2004 one police officer told me that in 1978 he was six years old and lived with his family in Cowley County, south of Wichita. On Saturdays his mother would usually go shopping in Wichita. He understood enough about BTK that he feared for her life. He never wanted to go with her to Wichita, but for the hours that she was gone he stood by the door or looked out the window in distress, watching for her return. He always cried when she left and was always so relieved when she returned that he cried again. He thinks that BTK was in part responsible for his decision to become a cop.

In 2004 many Wichita residents told me that they still habitually checked their phone for a dial tone as soon as they arrived home. One professional woman told me that she had always slept with her cell phone beside her even before BTK's reappearance in March.

One professional couple told me that they did not know until 2004 how much the 1978 BTK episode affected their eleven-year-old daughter. She understood that she was the same age as Josie Otero and did not want to have her family die like the Otero family. Because of their work schedules Mom went to bed at midnight and Dad was up at 5:00 a.m. Their daughter told them that she always stayed awake and on guard from midnight to five. She said she thought every family did that.

The two daughters of another professional couple told me that when their mother brought them home from school, even in the bitterest cold of winter, she made them stand outside on the front porch while she went inside, checked the windows and doors, checked the closets and under the beds, and checked the phone. Only then would she let them enter. Their mother verified their story and said that was not uncommon behavior for families living on the east side of Wichita.

Another woman told me that she married in 1976 and her husband worked nights. She slept at night until February 10, 1978. After that, she never again slept at night. She would stay awake and on edge all night, sleeping only when morning came.

Chapter 12

The Trail Grows Cold

After serving as an M.P. in the U.S. Air Force, Bernie Drowatzky returned to his home town of Blackwell, Oklahoma, and applied to the small police department. He was hired as a radio dispatcher. One night the chief was out of the district, and a hijacked shipment of nitroglycerin was located. When the chief was told, he ordered the only officer on duty to stand by the nitro to keep people away from it. The officer, fearful, refused.

Enter dispatcher Bernie Drowatzky. He offered to stand by the nitro if the officer would man the radio dispatch shack. They swapped jobs. When the nitro situation was resolved, Bernie was commissioned as a police officer and the officer was assigned to the radio dispatch shack.

In 1966, after ten years as a police officer in Blackwell and in Ponca City, Drowatzky was hired by the Wichita Police Department and, because of his experience and obvious competence, quickly became a detective.

In 1973 Detective Bernie Drowatzky was named Wichita's Police Officer of the Year largely because he solved the ten-year-running serial killer case of Thomas Leo McCorgary. McCorgary murdered Earl and Ruth Bowlin on their farm just outside of Wichita on April 12, 1963. While Earl was standing in his kitchen, McCorgary shot Earl twice through the head and five times in the chest. Ruth's body was found in a shallow grave near their home. Her head and arms were missing. On

April 26, 1963 her head was found in a pillowcase in a pond near their farm. Wayne Platt, a service-station attendant, was found shot through the head on April 12, 1963. McCorgary was convicted of that murder as well. McCorgary had stopped for gasoline and Platt saw one of Ruth Bowlin's hands fall out of McCorgary's car and then Platt noticed the blood on McCorgary's clothes, so McCorgary shot him.

At the time McCorgary was arrested for those murders, but there was not enough evidence to charge him. However, because McCorgary was then on parole for an armed robbery, his parole was revoked and he served the rest of his time. He was released in March 1968.

On July 15, 1972, Karl R. Williams was murdered. On October 15, 1973, McCorgary was convicted of Williams's murder.

Detective Bernie Drowatzky had developed the leads that led to McCorgary's arrest and conviction for the Williams murder. Three of McCorgary's former cellmates testified against McCorgary. Bernie also developed the leads that led to McCorgary's 1974 conviction for the Bowlin and Platt murders.

In 1979, Drowatzky would again be Wichita Police Officer of the Year. He talked a gunman into exchanging himself for the hostages. Drowatzky maneuvered the gunman near a small window. When the gunman realized he was visible, he angrily raised his gun to shoot Drowatzky, but the gunman was then killed by a police sniper.

On February 10, 1978, Bernie Drowatzky was lieutenant of a group of the six to eight detectives colloquially known as "the Hot Dog Squad." These were the best detectives and handled the toughest cases. They were confident of their skills, but they had never had to deal with a sexually motivated serial killer before, so they sought out some advice. They contacted detectives in New York who had investigated the Son of Sam case. Then they called the Los Angeles Police Department, who was at that time searching for the Hillside Strangler. The "Strangler" turned out to be a two-man team, but that was not known at the time.

"We've talked with other agencies to solicit how they have handled their investigations, basically, just to shed some light on methods," said Chief LaMunyon. "Those conversations were simply to be sure that we are covering everything, and the general feeling is that we are doing the best that we can."

As the city struggled to calm its nerves, overworked police detectives tried to find something, anything, that would link all the victims.

They needed a common thread, some sort of insight into how the killer went about choosing his victims.

Some police came to believe that BTK chose his victims by the way they looked. Noting that the female victims tended to have long brown hair, policemen with wives with long brown hair often strongly suggested a haircut.

As this search for a common denominator continued, LaMunyon considered how to keep his men from burning out. Everyone was working overtime, everyone was fatigued, but no one wanted to quit, no one could relax as long as this maniac walked the streets of Wichita.

"While we are using a lot of people to gather information," Chief LaMunyon said, "you have to use a small nucleus of individuals to consume that information—a nucleus of six to eight individuals. And after a while they get kind of numb and you have to give them a break." In some cases, he had to force them to take time off. "Our officers are very flexible in a crisis, and they have recognized the seriousness of the situation and are ready to jump in and go. Meanwhile crime goes on in other areas and we can't ignore that. Of course, this is the priority and we let slide what we can."

The police telephone hotline was still busy. Played back to back, all the tips received through Monday, February 13, 1978, would have taken thirty hours to hear.

Not all the calls police received were from sincere citizens hoping to help the police investigation. The fear that swept over Wichita led to an annoying number of crank calls as well. Some of the callers gave false tips, either implicating fictional individuals as the killer or trying to get back at an enemy by anonymously telling police the individual was BTK. Many man hours were lost on wild-goose chases because of these calls. Then there were those who would call up and say "I'm BTK," and then laugh.

"When you have a case like this, you have more than your share of cranks. It's disgusting," said Chief LaMunyon.

Some crank calls were made to the police, but most were made to citizens, who then reported the calls to the police. One man reported that a note had been left on his son's car. It said, "You're next," and was signed "BTK."

One woman told police that she knew who BTK was. Interested, police started taping the conversation, but when they asked the woman how she knew this individual was the killer, she said she had seen it in a vision.

The chief said that part of the fatigue factor was caused by the acquisition of new leads that led to dead ends. "All this weekend," he said on February 13, 1978, "we'd get something and our hopes would go up, our adrenaline would start pumping, and then it would turn out to be nothing."

By this time the Wichita police were definitely leaning toward the stabbing death of Kathryn Bright as the killing that went unnamed in BTK's letters.

In public statements, the police noted that they "could not be positive" that Kathryn was murdered by BTK because there were "extreme differences" between the way she was killed and the way BTK's other victims were killed—that is, she was stabbed while the others were strangled. But, Chief LaMunyon said, "it is the most logical, but that does not rule out other possibilities."

Police believed that BTK planned to strangle Kathryn Bright but that she unexpectedly came home with her brother. The brother, though shot twice in the head by the killer, still managed to flee the house. This caused the killer to be in a hurry to kill Kathryn, so he stabbed her three times in the abdomen.

In trying to figure out which murder was the seventh victim that BTK was taking credit for, police looked at all eighteen unsolved murders in Wichita since 1970. All but three were eliminated as possibilities. That left Kathryn Bright's murder and the murders of Sherry D. Baker on November 12, 1974, and of Denise Rathbun in November 1977.

Unknown to the public, police and prosecutors took a vote as to which victim—Sherry Baker, Denise Rathbun, Kathryn Bright—could have been BTK's victim between the Oteros and Shirley Vian. The votes were never unanimous.

One possibility was that BTK could have lied about the number of his victims and might not be taking credit for crimes he did commit, so that more than one of the unsolved Wichita murders could have been BTK crimes.

The other possibility was that BTK, perhaps like the Zodiac Killer in California, was taking credit for a crime he didn't do. It has been suspected that Zodiac took credit for murders that had been committed by others. If BTK did the same thing, then all of Kevin Bright's recollections were of possible value to the search for his sister's killer but useless in the BTK investigation.

By March 1978 the daily number of tips coming into police was dwindling. Detectives were becoming increasingly frustrated as lead after lead failed to pan out.

Since the press conference a few weeks before, more than fifty men had been identified as suspects. By March most of them had been eliminated from the suspect list for one reason or another. For example, police were very encouraged when they received a tip about a man who had the letters "BTK" tattooed on his forearm. Detectives were even more encouraged that the case was about to break when they learned the man had once attempted to strangle his wife.

Then the case against this guy began to fall apart. First, the man told detectives that the letters on his forearm did not mean "Bind, Torture, Kill" but rather "Born to Kill," a common saying made popular by American troops fighting in Vietnam.

This alone would not have gotten the man crossed off the suspect list. He didn't have to be telling the truth about what the initials meant. There was always the possibility that BTK could have more than one meaning to the killer.

A further search of the man's background, however, revealed that he was an ex-con who had been in prison at the time that at least one of the BTK victims was killed. Police were forced to rule him out as a suspect.

Bill Cornwell showed signs of that frustration when he told the press, "If the BTK Strangler died tomorrow, of natural causes or some accident, society might never know who he was."

The mentally disturbed man, the duck lover who had confessed to the BTK crimes back in 1974, confessed again. And again the guy had police going for a spin of the yarn or two until someone realized it was the same kook from the Otero case, and he was let go.

Cornwell said, "The leads are still so skimpy that we may have talked to [BTK] and not even known it."

Due to increased drug traffic, Chief LaMunyon had recently increased the Wichita Police Department's suspect surveillance capabilities. The film *The French Connection*, which received the Academy Award as best motion picture of 1971, portrays a true case of police surveillance that resulted in a successful interception of a large shipment of narcotics. That film influenced police departments across America. By 1978 the Wichita Police Department had acquired experience in suspect surveillance in drug cases. They applied everything they had learned about surveillance to the BTK investigation.

Although the public did not know it, LaMunyon ordered twenty-four-hour undercover surveillance of several BTK suspects. These included suspects I call Suspect Barbara, Suspect Cesare, Suspect Ferison, and Suspect Camenes.

Chief LaMunyon now did not believe the Otero murders were drug related. He believed the murderer was a sexually motivated serial killer who had also killed Shirley Vian and Nancy Fox. He wanted the prime suspects followed.

Among the surveillance detectives was John Garrison. He would later gain some fame as one of the men who helped solve "the Poet" case. The tough, rugged Garrison had worked a lot of drug cases in which he did undercover work and surveillance work, so his team was assigned to follow the prime suspect, Suspect Barbara.

The suspect was followed twenty-four hours a day with three cars and a helicopter. Garrison's car tailed the suspect at a distance. Two other cars drove parallel to the suspect, one block to the left and one block to the right. This way, no matter which way the suspect turned, there was always a car near him. The detectives rushed to stay in position. The helicopter went airborne whenever he made any unanticipated departure. With binoculars and telescopes the helicopter could keep the suspect's vehicle in sight from a great distance.

For the most part surveillance work consists of hours of tedium. The detectives generally watched the building that the suspect was in for signs of entry or departure. This surveillance began in February, in the coldest month of the Kansas winter, and all night long the detectives were cold. They intermittently ran the heater but only did so to defog the windows. They talked some but mostly they remained quiet. They could not read or engage in any activity that might distract them. They were discouraged from smoking because the light from the cigarette might reveal them, so some officers took up chewing tobacco.

And, although this is not something the officers necessarily want published, with hours of nothing to do, sometimes the surveillance detectives pulled pranks on each other. On at least one occasion in the dead of night a pair of the surveillance officers sneaked up on the other pair and scared the heck out of them. On another occasion, in retaliation for a prank, one of the officers who spit her chewed tobacco into a large cup drove by and tossed the contents of a full cup into the side window of another detective's car. It froze and was still there at shift change. The detective said he didn't know how it got there.

On another occasion, when the detectives were out of their cars, one sneaked back to the car of a detective who feared snakes. He brought a dead snake and some string. The snake was coiled on the passenger's seat with the string tied to the driver's door. When the driver's door was opened, the detective would see the snake apparently striking at him and was expected to jump and scream. What the three watching detectives saw instead was a muzzle flash. The quick-draw detective shot a hole through the snake and the floorboard of the car.

This massive surveillance required three shifts of officers, plus considerable overtime and the use of a variety of automobiles.

Wichita city government made a deal with an out-of-state automobile wholesaler to lease thirty cars for $3,000 a month. During the initial BTK panic, these expenses were not considered overly burdensome, but later there would be battles over budgets.

Many suspects were followed. Searching for biological samples (this was still the days before DNA) to be used for comparisons now considered primitive by today's standards, police always kept a close watch on the suspects they were watching. If a suspect blew his nose on a tissue and threw it into a waste container, that tissue would be retrieved. Discarded cigarettes were retrieved for the saliva they might contain. Coca-Cola cans were pulled out of the trash bin in hopes they would contain some of the suspect's saliva. Police were looking for a sample that could match a PGM-1 nonsecreter, which they knew BTK was because of the semen samples left at the crime scenes.

One of the suspects was followed twenty miles from Wichita to Newton, Kansas, where he looked in a book in the Bethel College library and then drove back to Wichita. The detectives said that they felt their parade of Dodge Darts following him was comical.

Although much of the time surveillance work was routine, John Garrison reports there were moments of terror. On rare occasions they would lose a suspect in traffic or on foot. When that happened they could never believe it. How could you lose a suspect with all these experienced officers following him? But, fortunately, none of these moments of terror lasted long. The police always quickly reconnected with their suspect.

Also keeping BTK suspects under surveillance was my friend Detective Pete Dubovich. I met Pete in 1978 while he was on BTK surveillance. At this time I was working with pre-op and postoperative patients at Wesley Medical Center, and Pete came into the hospital for some orthopedic surgery. Pete has been acknowledged by everyone with whom I have discussed him, even those who did not like him, as Wichita's most flamboyant detective. Wherever Pete was, that was where the action was. Nelson Shock, KFDI radio's top field reporter, reported on whatever Pete Dubovich was doing each shift. In August 2004 Pete's widow Rita told me that she knew when Pete would be home late because she would hear what Pete was doing by listening to Nelson Shock's radio reports.

A career surveillance detective and Vietnam combat veteran, Pete still holds the record for most days suspended without pay (365) and most times busted back to a lower rank (the exact number is in dispute, but averaged around one promotion and one demotion a year). Rita told me that Pete kept them poor, but life was never dull. Pete did not always follow police protocol, and even when Chief LaMunyon and his other supervisors personally approved of Pete's behavior, they were often bound to discipline him.

While Pete was on the orthopedic floor at Wesley, he started talking to me about BTK. Maybe he was not supposed to talk as much as he did, maybe the pain medication he was taking helped loosen his tongue, but for whatever reason he told me a lot about the BTK case and its investigation. At one time he paused in his narration and grabbed the orthopedic rope used to elevate injured arms and legs. He said, "We had determined that the rope used on the Oteros was Venetian blind cord, but I keep looking at this and I'm going to have to check to confirm that it is not orthopedic rope. It looks just like this."

Pete believed that he had identified BTK, and he spent years following and investigating his suspect. Pete would be obsessed by the BTK case to the end of his life in 1996.

The suspect that Pete had decided on was a night prowler. After a while he knew he was being tailed and from time to time talked with his "shadows," Dubovich and Pat Taylor. On one occasion Pete hid in the backseat of the suspect's car. When the man entered his car near midnight to go prowling, Pete sat up, almost "scaring the piss" out of the suspect.

"Dubovich, what the hell are you doing in my car?" the suspect screamed.

"Due to the energy crisis," Pete answered, "it makes no sense for us to use two cars. So tonight we'll use your car. Tomorrow night we'll use our car."

The suspect paused thoughtfully, then said, "When you can prove I'm BTK, then you'll do it. Until then, get the hell out of my car."

The man then drove to Nancy Fox's old residence and masturbated on her front lawn. Detectives decided not arrest him but agreed they did need to collect the semen for testing.

"You collect the semen," Pete said.

Pat replied, "You provoked him. You pick it up."

Pete, who claimed he cut the ears off Viet Cong in Vietnam, said that this was the most disgusting chore he ever did. Worse, from Pete's point of view, the test did not convince his supervisors or the district attorney's office to permit him to arrest the suspect.

During the height of BTK "fever," some detectives continued to keep surveillance on suspects even when off duty. Everyone wanted to be the man to arrest BTK. During surveillance, a very high ranking officer in police administration noticed two detectives who seemed to be watching him when he entered and exited a residence. Unfortunately, this high-ranking officer was entering and exiting the residence of his mistress. He ordered the surveillance to cease.

As far as I have been able to determine, there was only one location where undercover detectives worked for two years. It was Scene Seventies at 2313 South Seneca. This was an L-shaped bar in a strip mall in southwest Wichita.

The police thought that there could be something to Dale Fox's claim that Nancy's murderer came out of Scene Seventies. For two years, on Friday and Saturday nights, at least one undercover detective patronized Scene Seventies, later The Foundry, looking for BTK. A detective who had this job for a while told me that from time to time he would overhear something that made him suspicious. He would engage in conversation someone he wanted to learn more about. On rare occasions he would signal an undercover officer in the parking lot to tail a suspect.

I also interviewed a second-shift police lieutenant who regularly checked Scene Seventies/The Foundry on weekends and a former drug dealer who said that he often worked out of there.

I asked the dealer if there was ever anyone he suspected of being BTK. He paused only for a moment before answering Cue Quilty.

Beat officer Jim Carney patrolled the second-shift beat in the neighborhood where most of the murders occurred. Typically, two or three times a shift he would receive a call to "check the residence." On arriving he would find a frightened woman who had just arrived home after dark, and she would insist either that she had left a closet door open or a light on, or that something that was different now that convinced her that BTK was in the house. So Carney would call for three officers for backup. One would stay outside with the woman, and the other three officers, two with a flashlight in one hand and a handgun in the other, the third with a gun in one hand and walkie-talkie radio in the other, would enter the residence. They would search the apartment or house, ultimately arriving at the woman's bedroom last. At every shift exchange squad meeting, the sergeant would remind the officers that BTK was out there, he was hiding in a woman's closet, and they should be careful when checking a residence. BTK was known to be armed at minimum with an automatic pistol and a knife.

So, with their blood pounding in their ears, their bodies surging with adrenaline, at highest tension, the officers would finally give the signal. . . .

Guns pointed, they would fling that closet door open . . .

And there was never anyone there.

The police weren't the only ones out on surveillance. News reporters were on the hunt too. A group from KAKE were seeking the scoop on BTK.

They were led by Ron Loewen. His path to journalism was unusual. Loewen graduated from the University of Virginia with a degree in political science. He then earned a master's degree in educational counseling from Emporia State University. Later, he earned a law degree from the University of Kansas. But it was during an interim while he was attending a class at Wichita State University that his life turned to journalism. There he happened to sit next to a scruffy-looking guy named Darrell Barton.

Darrell Barton was a television cameraman for KAKE television. Loewen and Barton happened to strike up a conversation and Loewen came out with an interest in Darrell's career as a television photojournalist. Ron Loewen did not then know it, but he was talking with a man who would later be recognized as one of the world's finest television photojournalists. In 1974 and 1981 Barton would be honored with the National Press Photographers Association Television News Cameraman of the Year award. Sometimes running with his camera on his shoulder, he was the first cameraman for the television programs CBS's *48 Hours* and *Cops*. He has done a lot of work for *America's Most Wanted*, and if you have seen the footage of Saddam Hussein's "hidey hole" that was broadcast on Dan Rather's CBS *Evening News*, then you have seen footage shot by Darrell Barton. Barton and Loewen became good friends, and over the years they would often talk of journalism and BTK.

Ron Loewen learned journalism by doing it. While working for a short time at *The Wichita Eagle*, Loewen met the weekend editor Randy Brown, who would become the second member of the KAKE TV BTK team. Brown left Wichita for a short time to work for Nebraska's *Omaha Sun*, where he would be part of the team awarded a Pulitzer Prize for investigative journalism in 1973. *The Omaha Sun* revealed the financial resources and soliciting practices of the famous Boy's Town, a school for troubled young males that once housed Charles Manson.

Brown returned to Wichita to become editor of *The Wichita Sun*, and while Ron Loewen and Randy Brown worked at the *Sun*, they became fast friends.

Another friend in this clique was television photojournalist and reporter Larry Hatteberg. Larry started at KAKE in 1963 and was still there in 2005. He has held every job in the newsroom including writer, photographer, director, film editor, reporter, and anchor. Like Darrell Barton, Larry has *twice* received the National Press Photographers

Association Television News Cameraman of the Year award. He's also received a regional Emmy and an Edward R. Murrow Award.

In February 1978, Ron Loewen was news director at Martin Umansky's KAKE TV. Randy Brown was now an on-camera reporter. Larry Hatteberg was a photojournalist and occasional reporter. This extraordinary group of journalism colleagues wanted to solve the mystery of the BTK Strangler and break the story identifying him.

On February 10, Police Chief Richard LaMunyon appeared with news director Ron Loewen on the KAKE TV evening news. What the viewers did not know is that this was at the request of the police department. They wanted both LaMunyon and Loewen to be on camera, particularly Loewen. The killer had contacted KAKE TV, and they thought BTK might want to contact someone like Loewen. In a June 2004 interview broadcast on *Dateline NBC*, Loewen said, "The police said, I guess based again on their talk with their behavioral people, that this is a cry for help. This guy has more that he wants to say. We suggest that you do the story, so that it has someone that he might choose to communicate with again. It was a crazy time. The police looked after me. They checked my apartment out every night when I went in, and they followed me to my car, which after a while became so nerve-wracking for me, after a number of weeks I just asked them to stop doing that."

The police also provided Ron Loewen with a police revolver, to protect himself from BTK.

Randy Brown told me that for a period of time, after the conclusion of the 10:00 Central Time news broadcast, it was typical for Loewen and him to tool around in Brown's Saab and park near crime scenes, near suspects' residences, and any other place that had come up in reports or in speculation.

On at least one occasion, when they parked near a suspect's home near midnight, down the street were two on-duty undercover detectives in their monthly car, and also nearby there were two off-duty detectives in a private car, all of them staking out the same suspect, all of them believing that all it took was one good break and they could be the team that learned the identity of the BTK Strangler.

In their increasing desperation, the police even turned to a college professor to help provide leads.

Wichita police officers were encouraged to obtain college educations, and all who expected to reach command ranks did so. They had noticed that in 1976 when Richard LaMunyon was promoted to chief over men of much greater experience, LaMunyon had one thing no other candidate for chief had—a master's degree.

For many years WPD officers had enrolled in a folklore course taught by English professor P. J. Wyatt. Professor Wyatt had the reputation of being direct and honest. She understood that officers sometimes had interruptions in their schedules—detective undercover work was rarely a nine-to-five job—and she always gave them the benefit of the doubt.

Detective John Garrison took the folklore course in 1977, and in February 1978, Garrison, on his own initiative, asked for permission to take "Oh! Death to Nancy" and other BTK writings to Professor Wyatt for her opinion. He thought that perhaps she might recognize something the police did not: maybe she could tell what part of the country this guy was from by his word choice, or something else to help the case.

He made an appointment to meet privately with her in her office. He told her why he was there and, before showing her anything, requested that she keep their meeting confidential.

The first document he handed her was "Oh! Death to Nancy." Professor Wyatt looked at it only a few moments before exclaiming, "He's a plagiarist!" She immediately picked a book off the shelf behind her and turned to the page where the lyrics of an old Kentucky folk song were printed. She showed Detective Garrison the song "Oh, Death." The words closely paralleled the BTK version:

Oh, death
Oh, death
Won't you spare me over til another year?

Well what is this that I can't see
With ice cold hands taking hold of me
Well I am death none can excel
I'll open the door to heaven or hell . . .

These lyrics were in the text that P. J. Wyatt used to teach her folklore courses.

Garrison took the information to the detectives assigned to the case. Arlyn Smith, Bernie Drowatzky, and others went back to WSU. The photocopy machine in the basement of the life sciences building was used to make the 1978 photocopies. While the semester-long folklore course was taught in Jardine Hall from 1964 to 1973, Wyatt's folk song course, where she also used the "Oh Death" lyrics, was taught in the life sciences building, not far from where the photocopy machine was.

Detective Arlyn Smith told me that they did not have probable cause to obtain a court order for class rosters, library records, or employee records, but when they explained the situation to the WSU administration, such was the climate of fear of BTK in Wichita that every record requested was provided.

The Wichita Police Department then conducted an investigation of current and former WSU students, faculty, staff, and vendors that stretched out for more than a year. A detective had first investigated WSU students in connection with this case in 1974, when Pat Taylor infiltrated a campus organization. The police checked work and class attendance records. They asked a lot of people a lot of questions, and some were interrogated. They obtained biological specimens from a few. But, as with every other avenue investigated, they either eliminated everyone they looked at or did not develop enough information to continue the investigation. When they had thoroughly investigated every lead, they had exhausted their investigation at WSU.

Every trail they followed seemed to peter out in another dead end.

Chapter 13

Burglary on Pinecrest

Just as his most recent letter had promised, BTK had indeed chosen his next victim, but he was not to claim her. On Saturday night, April 28, 1979, he cut the phone lines and then broke into the home of sixty-three-year-old Anna Williams, who lived at 615 South Pinecrest, six blocks from Nancy Fox's home.

Some police later believed that the intruder was stalking the woman's granddaughter, who often stayed with her. She worked for the Kansas Turnpike Authority at the Forty-seventh Street South toll-booth. Her residence was in a town south of Wichita, but more often than not she stayed with her grandmother. The intruder entered Anna Williams' house sometime after 6:45 p.m. and departed sometime before 10:45.

The intruder broke a back window, entered through the window, and then swept the broken glass into a tidy pile. He waited in the master bedroom closet.

No one came home while the killer was there. He took one of the woman's scarves, along with other clothes, jewelry, and $35 in cash, and left frustrated. When Williams did get home at approximately 11:00 that night from the dance she had been attending, she discovered the broken window, the cut phone lines, and the items missing. Sinisterly, BTK had left behind some rope and a wooden broomstick handle together near Anna Williams' bed. She called police and reported a burglary.

In one of BTK's letters, he expressed admiration for the man credited as being the first American serial killer, Dr. H. H. Holmes. BTK's intended victim, Anna Williams, shared the first and last name of the second-to-last of Holmes' victims. Was BTK once again paying homage to his own perverse role models?

On Monday, June 15, 1979, Anna received an envelope from BTK. It was addressed to her late husband, Clarence. The woman and her daughter were returning to her home and arrived at the same time as the mail carrier. The daughter opened the envelope, recognized the contents as being from BTK, and called the police without telling her mother what was in the package.

The manila envelope was eight and a half by eleven inches and had been addressed in printed block letters. The missing scarf and jewelry, a nineteen-line poem, and drawings were included.

The drawings, showing how the woman would have been found dead, were in the same style as those included in previous BTK letters, helping verify that this package was actually from BTK.

In the drawing, the woman has her upper body resting on a pillow and is kneeling beside the bed. She is bound at the ankles, a single piece of rope holding her feet together, and putting tension on some sort of rod that is under her and runs from her torso down between her legs. She is gagged. Most disturbingly, the victim rests with her face toward us, so we can see that her eyes apparently have mirrors over them.

According to FBI profiler John Douglas, publicizing this drawing could have helped find the killer: "A guy just doesn't start doing that kind of art, that graphic kind of stuff, that violent artwork, someone would have been looking over his shoulders over the years, and seeing that stuff."

The killer wrote in the letter that he was upset that she had taken so long to get home that night because he had really been looking forward to killing her.

The package contained a typed poem. The original title was "Oh Louis, Why Didn't You Appear" but the word "Louis" had been crossed out and handwritten above it was "*ANNA."

The poem read:

I was perfect plan of deviant pleasure so bold on that Spring nite
My inner felling hot with propension of the new awakening season.

Warn, war with inner fear and rapture, my pleasure of entanglement, like new vines at night.
Oh, Why Didn't You Appear
Drop of fear fresh Spring rain would roll down from your nakedness to scent the lofty fever that burns within.
In that small world of longing, fear, rapture and desperation, the games we play, fall on devil ears.
Fantasy spring forth, mounts, to storm fury, then winter clam at the end.

*Oh, * Why Didn't You Appear*
Alone, now in another time span I lay with sweat enrapture garments across most private thought.
Bed of Spring moist grass, clean before the sun, enslaved with control, warm wind scenting the air, sun light sparkle tears in eyes so deep and clear.
Alone again I trod in pass memory of mirrors, and ponder why you number eight was not.
*Oh, *Why Didn't You Appear*

"It is our opinion that BTK was in fact in her home," said Deputy Chief Bobby Stout. "It is our opinion that had this lady been at home, she would have been killed. We quite definitely believe that that was the intent, and we feel very fortunate that no one was killed."

Terrorized, the intended victim stayed with relatives for a time before moving away. Even before the burglary she had not been in good health. Her husband had died less than a year before, and she had been treated for severe depression.

The letter caused the BTK task force to be reactivated. The police called the local media outlets and told them to be on the lookout for BTK packages.

The following day, June 16, KAKE-TV received a similar envelope from the killer. The television station turned the envelope over to the police unopened.

This envelope contained more items from the South Pinecrest burglary and a letter in which BTK claimed to have committed the April burglary. Also included was BTK's special feature so the press and police would know it was him.

* * *

In December 1977, at age twenty-six, Arlyn Smith was promoted to detective. He was the youngest detective in Wichita's history. Arlyn says that he was fortunate to be taken under the wing of Master Detective Gerald Oakley, "a prince of a fella," who in 1976 had been assigned as lead detective on the Otero murders. Well-educated and intelligent, Arlyn Smith was dubbed "Dietrich" by Detective Ron Davenport, after the genius detective Arthur Dietrich, portrayed by Steve Landesberg on the popular cop show *Barney Miller*.

With his reputation growing after only six months as a detective, Arlyn Smith was assigned in June 1978 to Captain Al Thimmesch's Major Case Squad and specifically to Lieutenant Bernie Drowatzky's "Hot Dog Squad."

Along with another young, intelligent detective, George Scantlin Jr., Drowatzky assigned Arlyn Smith to the BTK investigation. The two new detectives were taken to a room where all the evidence was stored and told, "You have a fresh eye, having not previously worked on the case, and not previously been detectives. And you're supposed to be smart guys. Here is the evidence. Go to work."

For the first two months they combed through the thousands of pages of reports. A tremendous amount of investigative work had been done on the BTK cases, but it was not in coherent order. After familiarizing themselves with the evidence, Scantlin and Smith made several false starts. Looking at the Otero crime-scene photos one day, Smith had a revelation that excited him. A photo of the kitchen showed an ice tray with ice still in it! The killer was thought to have departed early in the morning, but he must have returned and made use of the kitchen in the mid or late afternoon. How had this been missed?

Straining to contain his excitement, Detective Arlyn Smith showed Drowatzky the photo and explained his analysis. Drowatzky dismissed it quickly. He said that one of the boys—it must have been Danny—came in from school and went straight to the refrigerator. He took out the ice tray and started to make himself a cold drink. He never finished. Taking out that ice tray was the last normal experience any of the Otero children had before their lives were irrevocably altered. Bernie told Arlyn that there was a report about this somewhere, but it must have been missed or misplaced.

Arlyn Smith nodded. He went back to his fifth-floor office.

First, the two new task force officers looked into every aspect of the ropes. That took some time but did not produce any breakthroughs.

Then they went upstairs to the sixth floor to see Lieutenant Pat Glenn in the Wichita Police Department Crime Laboratory.

Arlyn Smith said, "Pat, is there something more we can do with these letters? These are photocopies. Can we determine which photocopy machine made these photocopies? Can't we determine what type of toner was in the machine that made these copies and trace the brand?"

"No," answered Glenn, who was much admired as an excellent criminalist, "can't do that. Making photocopies is a process like making gasoline. They all end up the same and you can't tell where one was made unless there is an identifying mark on the glass, and we checked and there is no identifying mark on the glass."

"But," Smith replied, "making photocopies is a mechanical process. It's like making an airplane. This paper had to be manufactured, packaged, and sold. Trees had to be grown. Chemicals are used in the pulping and paper-making process. Maybe this paper can be identified. Maybe the paper seller can be identified. And the manufacture of ink is a mechanical-chemical process. Maybe the ink toner can be identified. Maybe there's something special that an expert in photocopies will see that we do not. Are you sure there's nothing that can be done?"

This avenue had already been explored. The letters had been sent to the FBI laboratory. They came back pinkish-red, because the FBI had sprayed the letters with a red iodine-based solution to look for fingerprints. The FBI reported that they were unable to find any fingerprints, or identify the paper, or identify the type of copy machine.

So Arlyn Smith and George Scantlin went back to their fifth-floor office and talked some more. Smith was firm in the belief that they needed to try to identify the photocopy machine. They had to ask photocopy experts outside the FBI if they could identify a particular photocopy machine to the exclusion of all others. Maybe they could catch this guy that way.

So they went to Bernie Drowatzky and made their pitch. At that time photocopy machines were not as ubiquitous as they are today. Most schools still used mimeograph machines because good-quality photocopy machines cost $25,000 each. Few companies owned their machines and most were leased. Arlyn thought that copy machines were few enough in number that each could be checked. Drowatzky thought that they were nuts, but they were enthusiastic, and the idea was plausible, so he gave the okay.

Going through the Southwestern Bell Yellow Pages, they made a list of all the copy machine brands and companies in the Wichita area. Then they called each company, told them who they were and what they were doing, and asked if each would send a service manager to City Hall and meet with them and look at these BTK photocopies. A service manager from each company agreed, and approximately twenty managers attended the meeting.

They talked quite a while and kicked around a lot of ideas. Some things were fairly obvious. One copy was on twenty-pound Hammermill Bond. It was a better quality, more expensive copy paper and came in reams, not rolls. In 1978 this paper was not typically used in low-cost, high-volume public machines. The service managers agreed that this was more likely used in a copy machine in a private office.

The four pages of the second letter, however, were on thin, cheap copy paper from a 1,000-foot roll. The thin cheap paper fed into the machine, and the paper was cut from the roll for each copy. This type of paper was now rare because it tended to gum up the machine.

At the end of the meeting the service managers all agreed on three things:

First, there was one mark caused by a spot on the glass, but this was almost certainly a mark that would be cleaned off and was not a permanent feature of the machine.

Second, another mark had been caused by a spot on the copy machine's internal mirror, and this might possibly be of help in identifying the machine, but this, too, would not be a permanent feature as the spot would eventually be cleaned.

Third, several splotches on the paper had been caused by the FBI being sloppy with their iodine fingerprint solution. They were very disappointed with the FBI laboratory.

At the conclusion of the meeting Detectives Arlyn Smith, George Scantlin, and Richard Vinroe stood and shook hands with each of the men. As the service managers filed out, Smith noticed that two of them, men in good suits who had said nothing during the long afternoon meeting, stayed behind.

The two mystery men introduced themselves. "Sirs, we are authorized to tell you that the Xerox Corporation research labs are at your disposal to do whatever it takes, to glean whatever information we can, to help in any way we can to help identify the source of these photocopies. Whatever we can do, we will do."

Smith, Scantlin, and Vinroe thanked the men, took their names and saw their identification, and discussed some specifics. Then the men departed. The detectives talked about the evening's meeting and decided that they would propose taking the photocopies to the Xerox Corporation research labs in Rochester, New York. They could not risk sending the BTK letters and drawings through the mail. Someone would have to take them back East. As soon as it could be arranged, the Wichita Police Department sent Detective Tom Allen with all of BTK's photocopies to the Xerox Corporation research labs in Rochester, New York, for a week.

With graciously volunteered help from Xerox, Potlatch Paper, Great Northern Nekoosa Paper, and Nashua Toner laboratories, and diligent work by the detectives, the investigators determined the brands of copy machines, toner, and paper used to make the photocopies from BTK. Then the detectives searched for photocopy machines with these particular combinations of brand-name products that were working in February 1978 and June 1979. That meant that the detectives had to ask many companies to look into their purchasing and use records for 1978 and 1979.

It was determined that only three Wichita area photocopy machines could have been used to make the BTK letters.

The coin-operated Pitney Bowes PBC copy public machine near the stairway on the mezzanine of the downtown Wichita Public Library was likely to have made the June 1979 copies. It used the Pitney Bowes toner. It did not typically use the more expensive Hammermill Bond paper, but the library clerk who put the paper in the machine remembered that in June 1979 that machine had run out of paper. There was none of the less expensive paper typically used in the machine available, and a woman wanted to use the machine right then. So the machine was filled with the more expensive paper. Because it was a woman who wanted to use the machine when it was out of paper, the library employee did not think that she saw BTK. He must have come along later and used the machine.

The five-cents-a-copy basement IBC Copier II public machine in the stairway of Wichita State University's life sciences building, now Hubbard Hall, was likely to have made the February 1978 copies. The clerk who serviced that machine remembered that in February 1978 the toner cartridge was empty, and he remembered that he used the very last cartridge of a different toner than they had been using. It was Nashua toner. The only time that toner was used in that machine was in the first part of February 1978. This was the machine that used the inexpensive electrostatic paper in 1,000-foot rolls that gummed up the works. From the manufacturer, the detectives determined that this type of paper was purchased in Kansas only by the government of the State of Kansas. Checking with the state purchasing agents, they traced the paper to the University of Kansas, which had discovered the paper gummed up their copy machines and stopped using it. To get rid of the paper the university shipped it off to WSU, where it was put in a little-used machine in the basement stairwell of the life sciences building, and BTK used it to make copies.

There was one other machine that matched the characteristics. The second floor controllers' office in WSU's Jardine Hall had a Pitney Bowes PBC copier, used the Nashua toner, and routinely used the more expensive Hammermill Bond paper. It was removed from service ten days after the June 1979 BTK letter was received.

BTK must have stood at public machines, put in a nickel, made a copy of his letter, made a copy of his drawing, then made a copy of each copy, then did so again and again, until he had made at least fifth-generation copies of everything. Each copy would have "fuzzed up" a bit more than the previous copy and made indistinct the distinctive typewriter imperfections of the letters, thereby making it more difficult to identify the typewriter.

Either the killer used these machines during normal business hours, repeatedly making copies of, for example, the obscene drawing of what he had intended to do to the victim on Pinecrest with the rope and broomstick, when anyone could have walked up and waited next to him, or he had access to the machines outside of normal business hours. The detectives looked at people who might have had access to these copiers outside of normal business hours, but this did not develop good suspects.

For all the terrific detective work, they were no closer to catching the BTK Strangler than before.

After the BTK case had made big news in Wichita, Dr. Tony Ruark, Ph.D., received a letter from the Wichita Police Department. Dr. Ruark was a respected psychologist, and the department wondered whether he would consult on the BTK case. He agreed and for more than two years worked closely with Detective Arlyn Smith and others. As done for Dr. Harrell and Dr. Porter, he was given access to all the files and case information. Among the things the police wanted to know was how old BTK would be.

Dr. Ruark believed that BTK would have been treated for psychological disturbances as an adolescent. Dr. Ruark arranged for case review of male adolescents in the Wichita area who exhibited behavior that would today be diagnosed as aspects of BTK's pathology. The final count surprised him, as there were 114 men who met the criteria.

Instead the Wichita police turned to a more practical type of psychological assistance. In the 1970s the FBI had started its Behavioral Science Unit, which soon included Howard Teten, Robert Ressler, Roy Hazelwood, and John Douglas. Douglas and Ressler, with Ann and Allen Burgess, later coauthored *Crime Classification Manual: A Standard System for Investigating and Classifying Violent Crimes*. The FBI began trying to define and classify criminal behaviors, now colloquially called "profiling."

Psychological profiling became popular in part because of its astonishing accuracy the first time it was ever used. For sixteen years, from 1940 to 1956, the Mad Bomber terrorized New York City with thirty bombs. As BTK would do, this serial bomber sent letters to the authorities. Although many were seriously injured by the bombs, none of the explosions resulted in fatalities. Frustrated at their inability to catch this bomber, grasping at straws, the police consulted a psychiatrist. They showed him the evidence and asked him to tell them what he believed about the bomber.

The man the police consulted was James Brussel, M.D. He was very specific in his December 1956 profile. He concluded that the Mad

Bomber was male, middle-aged, meticulous, largely self-educated, Slavic and Roman Catholic, had an Oedipus complex, and lived in Connecticut. He worked for Consolidated Edison or one of its subsidiaries. Dr. Brussel said that to draw out the bomber, the case and the profile should be widely publicized. He also suggested the police have Con Edison search its files of past employees. As the detectives were leaving, Dr. Brussel stopped them. One more thing, he said. When you catch him, and I have no doubt you will, he will be wearing a double-breasted suit. And it will be buttoned.

The police were skeptical but asked Con Edison to search their files for anyone who might match that description. Within hours a clerk named Alice Kelly found a match. His name was George Metesky. When the police went to George Metesky's home, they did not expect to find the mad bomber, but were simply following up the lead. They had already questioned hundreds of suspects over the past sixteen years. But shortly after they arrived, Metesky politely confessed.

When police showed up at his door, Metesky was wearing a bathrobe. He asked if he could change, and the police consented. George Metesky put on a three-piece suit and buttoned it. It was January 22, 1957, only about a month after Dr. Brussel gave his profile to the police. Sixteen years of detective work was unsuccessful, but a month after being given a psychological profile, the police had their man. The profile perfectly described George Metesky and was directly responsible for the Mad Bomber's capture.

This astonishing success became legendary to those working in criminal psychology. Time and again profiling has demonstrated amazing accuracy. Quoting from Robert K. Ressler's book *Whoever Fights Monsters*, "When the Elverson-Calabro case was all over, Lt. Joseph D'Amico, Foley's boss and a former student of mine at Quantico, told a reporter, 'They [the profilers] had him [the suspect] so right that I asked the FBI why they hadn't given us his phone number, too.'" Ressler had perfectly described the criminal sought, and his profile was instrumental in solving that case.

Profiling serial murderers became an object of academic and practical study. According to Wichita psychologist Dr. Greg Smith, profiling can broadly be divided into interpretive and statistical methods. California professor Dr. Eric W. Hickey, author of the widely used text *Serial Murderers and Their Victims*, says there are seven basic types of criminal profiling. The first is offender profiling, gathering as much information about offenders as possible, then making checklists (statistical). The second is victim profiling, identifying victim traits and learning who is most likely to prey on them (statistical). Third is the psychological autopsy, applying heuristics (rules of thumb) to explain the psychological motivations of those responsible for deaths (interpretive). Fourth is DNA profiling, which is growing in use (statistical). Fifth is the crime scene profiling, comparing similar cases and offenders to create matches of "typical" offenders to similar crimes (statistical). Sixth is psychological profiling (interpretive). Seventh is geographical profiling (statistical).

Criminal profilers come from diverse backgrounds, comment either as academics or practitioners, and have varying degrees of success and respect. Some observers complain that profiling is as much art as science, but all experienced physicians tell me the same is true of medicine. Because medicine is as much art as science does not mean that one should not consult a doctor.

In the late 1970s, at two different times, two Wichita detectives working on the BTK case, Al Thimmesch and Bernie Drowatzky, brought the BTK letters, poems, and drawings with them and met in the FBI's Behavioral Science Unit with John Douglas.

Chapter 14

The Poet Attacks

On Monday, November 6, 1978, Ruth and Ed Finley visited the fifth-floor of the Wichita Police Department. The couple filed a report stating that Ruth had received threatening letters from a stalker who had accosted her. Detective Bernie Drowatzky took the report. In it Ruth said that she had received a letter in June 1977 from a man asking about something that had happened to her in 1946, when she was sixteen years old. The inquiry involved a news item in the Fort Scott, Kansas, *Tribune* from that year. The item stated that an unknown white male had attacked Ruth C. Smock and had branded her on both thighs with a flatiron.

Ruth had grown up in Richards, Missouri, but when she was fifteen, she moved to Fort Scott on her own to take sewing and typing classes that weren't available in Richards. Soon after she turned sixteen she got a job in Fort Scott with the phone company.

On October 14, 1946, she reported being grabbed from behind by a white male soon after she entered the boardinghouse where she lived. A cloth soaked with chloroform was pressed over her face. When she awoke she found that her thighs had been branded. The man had apparently heated up the iron on the kitchen stove. She suffered first- and second-degree burns on her thighs and some light scratches on her face. There was no evidence of sexual assault and her clothes were not torn.

Back in the present, 1978, the Finleys received so many harassing phone calls that they had to change to an unlisted phone number. After their number was changed, the man began to write letters. He had first accosted Ruth while she was walking along a street in downtown Wichita. She later told the story of how he had followed her into Henry's Department Store and had said to her: "I like your face—I'll see you again, you can count on that."

Ruth next saw the man in September 1978 in front of Wichita's downtown Macy's store. He grabbed her arm and she broke away from him. He had said, "Ruth, get back here, you stupid bitch!"

Ed and Ruth were a soft-spoken, sober, middle-class couple who had been married since June 1, 1950. Ed was an accountant, and Ruth was the secretary for the head of security for Southwestern Bell Telephone Company and was among their most trusted employees. They lived in a quiet neighborhood. Ed was fifty years old, his wife forty-eight. They had two grown sons who had moved away.

To Drowatzky, they didn't seem at all like the type of people who would be harassed by a stalker.

The first and second letters from Ruth's stalker arrived a week apart. The second letter read:

> Ruth: How would you like to put about $100 in a tablet under the seat in yor husb. p.u. I used all the other tab up & the notebook you can save you a lot of truble if you will. I no how to get you truble. Don't tell no one you can get that much without yur husb. To no it. I can find that Lt name on yur car . . . Don't tell him neither. I will call you and tell you when I will get it. I can tell if anybody is watch me. Don't be a dum bitch agin & blow this. I will have to see you soon if you do Don't think yur fucking frends at that tele ofs can get away with any stuff they shudnt I can tell if you have them try & I will see you for it. I will try to be yur frend but when you are a dum bitch I don't like you and I have some dum things you wold not like just keep yor smart ass mouth shut & have the $100 in the tablet under the seat and you wont have

to take a ride & you and I no I can do that & I will not let a dum smart ass bitch let my buddy laff at me. This time you talk to me when I call you soon. I may have to tell some people that yo see yur brand how wuld you like that.

Where ever you go on water or land
You still got to pay or I tell about yur brand
I am smart and no things to do
You talk to people I dispise
Like police Lt & tele spies

A little over two weeks after the Finleys had made their report, on November 21, a cold, misty day, Ed Finley called the police to report that Ruth was missing. Detective Richard Zortman immediately began a missing-person investigation. Later in the day, however, Ruth turned up.

Ruth told police that she had been abducted by two men. One of the men kicked her hard in the shin and struck her with a "piece of concrete." Then both men had forced her into a car.

She never saw the driver, who always looked straight ahead while she was in the backseat with the other man, who showed her his switchblade menacingly. They had driven around for four hours before she had managed to escape. She told the men she had to go to the bathroom and they let her out of the car near the Twin Lakes Shopping Center and escorted her into a woods. She managed to get her bottle of mace out of her purse, sprayed both men in the face, and escaped on foot.

She was unable to give a description of either of her abductors.

At the scene of Ruth's escape, police found many footprints in the mud that matched Ruth's, but none that could be matched to her adult male abductors.

The stalker began sending Ruth letters with greater frequency. The poems contained lines such as these:

The river is searched for the perished
Whores will hate me but by men I will be cherished
Viper thoughts coil round my mind
Torture and agony are unkind.

The stalker was referred to by the Wichita press as "the Poet."

Following her abduction, police placed Ruth under surveillance for five weeks, but there were no further attacks. Detective George Anderson accompanied the Finleys on a two-day trip to Fort Scott. Friends and family were interviewed, with no useful results. A second trip to Fort Scott was made without the Finleys by Anderson and Detective Mike McKenna, again without success.

The police staged a talk show on KEYN radio about Ruth's problems and invited listeners to call in. Ruth and police monitored all the calls, but she could identify none of the voices as that of the Poet.

On Wednesday, December 13, 1978, Drowatzky received a letter addressed to him at the police station by a person alleging to be the Finley stalker.

On January 25, 1979, Ruth received a call at work from her stalker.

"I have a surprise for you in the lobby, Ruth," the man said.

Police searched the lobby and found a knife wrapped in a red bandana in a phone booth. Witnesses said they saw a man in the phone booth who resembled the composite sketch based on Ruth's description.

On January 27, Ruth received a poem in the mail:

There was a female named Ruth
Who thought nothing of calling a sleuth
I have no doubt
My call was checked out
I didn't tell you your present was in a booth.

On February 28, 1979, the Poet sent a florist five dollars and a note that read: "Wud you send one black flower with this note. If this is not enuf for a delivered one call [the Finley phone number] & tell her to come & get it."

On March 5 a man called KARD-TV3 in Wichita and identified himself as Buddy, the driver who had accompanied Ruth's abductor and whose face, according to Ruth's story, she had never seen.

Buddy said he knew who the Poet was and asked if it was true that the police were willing to make a deal. Ten minutes later the same man called KAKE-TV. He promised to call back the next day. Two policemen readied themselves to intercept and trace the call, but Buddy never called back.

On Monday evening, August 13, 1979, Ruth was admitted to St. Joseph Medical Center. She had been stabbed three times in the back, with one of the stabbings coming very close to puncturing her kidney. A man had attacked her, she said, in the parking lot south of the Penney's store in the Towne East Square shopping mall.

According to the After-Action Police Report on the Poet Case:

> "[S]he had just returned to her parked car when a voice from behind her said: 'Hey, Ruth! I didn't know you would make it so easy.'
>
> She frantically attempted to unlock the door of her car in order to escape. In her haste, the wrong key was inserted in the lock, causing it to jam. She was grabbed from behind and a struggle ensued. Ruth broke free and ran to the opposite side of the vehicle where she managed to enter the car through the passenger door. The suspect tried to reach through an open window to grab his intended victim but Ruth quickly rolled the window up, catching the tip of her assailant's glove where it was held securely between the glass and window frame of the door.
>
> Starting the engine, Ruth drove to a service station where she immediately established telephone contact with the Major Crimes Unit and reported the incident. She was advised to go home to her husband and wait there until officers arrived. For the first time since her encounter with her assailant, Ruth experienced a twinge of pain in her lower left side.

She looked down and saw a boning knife protruding from her back. She drove home and Ed called an ambulance.

Ruth was hospitalized for nine days.

Wichita Eagle editor Susan Edgerley told reporter Fred Mann, who expected to be on the police beat for only a couple of weeks, to "stay on the stabbing story." With his byline attached to the stories, Fred Mann began to receive letters from the Poet.

Ed Finley's employer offered a $3,000 reward for information leading to the capture of the man who had attacked Ruth. Police put an eight-man surveillance team in Towne East Shopping Mall. Police placed the first of fifty-four personal ads in *The Wichita Eagle*, hoping to draw out Ruth's attacker.

Copies of the stalker's poems were sent to psycholinguistics consultant Dr. Murray S. Miron, who had worked on the Son of Sam case in New York City in 1976–77. Dr. Miron said that Ruth's stalker was "severely psychotic, schizophrenic, wily, pathological, paranoid, and a loner with a deep feeling of persecution."

The day of Ruth's stabbing, KAKE-TV and radio were advertising that the next day they would broadcast an enhanced audio of BTK's voice—the tape of the killer reporting Nancy Fox's "home-icide."

Police had sent a copy of the tape of BTK reporting Nancy Fox's murder to Professor Mark Weiss of Queens College in Flushing, New York, who had invented a computer process to eliminate extraneous noises on tape recordings.

Unfortunately, there wasn't much to work with in the first place. The quality of the recording was very poor. It had been recorded on a slow-speed police tape recorder. Plus, there was much background noise, including a loud sound that was thought to be a bus accelerating.

About the computer enhancements, Police Chief LaMunyon said, "We didn't want to do it just for news. But we thought there might be some possible benefit to the investigation. We didn't want to do it just for show, but I discussed it with the detectives and we decided we had nothing to lose. It's a long shot, but there's a possibility."

After the enhancement was completed, LaMunyon said, "We didn't learn anything additional from the processed tape than we had from the original we had."

Regarding the broadcasting of the tape, LaMunyon said at the time, "I'm very hopeful for positive results, but I'm very doubtful. Even if you know the individual, to identify him will be very difficult unless he's very close to you."

The telephone call played initially only on KAKE television and radio—beginning on Tuesday morning, August 14, 1979—but one day it was released to all the local broadcast press and widely played. Police received more than 100 tips in the first day alone. The frequency of responses increased each time the tape was broadcast and then tapered off.

KAKE aired the tape during every radio news broadcast between 4:00 p.m. on Tuesday the 14th and 9:00 a.m. on Wednesday. After that, the radio station continued to play the tape regularly as part of a public-service announcement.

KAKE-TV broadcast the tape at 5:30 and 10:00 p.m. on Tuesday and at noon on Wednesday. On Wednesday afternoon copies of the tape were sent to other media outlets in Wichita, so that they could broadcast the tape as well.

Ruth's harassment by the stalker became increasingly bizarre. The Wichita Health Department received a letter stating that Ruth was spreading venereal disease. A mortuary received a message that Ruth was seeking more information regarding their services. A container of urine was left on the Finleys' front porch. An unlit Molotov cocktail was left at the rear of the Finley house. On Sunday, December 21, 1980, the Finleys' Christmas wreath was set on fire. The fire destroyed the Finleys' picture window.

On Christmas Eve, their phone lines were cut. This started speculation that Ruth's stalker might be the BTK Strangler.

The Poet sent Ruth pieces of a red bandana. The small pieces of red cloth became her stalker's trademark. Eggs and feces were found splattered against the outer walls of the Finley home.

On January 8, 1980, the Finleys' phone line was cut for a second time.

On Tuesday, February 19, 1980, Ruth Finley received a threatening rhyming Valentine from her stalker.

Here's to you tender valentine
Red with blood and tied with twine.
Nothing too much for a valentine
Gone from here by a whim of mine.

The envelope contained a swatch of red bandana. The Poet letter fit the BTK pattern in two ways. It was in the form of a Valentine, as was the "Shirleylocks" poem mailed near Valentine's Day, and it contained a piece of clothing, as did the packages mailed after the Pinecrest burglary.

And poetry was part of the BTK profile. When he had given the press a list of names that he could perhaps be known by, the BTK Strangler was the one that stuck, but among the options he offered was the Poetic Strangler.

This caused the police, especially Bernie Drowatzky, to believe that the Poet and BTK could be the same man. Family members and friends of known or suspected BTK victims, including Nancy Fox's friend Gloria Patterson, were shown the bandana swatch and asked if they could identify it.

On March 5, 1980, KAKE-TV received its first letter from the Poet. The letter contained threats against Wichita police detectives, including Detective Drowatzky. The television station turned the letter over to the police.

Suspects were interviewed and released.

Memories vary on the precise time, but all interviewed agree that during the Poet investigation both *The Wichita Eagle* and KAKE-TV agreed to cooperate with the police. General Manager Martin Umansky of KAKE-TV and Editor-in-Chief "Buzz" Merritt made agreements that, in consideration for exclusive stories, they would not open any communiqués from the Poet or BTK, and, upon recognizing them as communiqués, would immediately turn them over to the police. Station Manager Ron Loewen was the inside man at KAKE-TV.

Eagle reporter Fred Mann, who according to former *Eagle* editor James Preston Girard was the best writer on the paper, went inside the police investigation of the Poet.

The negotiations with the *Eagle* were long and loud. When Buzz Merritt finally consented to LaMunyon's requests, he said "We'll do it if we get the exclusive. But if we're going to get in bed with you, we don't want to be screwed in the morning."

"You won't," LaMunyon reassured him. It was in everyone's interest to have this case solved. The police and press would work together.

For several years Fred Mann had a periodic column in the *Eagle* titled "Mann at Work." He would work along with citizens at their daily occupation and write about the experience. One thing that Mann learned almost immediately when he was let inside the Poet investigation was this: some of the police suspected Ruth was playing a hoax on them. Detective Mike Jones immediately said, "It's her." Chief

LaMunyon said, "Of course, I don't believe any of this because I think she is doing this." When Mann asked why they were conducting this elaborate investigation if he thought it was all a hoax, LaMunyon answered, "Because I trust my people and they don't think it's a hoax."

Fred Mann then received a letter from the Poet asking Fred to meet him at the corner of Broadway and Douglas on St. Patrick's Day during the annual parade, and another letter from the Poet made references to Shirley Vian. The police asked Mann to make the appointment. A team of detectives staked out the area where the Poet was to meet Mann. Under his clothing Mann wore a police bullet-proof vest. On March 17 Fred stood on the corner throughout the St. Patrick's Day parade, occasionally catching glimpses of undercover officers he recognized on nearby roofs or walking along the street. If BTK and the Poet were the same man, March 17 may have a special meaning to him. Shirley Vian was murdered on March 17. March 17 was St. Patrick's Day. And it was the day that Albert DeSalvo was arrested and confessed to being the murderer Boston's press then called the "Phantom Fiend," later better known as the Boston Strangler.

Among the detectives who worked on the Poet case were Drowatzky, Zortman, Arlyn Smith, Richard Vinroe, Gary Caldwell, Don Goseland, and, to his irritation, Sergeant Al Stewart. Each had his turn protecting Ruth and partaking of her homemade pies, which everyone liked.

For reasons known only to Ruth and not disclosed to this day, Ruth Finely took a shine to Al Stewart, who was polite to her but was never fond of her at all. The other guys found amusement in the situation, and when Stewart entered the office they would yell, referring to Ruth Finley, "Al, your girlfriend called," even when not true. Stewart would reply "Goddamn it. I don't want to see her anymore."

Between December 16, 1979, and May 20, 1980, more than fifty letters were received from the Poet by a wide array of persons. Among these letters was a threat against KAKE-TV anchorwoman Rose Stanley. As a result of this, combined with the fact that Stanley had recently been threatened by an ex-boyfriend, for several weeks she was provided twenty-four-hour police protection.

Stanley apparently still believes her round-the-clock police protection occurred because of a threat from BTK. That protection, however, seems to have been spawned by two concurrent events—a threat by an ex-boyfriend and a letter from the Poet.

A handwriting expert was given the Poet's letters and determined that they had not been written by Ed Finley. Other tests were inconclusive.

A police chaplain, Robert C. Ely, did a linguistic analysis of the letters and found that the letters contained 107 terms that were not in the average vocabulary. The first letters had been written as if to sound semiliterate, but the later letters had clearly been written by an educated person.

The 107 unusual terms broke down this way:

Literary, 65
Psychological, 23
Philosophical, 11
Theological, 5
Archaic, 3

Because of this analysis, Ely said that both Ruth and Ed Finley could be ruled out as the writer of the letters because each lacked the necessary educational background.

On June 3, 1980, Ruth received a threatening letter with an Oklahoma City, Oklahoma, postmark, the first letter received from outside Wichita.

Based on an anonymous tip, a suspect was taken into custody at the Foss reservoir in Washita National Wildlife Refuge. The man was brought to Wichita. Ruth Finley said he looked like the stalker, but was "different." He was released.

By this time, Ruth Finley had round-the-clock police protection. Drowatzky, who attended the same church as Ruth, virtually became her bodyguard.

Three years earlier, in 1977, Detective Bernie Drowatzky remembered Gloria Patterson's outburst: "She has a name. Her name is Nancy." Drowatzky held to the traditional view that cops could never let themselves become personally involved with the victims or with any others on the cases they worked. With the Finleys, however, especially with Ruth, Drowatzky let his guard down and became emotionally involved with protecting Ruth. Ruth was a victim. Drowatzky wanted to capture the Poet, the criminal. Drowatzky knew as much about BTK as anyone, having worked the case from that horrible first day at the Otero house.

On September 4, 1981, Drowatzky received a letter that unambiguously implied that the Poet and BTK were the same man. He used the words "fox" and "petticoat" in his letter, which led some to believe that this was a reference to the December 1977 murder of Nancy Jo Fox and subsequent ejaculation.

The letter also said that victim #8 would be Ruth Finley, and victim #9 would be Sharron LaMunyon, the Wichita police chief's wife.

According to Assistant District Attorney Steve Robison, many detectives, including Bernie Drowatzky, believed the Poet was BTK. Robison recalled Bernie telling him of all the similarities between the two and why he was convinced they were one and the same.

After Robison left the D.A.'s office, his private practice office was initially in the Sutton Place building, which is near the Southwestern Bell offices where Ruth Finley worked. When he went outside, on occasion Robison saw Wichita detectives. They told him they were part of a surveillance team for the Poet. Steve Robison told me that he often wondered if they would come up with the Poet and get BTK in the same arrest. It was a reasonable conclusion under the circumstances.

The letter to Drowatzky, like all of the others received from the Poet, failed to yield a single fingerprint.

On September 5, Chief LaMunyon brought home all fifteen volumes of files regarding Ruth's stalker and began to study them. The chief noticed some odd patterns in the evidence:

- During the abduction only Ruth's fingerprints were found at the scene
- Activity in the Finleys' backyard stopped (and even switched to the front of the house) as soon as the video camera was installed in their birdhouse, in spite of the fact that the police and the Finleys were the only people to know the camera was there

"It didn't make sense," LaMunyon later recalled. "I didn't say it out loud, but I figured she must be crazy."

On September 8, 1981, Wichita Police rented an entire floor of the Wichita Hilton Hotel, near the intersection of Kellogg and Rock Streets, where they could observe the Finley home, two blocks away, at all times.

The floor also served as headquarters for a small army of surveillance detectives, including Detective John Garrison. Lieutenant Garrison was in charge of the midnight to noon shift of surveillance detectives. Lieutenant Gary Stokes was in charge of the noon to midnight shift.

Chief LaMunyon suspected that because Ruth Finley was such a passive person and her husband Ed Finley was so dominant, it was possible that Ed Finley could be the Poet.

After Ruth's stabbing in August 1979, doctors swore that Ruth could not have possibly stabbed herself. In the first place, the wound could have been fatal. In the second place, there was no way for a person to stab oneself in the middle of the back. It was impossible.

There was a secret meeting in the basement of the Sedgwick County courthouse where everyone who worked on the Poet case was present, including Fred Mann, who told me the story. One by one each person expressed what they thought. Some thought the letter writer was Ruth, some thought it was Ed, some thought both, but many said "No! There is this guy who is writing letters and that is who we are after." Chief LaMunyon ordered a full-scale twenty-four-hour surveillance of the Finleys. "The first thing we shall do is eliminate the Finleys." All vice, narcotics, and other surveillance activities were halted and all resources were put into keeping constant coverage of the Finleys.

Helicopter and motor surveillance on September 17, 1981, observed the Finleys mailing letters. Ed and Ruth had driven to a mailbox and Ruth mailed five letters.

Detective John Garrison was following the Finleys. After observing them mailing letters, he pulled his unmarked car up to the mailbox, popped the hood of his car, pretending to have car trouble, and obstructed the mailbox and kept citizens away until postal inspectors could arrive.

When the inspectors collected the mail, among the letters identified as being from the Finleys were two paid bills, an unrelated letter—and two letters from the Poet.

A short time later Ruth was spotted mailing more letters, and these turned out to be letters from the Poet as well. Police checked the fracture marks on the stamps and determined that they had all come out of the same book of stamps.

Without the Finleys' knowledge, police obtained search warrants and checked the Finleys' home. They found the remaining part of the red bandana and other materials hidden in a rolled-up blanket in a storage area of the Finleys' home. Also found at that time were a book of poems called *Maniac and Other Poems*, pencils, pens, letters, carbon paper, and an empty stamp book.

The police concluded that Ed Finley was the Poet. On October 1, 1981, Ed was given a polygraph and passed. This puzzled the police.

Ruth Finley worked as the secretary to the head of security for Southwestern Bell Telephone. This was a position of great trust—but police obtained a search warrant and searched her desk and work area. On September 18, 1981, Wichita police located items that appeared to be from the Poet in Ruth Finley's trash can.

They found the rest of the Poet materials.

Ruth was confronted with the evidence.

Detective Mike Hill said to her, "Ruth, it's time you tell me why. Ruthie, look at me. . . . I am not mad at you. Ruth, I don't know why you are doing this, but we got to find out why."

"No," she said.

"Do you need help?" the detective asked.

"I wish I were dead," she said. "I guess I am just crazy."

Ruth later recalled, "I wasn't sure I was guilty. But I did know that there was something very wrong with me."

With reporters from KAKE and the *Eagle-Beacon* listening in, Ruth confessed that she must be the Poet and voluntarily entered the St. Joseph Medical Center for psychiatric treatment.

Four days later, Dr. Andrew Pickens, a psychiatrist, issued a report explaining that Ruth Finley's behavior was attributable to the limitations of her personality, repressed childhood trauma, and attempts to ward off anxiety about BTK.

Dr. Pickens concluded that Ruth was another example of Wichita women's extreme anxiety over BTK. She wanted round-the-clock police protection from BTK, and this was her subconscious method of obtaining that protection. Dr. Pickens concluded that Ruth had not consciously perpetrated a hoax.

Ruth and her doctor disagreed on one point. Ruth was always convinced that the Poet and BTK had nothing to do with each other and always denied that she had felt any anxiety at all about BTK's presence in her city.

Another person who disagreed with Dr. Pickens' diagnosis was Chief LaMunyon. The chief wanted to prosecute Ruth. After all, it had taken the police three years and cost the taxpayers $370,000 to determine that they were all victims of a hoax. The district attorney's office refused to prosecute, however.

Detective Drowatzky, embarrassed, was removed from the Major Case Squad, and reassigned.

On Thursday, May 26, 1988, Larry Hatteberg and Randy Brown of KAKE-TV broadcast a program about Ruth and the Poet. The show ran without commercials. No one at the station believed anyone would want to sponsor the program, so no commercials were solicited.

Afterward, author Gene Stone came to Wichita, interviewed many of those involved with the Poet episode, and wrote a sanitized version of events—essentially Ruth Finley's version of the Poet story. The book was published by Pocket Books and called *Little Girl Fly Away*.

In respect to the BTK investigation, the Poet case was so embarrassing it caused a diminution of resources into the BTK investigation for several years—until, secretly, it was rekindled by federal funding.

PART THREE

THE GHOSTBUSTERS
1982–1986

Upon this point a page of history is worth a volume of logic.

—Justice Oliver Wendell Holmes Jr.

Chapter 15

The New Hunters

When a hunter plans to stalk a specific prey, he learns the prey's habits. Where does the prey sleep? Where does it drink? Where does it find what it seeks? Once a hunter knows where the prey travels, the hunter knows where to wait, and then it is generally a matter of patience until the prey travels into the hunter's trap.

The BTK Strangler is a predator on society. He preys on women in their own home and hearth, where they feel the safest. He practices deception and then he springs his trap to terrorize them. Too late they realize they have become victims.

But BTK is not the only hunter. Some social scientists, military officers, and police have long theorized that our human species gives birth to males who are natural predators of society and males who are natural protectors of society. Career police and military may be either. U.S. Army lieutenant colonel Dave Grossman discusses this in detail in his book *On Killing: The Psychological Cost of Learning to Kill in War and Society*. Grossman calls society's protectors "metaphorical sheepdogs" who protect the otherwise unprotected members of the social tribe from its aggressive predators.

In 1982, social scientists and the U.S. Congress recognized what statistics unequivocally showed—that a grotesquely disproportionate amount of crimes are committed by a small minority of offenders, and these are society's predators. These repeat offenders are not rehabilitated or deterred by incarceration and will continue to prey on society so long as they are free in society.

In our society, predators must be apprehended by law enforcement officers. In the USA there are at least six distinct governing authorities with criminal arrest power, depending upon the jurisdiction and nature of the crime. Officers of the federal government, such as FBI officers, may make arrests. Officers of a state government, such as a local police department, may make arrests. Federal military officers may make arrests on military reservations, and state military officers may make arrests depending on the situation. Tribal officers may make arrests on tribal reservations. And officers from other nations granted such authority by treaty may make lawful arrests. This is how we lawfully transfer fugitives wanted in other nations but apprehended in the USA to incoming foreign officers.

Jurisdictions are further divided into separate departments by local governing authority. Here in Wichita I have seen or been made aware of arrests by military police at McConnell Air Force Base; by federal officers from the FBI, ATF, or DEA; Kansas state officers (state troopers and Rangers and the KBI); Kansas National Guard officers (under the state militia authority of the governor); officers from seventeen local satellite cities; city and county fire marshals; the Sedgwick County Sheriff's Department, and the Wichita Police Department. Each of these departments has their own chain of command, funding, practices, history, and culture.

As with police departments everywhere, they do not routinely share information with each other about certain crimes. This has long been recognized as a problem. When serial criminals commit crimes in adjacent jurisdictions, the local officers might not recognize that they have a serial criminal because they are unaware of the similarity of the crimes. This has been true in some famous cases. Prosecutor Vince Bugliosi wrote about the appalling failures to communicate between the Los Angeles Police Department and Los Angeles Sheriff's Department in his bestseller *Helter Skelter*. Another California lawman, Detective Pierce Brooks, made famous in Joseph Wambaugh's book *The Onion Field*, is credited with first suggesting a nationwide computer database into which departments would enter basic information about violent crime so that any other interested department

The victims (*from top, left to right*): Joseph Otero, Julie Otero, Kathryn Bright, Shirley Relford (Vian), Nancy Fox, Vicki Wegerle, Dolores (Dee) Davis, Marine Hedge. Not pictured: Joseph (Joey) Otero, Jr.; Josephine (Josie) Otero. (Photos of Joseph Otero, Julie Otero, Kathryn Bright, Vicki Wegerle, Dolores (Dee) Davis, and Marine Hedge courtesy of *The Wichita Eagle.* Photo of Shirley Relford (Vian) courtesy of Steve Relford and KAKE TV. Photo of Nancy Fox courtesy of the Fox family.)

January 1974—Police remove the body of one of the victims from the Otero family house. (Courtesy of *The Wichita Eagle*)

September 1986—A police officer inspects Vicki Wegerle's abandoned car. (Courtesy of *The Wichita Eagle*)

P.S. Since sex criminals do not change their M.O. or by nature cannot do so, I will not change mine. The code words for me will be ... bind them, toture them, kill them, B.T.K., you see he at it again. They will be on the next victim.

October 22, 1974, letter from the BTK Strangler to authorities regarding the Otero murders

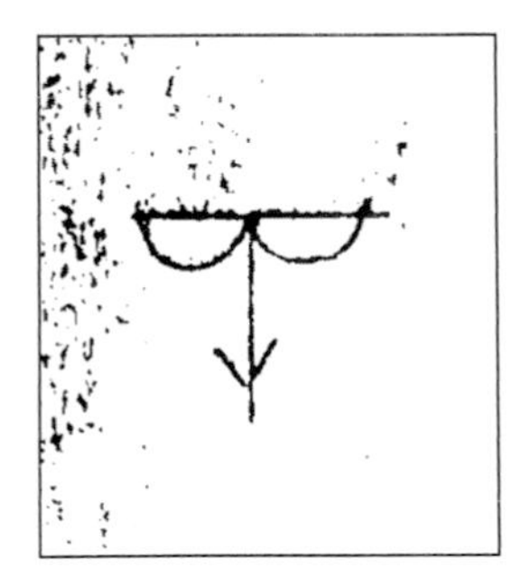

BTK's brand, taken from his 1979 message to Anna Williams

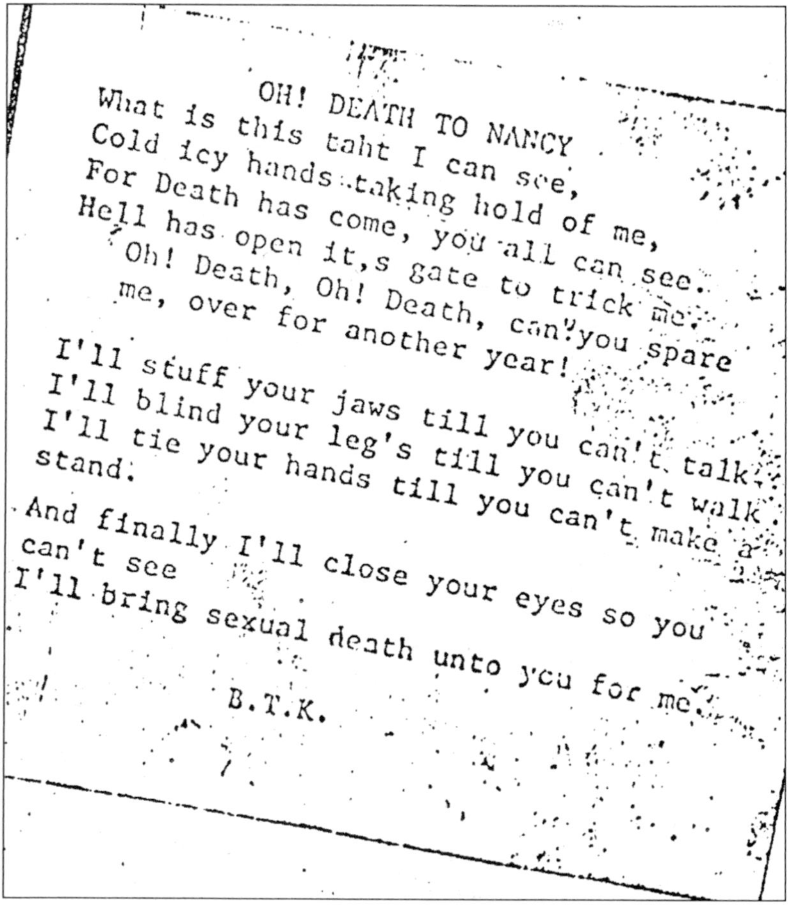

OH! DEATH TO NANCY

What is this taht I can see,
Cold icy hands taking hold of me,
For Death has come, you all can see.
Hell has open it,s gate to trick me.
Oh! Death, Oh! Death, can't you spare
me, over for another year!

I'll stuff your jaws till you can't talk
I'll blind your leg's till you can't walk
I'll tie your hands till you can't make a
stand.

And finally I'll close your eyes so you
can't see
I'll bring sexual death unto you for me.

B.T.K.

BTK's poem about Nancy Fox, derived from the "Oh Death" folk song. It was sent to KAKE TV 10 on February 10, 1978.

Detectives John Garrison and Terry Burnett tailing BTK suspects circa 1978 (Courtesy of John Garrison)

Officer Charles Liles of the Wichita Police Department
(Courtesy of Charles Liles)

Ghostbusters captain Al Stewart (Courtesy of Roger Stewart)

Wichita police chief Floyd B. Hannon, Jr. (Courtesy of Floyd B. Hannon, Jr.)

Wichita homicide captain Charles Stewart (Courtesy of Dan Stewart)

Wichita Lieutenant Colonel Jack Bruce (Courtesy of Jack Bruce)

CHAPTER 8

M	O	A	S	D	D	O	P	J
C	R	U	I	S	E	X	F	G
P	J	K	W	P	T	H	G	O
R	L	E	O	O	A	G	R	F
O	Z	F	L	T	I	J	Y	O
W	N	A	L	P	L	M	U	R
L	F	N	O	V	S	N	I	I
X	C	T	F	I	V	B	S	T
Q	I	A	M	C	L	D	D	L
W	O	S	R	T	T	B	L	S
T	P	I	N	I	P	U	I	L
Y	H	E	L	M	Q	E	U	F
X	N	S	T	E	A	M	B	X
I	D	T		6	2	2	D	X
	2 S	E	I		0 P	A	R	F
	5 U	L	A	R	R	Y	E	G
	9 Q	E	N		3	1	6 C	H
Q	W	P	D	S	D	F	I	J
A	E	H	E	Z	X	C	F	K
G	N	O	R	T	S	B	F	L
S	R	N	S	C	H	O	O	L
F	T	E	O	P	L	A	S	D
H	Y	C	N		2	0	4	3 L
L	U	O	D	F	G	H	J	K
K	I	A	T	I	H	C	I	W
X		2	6	6 M	N	B	V	X
R	U	S	E	T	Y	U	I	X
E	I	E	O	P	F	A	S	D
A	N	R	E	M	O	D	E	L
L	S	V	F	G	R	H	J	O
T	U	I	S	K	S	L	P	S
O	R	C	S	T	A	S	L	T
R	A	E	E	E	L	O	E	P
S	N	M	R	Z	E	X	H	E
Q	C	A	D	C	V	B	N	T
W	E	N	D	I	E	K	A	F
E	R		A	G	N	O	R	W
X	N	A	M	Y	D	N	A	H

BTK's "Chapter 8," received by KAKE TV 10 in May 2004

Dennis Rader (Courtesy of KSNW)

Former police chief Richard LaMunyon (*left*) shaking hands with author Robert Beattie after the news conference announcing the arrest of Dennis Rader (Courtesy of *The Wichita Eagle*)

could look for similar features and perhaps link crimes committed in different jurisdictions to the same offender.

Congress first funded the Violent Criminal Apprehension Project (VICAP) in 1982 as part of the funding for the National Center for the Analysis of Violence Crime (NCAVC), and the program was to be operated by the FBI. The FBI wanted the first two cases entered to be a solved serial killer case and an unsolved serial killer case. The solved case was the Atlanta child murders committed by Wayne Williams.

The unsolved case was Wichita's BTK Strangler.

After the embarrassment of the Poet episode, Wichita police chief Richard LaMunyon wanted to select fresh faces with unbiased attitudes to work on the investigation of BTK. LaMunyon went through the personnel folders and selected a group of men who had never worked together before, did not socialize with each other, had demonstrated competence and trustworthiness, and had never worked on the BTK investigation. He called them to a conference room, telling them to not tell anyone that they were summoned.

The official Wichita Police Department history book reports that eight men were summoned to that meeting, but other sources tell me that only six were summoned to that first meeting and two others were later added. The WPD history book does not identify the men, but as best as I have been able determine with this particularly tight-lipped and secretive group, the group that came to be known as the "Ghostbusters" were:

- Captain Al Stewart, who had been head of Internal Affairs and had worked as a street supervisor and in the police laboratory
- Lieutenant Erwin L. Naasz
- Lieutenant Mark R. Richardson
- Detective Gary Fulton
- Detective Jerry W. Harper
- Patrol Officer Paul C. Holmes, who would be promoted to detective during the Ghostbusters investigation
- Patrol Officer Kenny Landwehr. In the course of the Ghostbusters investigation, Landwehr was promoted to detective. He has declined to be promoted above lieutenant because this would take him into pure management, and he has wanted to

> stay an active homicide investigator. Landwehr has also worked hard off the job. With Lieutenant Charles Liles, Landwehr started the Wichita police branch of the Special Olympics. Kenny Landwehr had a retarded brother and Charles Liles had a retarded son.

LaMunyon told each man that they had been picked as members of a Special Investigative Unit (SIU). They were not to tell *anyone* what they were working on. They were going to catch the BTK Strangler. If anyone disclosed the project, they would *all* be fired.

Soon there was a non–law enforcement member of the Ghostbusters, a man described by one of the detectives as "the most intelligent man I ever met," Wichita State University mathematics professor Dr. Stephen W. Brady. Stephen Brady earned his Ph.D. in mathematics at Indiana in 1968 and came to teach at Wichita State University for a short session. He was contacted by the Ghostbusters in 1984 because they were seeking a computer consultant. They wanted to take all the information and computerize it so it would be instantly accessible and searchable.

One question Brady was asked early in the investigation was "Could we computerize a fingerprint?" At this time Wichita had a human examiner who still individually compared each suspect fingerprint with the crime scene fingerprints/palmprints. This took an enormous amount of time. The police wanted to know whether this could be done automatically. Doc Brady thought so and after a little research told them about AFIS—automated fingerprint identification systems that were already being used in Japan, by Scotland Yard in England, and in some American cities including San Francisco.

Soon, Doc Brady was a familiar face in the police department, but outside of those in the SIU none knew what he was doing there. He was some kind of consultant and everyone called him "Doc."

Another full partner in the investigation was FBI supervisory special agent and profiler Roy Hazelwood.

Hazelwood has been the subject, author, or coauthor of several nonfiction books about profiling and law enforcement, and he has been the apparent model, in whole or in part, of law enforcement characters in several crime novels, including Michael Connelly's *The Poet* and *The Narrows*. Psychiatrist Park Dietz, M.D., says that Roy Hazelwood's influence is everywhere when it comes to investigating sexual crimes. From the military's Criminal Investigation Division to the FBI's Behavioral Science Unit, Hazelwood has been where the action is virtually his entire life.

Hazelwood reports that learning of Harvey Glatman's crimes changed his life. He realized that some crimes, particularly sex crimes, had nontraditional motives. It was Hazelwood who first suggested dividing criminals into organized and disorganized offenders, and he researched the claim that the criminal behavior antecedent triad was bed-wetting, fire starting, and animal abuse. Hazelwood's research showed that more commonly a serial rapist's background would reveal that in his youth or teen years he demonstrated alcohol abuse, shoplifting or other stealing, and assaulting adults.

The FBI sent their most experienced sex crimes profiler to Wichita to work on the BTK investigation.

Soon a psychologist was brought into the investigation's inner circle. Dr. John Allen was given a police radio call sign. He was simply and cryptically identified as "90." He had earned his Ph.D. at the University of Missouri and ended up in clinical practice in Wichita. He was initially hired in 1982 to counsel police. Because he was known and trusted, the Special Investigative Unit brought Dr. Allen in to consult with them on their BTK investigation.

After evaluating all the available information about BTK, Dr. Allen then had a meeting with the detectives that changed the course of the investigation. To this point the police had been looking for a crazy sex maniac. They had investigated a lot of men who had been picked up for sex crimes. They thought BTK would be a guy who one move away from in elevators or street corners because he "puts off bad vibes." They thought he would be a crazed Charlie Manson type. Whom had they looked at before? Guys who had intercourse with ducks. Guys who had a history of violence. Disturbed Vietnam veterans. Known or suspected rapists.

Quoting the title of Hervey Cleckley's classic text on psychopaths,

Dr. Allen said that BTK wore "the Mask of Sanity." The guy being sought was not the crazy guy one avoids, but the personable guy who was ingratiating. This guy talked with his victims. Kevin Bright said his sister's killer was dangerous and firm, but calm, almost gentle. Shirley Vian's children said they heard their mother talking calmly and in an apparently friendly way for a long time with the man who then bound, tortured, and strangled her.

Hazelwood's subsequent FBI research revealed that of thirty serial sex criminals, including serial killers, whom the FBI studied, seventeen of them had no prior criminal record. Before they were arrested for being serial killers or serial rapists, they had no arrests. BTK might well be someone with no prior arrest record. He might be a respected businessman, or a competent business manager, or a reliable employee. His friends, family, and colleagues might never suspect him.

These eleven men formed the nucleus of a secret team that hunted the BTK Strangler. At the beginning not even their wives or former partners knew what they were working on. With Chief Richard LaMunyon available as needed, and Captain Al Stewart at the helm, they dedicated themselves to their solemn task. They were going to protect society from one of its predators.

They were the hunters, and their prey was BTK.

Chapter 16

A New BTK Murder Is Uncovered

The Ghostbusters were located in two offices adjacent to Chief LaMunyon's office. At any time Captain Stewart had direct access to Chief LaMunyon without going through the secretary, and Chief LaMunyon had direct access to the Special Investigative Unit's office. This, plus the strictest secrecy and the fact that Al Stewart had been head of Internal Affairs, led to rampant speculation initially that the unit was investigating the police department itself. That all major crime reports and any unusual reports were to be filtered through the Ghostbusters unit first only increased the rumors.

One morning the SIU crew showed up at work, and on their main office door was the "no ghosts" symbol from the movie *Ghostbusters*. The movie had been released in June 1984, just prior to the formation of this group. An insult had been spreading around the department: "They are not making any visible arrests, so they must be busting ghosts."

Finally Chief LaMunyon quietly let it be known what the detectives were working on. The resentment of the rest of the department faded away as they understood that they were not the target of a major internal investigation.

The team was divided into different tasks. Two men worked primarily on the Otero case. They examined every possible permutation of the case. They looked at each victim as if each was the target. Was

Joseph the target and the rest were in the way? Was Julie the target? They investigated each possibility independently.

Were none of the Oteros the target of murder? Was this a crime with a conventional motive that got out of hand? If someone was accidentally strangled in a burglary in which each of the Oteros was gagged, did the killer then think that the rest must be murdered as well?

Were the previous residents the target? The couple's first initials were *B* and *T*, and while their last name was spelled beginning with the letter C, it was pronounced with a hard *K* sound—B-T-K. And the man was a relative of a notorious Wichita crime figure.

What if it was the wrong address? What if the Oteros were never intended to be the victims of crime? What if it was the wrong street or wrong number or some combination—south instead of north, 3803 instead of 803? Each lead was investigated, yet none came to anything productive.

Two other men similarly worked the Vian homicide. Was Shirley the intended target? Or was it Stephanie, the four-year-old? Bud? Stephen? Richard, the husband who was at work? Was it the wrong address? Conventional motive but things got out of hand? Was it the number? The detectives consulted numerologists and studied numerology. Phase of the moon? The detectives consulted astrologers and learned astrology. Each of the detectives had his horoscope cast. None of their avenues led anywhere.

Two others studied the Fox homicide. Was Nancy the intended target? Wrong address? They went through the same routine as the others.

Two others reviewed the Bright murder and the Williams break-in. Same speculations. Everything was looked at carefully, patiently, over the course of months.

They looked at every adult who lived within one quarter mile of each crime scene. Several had connections to more than one location. Some lived near one crime scene but moved to a location near another, or had a relative living close to another.

With the FBI's help the task force also examined every homicide in the country that struck them as similar to BTK.

And they found one.

On Tuesday, October 2, 1984, eighteen-year-old Karen Minkin was murdered at 1320 Lower Lane, New Orleans, Louisiana. She was strangled with electrical tape and a plastic bag over her head. The murderer was a nonsecretor PGM-1, as was BTK. Minkin had semen on her buttocks but was not sexually assaulted, and her keys were missing.

Police found many circumstances that would appear to indicate that this was a BTK kill. Those circumstances were:

1) Minkin's killer was PGM-1, as was BTK
2) Nonsecretor, same as BTK
3) Victimology same as BTK
4) College connection: victim was a college student
5) Key chain stolen
6) No forced entry
7) Victim was not raped
8) Sperm on buttocks, which was mentioned in a BTK letter

On investigation, the Ghostbusters learned that Suspect Barbara was in New Orleans at the time of Minkin's murder. But a large number of Wichitans were visiting New Orleans at the time of the murder because of a WSU–Tulane football game there on Thursday, October 4, 1984. Another suspect was also attending that football game. Ghostbusters investigators went to New Orleans, and they concluded that the Minkin murder was committed by BTK.

But only the Ghostbusters made this conclusion. The New Orleans police said that they didn't want to hear about any Wichita serial killer. They did not want people avoiding New Orleans because of a possible serial killer. They wanted people to come to New Orleans and spend their money at Mardi Gras.

And the New Orleans law enforcement community was angry that if this was true, then this was the second mass murderer from Kansas to haunt them in just over a decade. Beginning on December 31, 1972, and continuing until January 8, 1973, Emporia, Kansas, native Mark Essex operated as a tower sniper and arsonist in downtown New Orleans. Moving stealthily from building to building, he murdered nine, wounded ten, and started fires that destroyed an entire city block and caused millions of dollars' worth of property damage. Essex finally died when a military helicopter and assault team of hundreds of officers and soldiers attacked the building in which he had secluded himself. His autopsy revealed he had two hundred bullet wounds in his body. Essex is buried in an unmarked grave in Emporia.

This event was international news at the time but it was quickly forgotten and is little remembered now except for by those tormented by the episode. Professor Elliott Leyton wrote a chapter about Essex's crime spree in his seminal 1986 book *Hunting Humans: The Rise of the Modern Multiple Murderer*, and journalist Peter Hernon wrote an entire book about it in his 1978 *A Terrible Thunder: The Story of the New Orleans Sniper*.

New Orleans officials did not want to hear about another mass murderer from Kansas and demanded this be kept secret, which was fine with the Ghostbusters.

Back in Kansas, Captain Stewart personally took action. One of the suspects in the New Orleans murder was employed by Dillons, so Stewart met with the chairman of the Dillons grocery store chain. Stewart wanted Dillons to permit a detective to work undercover alongside their suspect. He did not tell Mr. Dillon what the man was suspected of doing, or that they were investigating BTK.

Permission was given.

An undercover detective—not one of the Ghostbusters—worked closely with the suspect for two weeks. Surreptiously, a biological sample was obtained. It did not eliminate him as a suspect, but did not confirm him. Under the circumstances, the Ghostbusters did not remove him from their suspect list, but they did not have enough evidence for further action. The surveillance operation was terminated on Suspect Darii.

Karen Minkin's father, meanwhile, was bitterly angry. He accused the New Orleans police of incompetence. He knew nothing of the Wichita Special Investigative Unit working on trying to solve his daughter's murder. He would later appear on an Oprah Winfrey program devoted to unsolved murders.

As it turned out, the Ghostbusters were wrong. In 1996, DNA from a convicted rapist would be matched with the Minkin sample found on her body in the New Orleans murder. The rapist was Minkin's apartment handyman at the time of her murder. On Monday, January 10, 2000, in New Orleans, Donald Langlois pled guilty to Karen Minkin's murder.

Chapter 17

Revisiting Old Cases

Following up old and new leads took the Ghostbusters everywhere. They went to see men in custody in prisons and in mental health facilities to conduct interviews, interrogations, and to obtain biological samples. They went to graveyards to confirm information and, apparently in some cases, to obtain biological samples. They followed up likely and unlikely tips.

Dr. Allen concluded that the man they sought was a narcissistic sexual sadist. After reviewing old reports from the 1970s, they realized that the man they sought might have been the subject of a report that was not in the BTK files, someone accused of a sex crime or false imprisonment or window peeping or impersonating an officer but not prosecuted, so they expanded their search to look through every report from the 1970s that might lead them to the killer.

Thinking of the break-ins, such as Nancy Fox telling her friends that she believed someone had been in her place and had gone through her hosiery and left her bed throw pillows on the floor, they also looked through old reports of break-ins and "check the residence" calls such as those Jim Carney and others investigated.

Then they checked with Southwestern Bell for any old reports of cut telephone lines. They found more reports than they expected, one at a significant address.

Aware of all the suspicious character calls during the 1970s, they went through those as well. That's when they put two reports together and found another BTK hit.

On the day of Shirley Vian's murder, March 17, 1977, a telephone line had been cut at a residence virtually across the street. The cut phone line belonged to Denise Cheryl of 1243 South Hydraulic. Shirley Vian lived at 1311 South Hydraulic.

Almost a year later, on February 14, 1978, Denise's roommate or former roommate (the report is unclear) at 1243 South Hydraulic made a suspicious character report of a man who came to the door and asked for Denise. The roommate told the man that Denise was not there, and the man departed, ignoring the roommate's questions.

This suspicious character matched a host of other suspicious-character and break-in reports that the Ghostbusters collected. This suspicious character also matches the description of the man Captain Klein had arrested in the Wichita Public Library days after BTK's letter was deposited there. Description: About five feet, ten inches tall. Medium build. Dark hair and mustache. Wore an olive drab military fatigue jacket.

Was this man BTK?

After a meeting with everyone evaluating the evidence, they concluded it was.

Shirley Vian was not his target. His target, Denise Cheryl, had not come home as expected. But he wanted a victim and therefore "chose at random with some pre-planning" to go across the street and use the "lost pet" ruse, and strangled Shirley Vian. He intended to murder the children the way he murdered the Otero family, including hanging Stephanie the way he hung Josie.

Later, at Anna Williams' home, when again the victim did not appear when he expected, he must have been furious. That led to the lamenting "Why didn't you appear" poem.

But now the Ghostbusters had to reconsider the entire sequence again. Were the Oteros the intended victims? Was there any other report of a cut phone line in that neighborhood? Had this guy intended to kill someone else and went to the Oteros instead?

And if he went out and immediately strangled someone else after missing Denise Cheryl, why didn't he also strangle someone else in the neighborhood after missing Anna Williams?

In fact, directly across the street from Anna Williams lived a woman named Laura Johnnie. Laura and Anna's houses were the only two on the street that looked exactly alike, including the fact that they were painted light green. After packages arrived from BTK in June 1979, some police had told Johnnie that she should move.

"Immediately leave your home and stay elsewhere. You are in danger," she was told. What she wasn't told was that she looked just like the woman in BTK's drawing.

Officers disagreed whether Laura Johnnie was a prospective BTK victim. However, when I interviewed her in 2004 she told me that, like Nancy Fox and prior to Anna Williams' break-in, she had an odd break-in. Nothing of value seemed to be taken, but her personal things, including her panty hose, had been gone through.

They also found an old report by "Sandy." As with Laura Johnnie, an officer told her that she had almost become a BTK victim in 1979.

One day that year, Sandy came home from work early. She usually didn't get home from work until after 5:00, but on this day she came home around 3:30. She saw a light in her basement. That was unusual, so she went to investigate. She found broken glass on the floor and semen all over her walls. She was soon convinced that BTK was the man who entered her home.

"The police, they told me he has a thing for lingerie, so he went through all my drawers and with the semen on my walls in my basement it was a repeated type of problem that he would do," said Sandy, who lived in the 300 block of Old Manor, just blocks from the Otero house. After this possible visit from BTK, Sandy never went back. She moved, changed her name, and bought a gun.

On March 26, 2004, KSNW featured an interview with a woman whom they showed only in silhouette and referred to only as "Sandy." "I refuse to be his victim," she said to reporter Dana Hertneky. "He's a scary man. There's something definitely wrong with him."

She had also provided a similar interview to Chris Frank at KAKE-TV on Thursday, March 25. Chris Frank introduced me to Sandy at the KAKE-TV studios. I later conducted telephone interviews with Sandy.

With Denise Cheryl's and Karen Minkin's cases, the Ghostbusters had discovered two more cases where they concluded BTK had attempted murder and committed murder. With Laura Johnnie and Sandy's cases, they found two more where it was always considered possible that BTK had made a break-in.

With Sandy's case they had also had a description of a car.

* * *

Dr. Stephen Brady's background led him to think of this as what in mathematics is called an "inverse problem." Inverse problems commonly include operations such as reconstructing aircraft and automobile crashes. With this crash result, what must have happened before? Here are the pieces of the aircraft, they were found in these separate places, and we know that before they fit together in these places. What must have happened during the interim? Often, the answer cannot be made with precision. Sometimes, however, there can be a helpful answer.

In general, this way of thinking helped the investigation. What do we know? We know that while in Wichita BTK's letters and poems and drawings were received in Wichita in October 1974, January 1978, February 1978, and June 1979. BTK made telephone calls in October 1974 to Don Granger and in December 1977 to the operator. BTK was known to have been at the Oteros, Dillons Central & Oliver, the downtown library, a payphone at Central and St. Francis, the Vian, Fox, and Williams homes, and one or more postal pick-up locations, and he was believed to have been at Denise Cheryl's and possibly Laura Johnnie's homes. BTK drove the Oteros' and Wegerles' cars. BTK made photocopies at the machines on the mezzanine of the main public library or possibly in Jardine Hall at WSU, and in the basement of the WSU life sciences building. The Ghostbusters hoped that sufficient evidence, logical reasoning, and detective intuition would lead them to the killer.

The Ghostbusters had to develop a useful computer program that would track all the information, cross-reference the information, and make it accessible. Dr. Brady provided the greatest possible help in doing this.

Computers in the early and mid-1980s were still mostly expensive mainframes. Home computers were generally weak versions such as the Commodore 64. Although precise information is still classified, the Ghostbusters apparently used a midi-computer. It was much more powerful than a desktop but not as powerful as a mainframe. They did use mainframe computers for some work. They had to use computers that could process the information they obtained.

For example, from Wichita State University they obtained computer lists of students. That information came on a floppy disk with the program WSU used. The Ghostbusters had to access a suitable computer with a suitable program. Similarly, they obtained book check-out information from the Wichita Public Library. Therefore, they had to locate and confidentially use a compatible system. Because they did not have enough evidence to obtain court-issued search warrants, they simply asked WSU and the Wichita Public Library for the information, and it was willingly turned over.

After a time they created an enormous flow chart that they posted on the wall. I have seen the chart and made detailed notes. The chart was fascinating in what it showed.

They pored over reports of old suspects again, from all walks of life.

They looked at suspects who worked for Southwestern Bell Telephone, at Dillons, at Gas Service Company employees.

They again looked at everyone who had enrolled in P.J. Wyatt's folklore courses, at engineering students, especially aeronautical engineering students, at Wichita State University faculty, staff, and vendors.

They checked out plumbers, window blind company employees and customers, inmates/patients at Topeka State and Larned State Mental Hospitals, especially those who had committed sex offenses, present and past.

They followed up every lead and prioritized their investigation. Suspects were stacked from "Very Good" to "Good" to "Other" to "Eliminated."

They re-interviewed Kevin Bright, Denise Cheryl, Stephen Relford, Shirley Vian's oldest son, more people who were suspects or possible witnesses in Karen Minkin's murder in New Orleans.

They obtained a profile from the FBI, which I presume is by Roy Hazelwood. The FBI profiler concluded that BTK (1) is a white male, (2) he is still killing, (3) he has a military background, (4) he has some type of Wichita State University connection, and (5) he lived close to his victims.

They obtained a census of everyone who lived in Wichita. They looked at every male who lived within a quarter mile of each victim. They investigated all those who had moved away from Wichita in 1979, especially those who had been in the military.

They still didn't have enough, but they were about to learn of a new investigative tool that would expand their search.

* * *

Doc Brady's brother was a pathologist living in England, and from him Doc Brady learned about a technology newly developed in England in an attempt to solve a murder. It was called DNA testing.

The Wichita police had been using the best biological testing available, which was the phosphoglucomutase (PGM) grouping test. From this it could be determined that BTK was of a blood and tissue type possessed by only 6 percent of males. This narrowed the possible suspects down to approximately 1 in 20. The DNA testing promised to narrow the field down even more than a fingerprint would.

On February 28, 1953, two British researchers, Dr. James Watson and Francis Crick, had walked into a pub in Cambridge and announced, "We have solved the secret to life." It is DNA, deoxyribonucleic acid, and it is responsible for life and the replication of life.

In 1984, at Leicester University in England, Dr. Alec Jeffreys was studying evolution. He took a blood sample and fragmented its DNA molecules with enzymes. An electrical field separated the fragments, and capillary action blotted them on to a nylon membrane. Portions of the DNA were made radioactive and X-rayed. He had thought he might see one or two major bands, but he saw a series of black and gray bands that resembled the new computer-laser bar codes. He instantly realized that with the ability to look at large numbers of genetic markers, he could identify individuals.

The first legal matter Dr. Jeffreys' procedure was used in was a paternity-maternity determination of a child. The case was brought by the British immigration department. They thought that a youngster was not the child of the purported parents, but DNA testing proved that he was.

The Wichita police wanted to try doing DNA testing, though it took some time before Captain Stewart found a laboratory in the U.S. that was capable of confidentially conducting DNA testing. The first man tested in the United States in a criminal investigation was a Wichita police officer. He was not BTK.

The Ghostbusters set out to eliminate the remaining suspects one at a time, using DNA testing. This involved crosscountry trips collecting blood and saliva samples from the suspects.

Captain Stewart said, "This wasn't a walk-in, 'I'm a cop,' type of thing. It was all voluntary. There was no coercion or force. We simply told them what we needed and asked them if they'd be willing to cooperate."

When all the tests were done, twelve names remained. Five of them were on the suspect list because they had refused to provide hair and blood samples. The other seven were on the list because their samples had been checked in the lab and revealed them to be nonsecretors.

The Ghostbusters did not agree on which of the twelve suspects was their man. Each had their own favorite. According to Stewart, "We tried 100,000 theories. We checked house numbers, the victim's length of residency, the phases of the moon."

They had tried science and they had tried superstition. They used the new technology of computers and of DNA. They had not found their man. What was left to try?

The strain of the intense but unproductive investigation began to wear on the men. In no case was this greater than that of Ghostbusters captain Al Stewart. As a teenager in Dodge City, Al was a hell-raiser. After getting married and moving to Wichita, he was living in an almost totally black neighborhood when a USAF KC-135 Stratotanker 17513 jet crashed two blocks away from his house. He immediately joined in helping the police and fire crews as they engaged in rescue and firefighting. The experience captivated Al Stewart and inspired him to apply to the police department.

Mature, brave, and totally straightforward, Stewart rapidly rose in the ranks and made sergeant after only a few years. After ten years, he was made the lieutenant in charge of the WPD Internal Affairs division. In the early 1980s, when home computers became available, Al Stewart was among the first to learn DOS and begin programming his home computer.

Al Stewart was working in the police laboratory in 1984 when he was picked by Chief LaMunyon to head the Ghostbusters investigation.

Stewart lived the BTK case. When he was off duty and at home, he used his eldest son, Roger, as sounding board for his investigation ideas. His wife, Leyola, also learned a lot about the investigation by its effects on Al. Leyola had long dark hair, but when Al took over the investigation, Al made her cut her hair short. None of the women BTK killed had short hair. He also began to always accompany his wife when she went grocery shopping, which he had never done before.

Stewart nailed his back windows and doors shut, and the door to the garage. The house and cars were always locked up tight, which they had never been before.

Stewart began sleeping with a loaded handgun under the bed. He slept lightly rather than soundly.

One night Stewart woke and heard footsteps in the house. He had imagined hearing footsteps several times, but this time they were real. He quietly pulled out his gun and went to his bedroom door. The footsteps were down at the end of his hallway. Al was convinced that BTK was in the hall. He leapt into the hallway in a crouch, prepared to fire, both hands on his pistol.

The gun was aimed just over the head of his eight-year-old son, Kirk. Kirk had got up to get a drink of water.

Stewart's face contorted in grief and pain. He had almost shot his own child. Leyola said that Al knew then that it was time for a change in the operation.

The next morning he called everyone together and told them what happened. He asked how many others were sleeping with a handgun under their pillow or otherwise at hand.

Every hand was raised.

Several of the guys had been trying to "get inside the head" of BTK. All of them had disturbing dreams or insomnia. All had chronic suspicions, some bordering on paranoia. They had a talk about their situation. Al Stewart called a temporary halt to the investigation. He contacted the police chaplain, Reverend Bob Ely. Each member of the team spent some time in counseling with the minister.

After two weeks they resumed the investigation. Later, they each had a talk with a psychologist. For all their probing, they were drawing a blank. All of their exhaustive work was only leading to exhaustion.

When Captain Stewart thought of the spy satellites that periodically took pictures of the local Air Force base as part of arms control agreements, he was excited. Perhaps one would show a car repeatedly driving by Nancy Fox's home, just a couple of miles north of the base. However, when he tried to obtain the photos from the military authorities his inquiries were rejected, and not always politely. He was told by all that the information was highly classified and could not be shared.

Finally, Stewart was granted an appointment with the highest accessible authority, apparently a director-general in the Pentagon, probably a member of the National Reconnaissance Office. Although the National Reconnaissance Office had existed for as long as the spy satellites it monitored, it wasn't until September 1992 the government would acknowledge its existence. Stewart never told his family the name of the man he met with, referring to him only as "the general."

Stewart suspected that the general was going to give him the brushoff like all the other military officials Stewart had talked to so he decided to try a completely different approach. As the general explained step by step why the U.S. Government satellite photos could not be shared with a local police department, Stewart was pleasant and agreeable.

But while the general was talking, Stewart took the heartbreaking BTK crime scene photos out of his briefcase and began to set them one by one, like playing cards, on the general's desk. He also placed there photos of the victims taken when the victims were living, smiling, engaging in the joys of life.

The general stopped speaking. He looked at the photo of nine-year-old Joey Otero sprawled beside his bunk bed, a cord around his neck. He looked at the photo of Josie Otero, half-naked and hanging from a pipe in the basement. The general looked at the other photos, then gathered them up and handed them back to Stewart. Neither man spoke.

Then Stewart leaned forward and said, "This is what is continuing in Wichita. This is what I'm trying to stop. Can you help us?"

The general quietly said, "I'll see what I can do."

Photos were provided, but did not provide the needed break.

After more than two years and more than $500,000, the Ghostbusters investigation still had not captured BTK. They had traveled the country. They had used the newest resources of behavioral and medical science with psychology, profiling, and DNA. Finally the authorities wanted to know what they had bought with their money.

They held what detectives described to me as a "dog and pony show." Their secret presentation was to a group of local luminaries that included elected officials, representatives from the district attorney's office, and representatives from the city manager's office, including the new city manager Chris Cherches. The Ghostbusters told the truth. They didn't have BTK. If that was not BTK's fingerprint on the chair they found at the Oteros', they might never be able to obtain a conviction of BTK for the murder of the Oteros due to a number of unexpected problems. They believed BTK had murdered Karen Minkin in New Orleans, but they couldn't prove it. They believed BTK had murdered Kathryn Bright, but they couldn't prove it. They believed that they could get a conviction on Nancy Jo Fox's murder. They could probably get a conviction on Shirley Vian's murder. They were unsure about convictions for attempted murder on the other break-ins, including Anna Williams, Denise Cheryl, and Laura Johnnie. But they believed that they could catch him. They wanted more time.

They did not get more. The next morning the Ghostbusters were summarily disbanded and each member reassigned. Some remain angry about that to this day. They believe that they could have solved the case if they had been allowed to finish.

According to the *Seattle Times*, Detective Gary Fulton later said, "I think we gave it the best shot we had. We hit it for two years and we couldn't put it together. I look at the unsolved case as a black mark on my record. It makes you feel you're a loser. You want this guy bad. You want him to pay for what he did. I'd give anything to wake up and read he's been picked up. I don't care how old he is."

Al Stewart's family told me that Stewart retired immediately after the Ghostbusters investigation ended because he was angry that the investigation was disbanded without Chief LaMunyon consulting or notifying him in any way. He had his twenty years in. He could retire, and so he did.

On April 27, 1985, Marine N. Hedge, 53, was abducted from her Park City home. Her body was found eight days later, seven miles away, in a ditch along a dirt road.

Park City police initially investigated this as a missing-person case. Marine—a petite (100 pounds), attractive woman—had been last seen on Saturday, April 27. Capt. Steve Megerdichian said a telephone line to Hedge's home had been cut and that her front door was found open by relatives who went to look for her. Marine also had not shown up at her job at Wesley Medical Center, where she worked in the coffee shop as the second-shift supervisor. Marine had been the Cal Ripken of coffee shop workers. Before her disappearance, Hedge hadn't missed a day of work in thirteen years. When she didn't show up for work, her supervisor called her church, to see if she was there, then called the police.

Her 1976 Monte Carlo (same make of car as Vicki Wegerle's) was found in a Wichita shopping-center parking lot the following Thursday. It was found a little after four o'clock in the afternoon. The car was in the southwest corner of Brittany Center at 21st and Woodlawn. A blanket and bedspread were found in the trunk. There was mud on the wheels, and weeds and evergreen needles in the trunk. Police believed it had recently been taken for a ride along dirt roads in the country. The lower left corner of the windshield was broken. Police intensified their search for Marine.

Marine—who had become a widow the previous June when her husband, a retired Beechcraft worker, died—was last seen at one o'clock on Saturday morning at her home at 6254 Independence, by her longtime friend Gerald Porter, with whom she'd played bingo that night. Marine was in fine spirits when he left her, Gerald said. Six hours later, Marine's car was gone, her phone line had been cut, and her front door was left open (it was always kept locked). Marine had at least one child, a grown son, who was living in the state of Washington at the time of her disappearance.

On the day after Marine disappeared, her purse was found by a woman who took it home. Unaware of the purse's importance, the woman did not report the finding of the purse until that Friday, almost a full week after Marine had disappeared. The purse was found in a ditch near 143rd Street East and 37th Street North. None of Marine's identification remained in the purse, but there were papers inside that proved the purse to be Marine's. Police said that a towel with tiny specks of blood was found near the purse, but they didn't know if it had anything to do with Marine. On Saturday, one week after Marine disappeared, the Civil Air Patrol helped in the search with air surveillance over Park City.

Eight days after Marine disappeared, at 2:30 p.m. on the second Sunday since she had last been seen, her body was found—nude, decomposing, near a dirt road in northeast Sedgwick County. The body was found in a drainage ditch near a hedgerow of trees on 53rd North, about three-fourths of a mile west of Greenwich Road—between Webb and Greenwich.

According to Park City Police Chief Ace Van Wey, who discovered the body, a knotted pair of panty hose lay next to the body, which had been hidden by tall grass and an evergreen tree.

Van Wey described how he came upon the body: "This area is known as a dumping ground for bodies. On the way back to 143rd Street, I was driving by here real slow when I thought I saw a shirt in the trees. The cloth was a piece of curtain, but nearby I spotted what was the body of a dead dog, some debris, and then a foot. Under the tree and some cut grass was the woman's body, lying on her back, her head near a box culvert and the panty hose near her head. She was not bound. Although the body was only a few feet from the road, it was pretty well hid."

Marine's hands weren't tied, but a knotted pair of panty hose was found nearby. The autopsy, performed by county pathologist William Eckert, showed Marine had been strangled by hand and not with the knotted panty hose found next to her body.

A spent slug and cartridge were found on the road bed a few feet from the body, but those may have had no connection with the case.

According to Assistant District Attorney Roger Skinner, the decomposition was consistent with the body having been in the ditch for a week.

Police believed that the killer used Marine's car to transport her body. Re-creations of the drive revealed that the killer could have driven from Marine's home to the ditch where she was dumped and then to the parking lot where he dropped off the car, in just thirty minutes.

In addition to Park City police, two Sedgwick County homicide detectives were assigned to the case. The panty hose aspect of the crime seemed to be a signature of the BTK Strangler, not the strangling by hand. So police were unable to make a conclusive determination.

Chapter 18

Deaths by Strangling

On Thursday, September 16, 1986, just before noon, Bill Wegerle was returning to his Wichita home at 2404 West 13th Street North for lunch with his wife, Vicki, and twenty-five-month-old son, Brandon. About a block away from his house, he thought he passed the car his wife drove, a 1978 gold Monte Carlo. "Nah," he thought, "must be another car that's very similar." But moments later when he pulled into his driveway, his wife's car was gone. He entered his house, puzzled.

He found his son sitting on the floor crying. His wife was on the bedroom floor, bound at the ankles and wrists—and strangled. He tore the bindings from her and began CPR. He called 911 and asked for an ambulance because his wife was not breathing.

The ambulance and fire-rescue crews entered and began advanced life support. Bill Wegerle told the first officer to arrive, Richard Vinroe, what he saw. He had seen his car driving west on Thirteenth, and he thought the man who attacked his wife must have been driving it. He also reported having recently seen a brown van he thought was suspicious. He had seen the van at the Indian Hills Shopping Center across the street from his home, and he had seen the van in the parking lot of the apartment complex where he had been working. He wanted the police to find his car and the brown van.

The KAKE-TV crew photographed emergency personnel performing CPR as Vicki was moved to the ambulance. They also caught Bill

Wegerle carrying his son, Brandon, out to the police car to go to the emergency room. After Vicki was declared dead, Bill grieved.

Bill Wegerle left his son with his sister, Glenda. Then he spent the rest of the day at the police station. He was pleased to learn that at 12:10 p.m. Vicki's Monte Carlo had been found only a couple of blocks away, in the 1300 block of North Edwards Street next to Johnson's Garden Center.

The police went to the bank on the north side of the street, catty-corner from where the car was found. They examined the bank's surveillance photos. I have heard two different stories about what was discovered. One is that the driver was just outside the camera's range; the other that the driver was seen, but the image was so far away that it was a useless blur. Whoever it was, he was the killer, and his escape was lucky.

Brandon told his aunt Glenda that a stranger had come in the house. Bill kept repeating his same story to the detectives, including Detective John Dotson, and Detective John Blevins.

Meantime, the Ghostbusters were consulted. Could this be a BTK hit?

They were unanimous in agreement: No. That day, they gathered at 3:00 p.m. in the police station for Al Stewart's retirement party.

His last homicide investigation was his brief consultation on Vicki Wegerle's murder. He concluded the husband did it.

At 8:00 that evening Detective John Dotson accused Bill Wegerle of murdering his wife. At first Bill did not understand what Dotson was saying. Bill had been repeating his story about the suspicious brown van. Why was he being accused?

The police had confirmed that Vicki had returned from school and church and made at least two telephone calls by mid-morning. The police said that sometime after that Bill returned, strangled her, and then moved the car; or he moved the car, then strangled her. Either way, they wanted a confession.

Bill became very angry. Why were they wasting time with this nonsense? They needed to find the brown van. They needed to find the man who murdered his wife. This circuitous conversation repeated several times and finally, furious and bitter, Bill Wegerle announced he was leaving. "Am I under arrest?" When the police admitted he was not in custody, Bill walked out of the homicide office and out of the police station.

When he told his sister what had happened, she was horrified. Brandon had told her that a stranger had come in the house. She knew Bill was innocent. The stranger had been the killer.

No one in the family had any money. They had little education. They knew no one of influence or power. Glenda was a secretary. Bill was a maintenance man. They knew that Bill needed a good defense attorney. Bill was filled with the anxiety that the police might arrest him at any moment. The next day they hired Steve Robison, the former Sedgwick County lead trial prosecutor.

Because the police were looking only at Bill as a suspect and were not investigating others, as soon as he had the money Bill asked Steve Robison whom he should hire as a private detective to investigate the murder of his wife. Steve Robison recommended P.I. Emery Goad, who had been an investigator for the attorney general's office and was recognized as one of the best in the state.

Vicki Wegerle had been a woman who was happy with her life and her prospects. Her ten-year-old daughter, Stephanie, was a splendid little girl. Her son, Brandon, was a typical twenty-five-month-old boy. Her husband was self-employed as an apartment maintenance man. His contract work income varied, but apartment buildings were always in need of maintenance, and Bill always made enough to provide them a living.

Vicki attended St. Andrew's Lutheran Church. Reverend Arno Meyer said that Vicki enjoyed babysitting at church events. According to Assistant Pastor Robert Winslow, Vicki was the nursery supervisor for Asbury United Methodist Church, four blocks west and two blocks north of her home. She scheduled volunteers to take care of children during church functions.

Shortly before 9:00 a.m. on September 16 Vicki had taken Stephanie to school at OK Elementary, where she attended the fifth grade. The school's principal, Devin Stahl, said that Vicki was active in the school's Parent-Teacher Association. Vicki was also a Girl Scout leader. She had no known enemies and everyone described her as nice.

Neighbors report that around 10:15 a.m. they heard dogs near the

Wegerle home barking. One neighbor said she saw Vicki's car pull out of her driveway around 10:15 a.m. She did not see who was driving.

At Vicki Wegerle's autopsy, it was discovered that she had some tissue under her fingernails. This was carefully preserved, but it was not DNA tested.

At 2:50 p.m. on Sunday, Halloween 1987, a young woman was found almost nude and stabbed to death in a sand pit in an area zoned to be an industrial park, near the corner of Thirty-third Street and Hillside. She was found facedown by two fishermen. Her hands had been bound behind her back with her bra.

No weapon was found at the sandpit, and some of the woman's clothes were missing from the scene, said Captain John Dotson. Unfortunately for investigators, several vehicles had driven over the murder scene before detectives could inspect the ground for tire tracks.

It took police several days just to identify the body. An autopsy was performed on "Jane Doe" late Sunday. It was determined that the body was of a white woman between her late teens and late twenties, five feet, six inches tall, about 135 pounds, and with brown hair and brown eyes. She had been stabbed dozens of times in the throat and chest. Her throat was slashed. Her carotid artery and trachea had been severed by the frenzied attack.

"There was a five-point star [pentagram] tattooed on the outside of her right ankle," Dotson said, "and she was wearing two gold rings: a friendship ring with clasping hands on her left ring finger and another gold ring on her right little finger. The victim was also wearing a silver chain-link bracelet on her right wrist and silver dangling earrings with little stars at the ends of silver strands."

The description was broadcast over Wichita television and radio. On November 3, it was determined that the victim was fifteen-year-old Shannon Marie Olson, a.k.a. Shannon Earl. She was identified by her stepfather, John Allen Earl, who heard of the description from a friend who listened to a TV broadcast, police said.

Her mother, Jacqueline Earl, told police that Shannon was uncontrollable. She had dropped out of Southeast High School just after the school year started. In addition, Shannon had stopped going home very much. Although her mother and stepfather had moved into a new home in the 1100 block of South Hydraulic Street two weeks before the murder, they had not seen much of Shannon during that time. She preferred to stay with friends. That was why she was missing for so long before she was identified.

"She was given a pretty free rein," said Major Jerry Bullins of the police investigations unit.

Shannon's young friends confirmed to reporters that she "lived a little loosely and partied a little too much."

When asked if his daughter was sexually active, her stepfather said, "I know she experienced the joys of womanhood, but kids do a lot of things these days a lot earlier."

Police traced Shannon's last known movements. She was last seen when visiting a girlfriend's home in southeast Wichita about 11:00 p.m. She told her friends that she was going out to buy some liquor—but she left the house without her purse.

Chief LaMunyon said that they were investigating the possible "magic cults" angle to the crime. Students at Southeast High School told police that there was an occult group in which Shannon was deeply involved.

"She just got into the devil worshipping thing way too far," said one friend. "I was in the group for a while, but I got out because it kind of scared me. Shannon said she wanted out a few weeks ago, but they didn't want to let her out. I really believe they had something to do with what happened to her."

Shannon's stepfather, a mechanic with the Kansas Air National Guard, said the tattoo had nothing to do with devil worshipping.

"It [the pentagram tattoo] was just something her and a bunch of friends did a while back," said John Earl. "Shannon had nothing to do with this devil worshipping stuff. If her death had anything to do with the occult, it was because they grabbed her or something, not because she was involved in it."

The victim had lived only two blocks from Shirley Vian. Despite the fact that all the known BTK victims had been killed and left inside their own homes, this Halloween case rekindled BTK awareness in the city.

On December 31, 1987, Mary K. Fager—a wife and mother of two and close friend with Boeing security supervisor Carol Maxwell—returned to her upper-middle-class brick home in east Wichita at 7015 East Fourteenth Street North. She had been visiting relatives in Emporia,

Kansas, for the past two and a half days. She was horrified to find her husband and two daughters murdered inside their home. The Fagers had been married for eleven years. Mary had been previously married.

Her husband, thirty-seven-year-old Melvin Philip Fager, a financial analyst at Boeing Military Airplane Co., had been shot in the back twice. Both shots were from close range, one of them from point-blank range. One bullet pierced his heart and passed through his chest. Philip, as he was known, was found just inside the front door and had apparently been shot immediately after entering the house because he died while still wearing his overcoat. He was found lying on his back with his feet toward the door. The weapon was a handgun, most likely a .38 caliber.

There were no signs that the house had been broken into. The front door was locked when Mary Fager arrived at the house.

Mary's two daughters were discovered dead in the basement. When Mary entered the basement she found the lid on the hot tub down. Lifting the lid, she found both of her daughters, Kelli, sixteen, and Sherri, nine, dead in the tub. Semen was found in the tub.

Sherri had been bound at the wrists and ankles—her hands behind her back—with black electrical tape. Sherri had been found wearing light clothes, and the older girl was found nude. No marks were found on Kelli's body and she had not been bound.

On January 2, 1988, Sedgwick County coroner Robert Daniels said that Sherri had been nearly strangled with half-inch-wide black electrician's tape, then put facedown into the hot tub's ninety-two-degree water.

The tape around Sherri's neck was identical with that binding her wrists and ankles. Daniels emphasized that Sherri was very close to death when she was placed in the water. "There might have been enough of a wisp of life to take a breath [in the water] and drown," Daniels said.

Coroners were unable to determine the precise time of the deaths. Their best estimates were that the three members of the Fager family had died approximately twenty-four hours before Mary returned.

Captain John Dotson said, "I think it would be reasonable to say there was resistance. There is evidence in the home that something occurred."

He refused to say which victims resisted, or what form that resistance took. Dotson said that twelve to eighteen detectives had been working on the case.

The Wichita Eagle had the possible BTK connection on the front page near the beginning of the story. Police acknowledged the similarities between this case and the murders of the Oteros back in 1974 but downplayed any possible connection between the murders of the Fagers and the BTK Strangler. "At this point we don't think so," Chief LaMunyon said. "I don't think there's any connection whatsoever. It would be very unusual if it was, but by the same turn we have to look at it as a possibility."

Sherri was a third grader who had transferred for the 1987–88 school year to Jefferson Elementary School after a year each at College Hill and Kellogg elementary schools. Kelli was a junior at Southeast High School, where Charlie Otero had attended.

During the early hours of the investigation, one suspect was former WPD officer Charles "Chuck" Dearing, who lived relatively nearby. Dearing was reportedly a close friend of Mary Fager.

The Fagers' car was missing, as was the workman who had almost completed construction of their new sunroom, thirty-three-year-old William Thomas Butterworth. At first it was feared that Butterworth had also been a victim of the multiple murder. The car was a gray 1983 Volkswagen Rabbit four-door with a diesel engine and Sedgwick County license E353. A description of the car was distributed nationwide.

Butterworth's own vehicle, a van, was found on New Year's Day with the keys in the ignition seven blocks from the Fagers' house, in the parking lot of the McDonald's restaurant at Thirteenth and Woodlawn. Nothing unusual turned up in the search of Butterworth's van.

But Butterworth was not a victim. In fact, he had taken the Fagers' car and had fled the scene. Butterworth was arrested by sheriffs in Martin County, Florida, outside a Howard Johnson's motel in the town of Stuart on Sunday afternoon, January 3.

One of Butterworth's relatives reported to Wichita police that Butterworth was on the phone with his wife, Shelly. The call was subsequently traced. Wichita police teletyped the Martin County sheriff's office at about 1:00 p.m. that a man wanted in connection with a triple homicide was staying at a local motel.

Sheriffs responded immediately. Lieutenant Richard Youngblood was heading south on U.S. 1 and almost directly in front of the motel when he heard the radio report. He pulled into the motel parking lot and arrested Butterworth.

He was on a pay phone in the motel's parking lot, still talking with his wife when he was apprehended at 1:10 p.m. The Fagers' car was parked on a nearby street, and the car keys were in Butterworth's pocket. He had been driving the missing car and was in possession of the family credit cards.

According to Lieutenant Youngblood, Butterworth didn't say anything when Youngblood approached and placed him under arrest. He looked surprised and then hung up the phone. Butterworth had not checked into the Howard Johnson's motel.

He was unarmed when apprehended and did not resist arrest. He was wearing light slacks, a sport shirt, and a pair of loafers. According to sheriffs he appeared uninjured and was "very quiet." He had $1.45 in his pocket.

The district attorney since his 1980 election, Clark Owens, charged Bill Butterworth with the Fagers' murders. Assigned as prosecutors in this sensational high-profile trial were two tough assistant district attorneys, Judy Fowler and Julia Craft.

Shelly Butterworth, of 8313 East Morris in Wichita, said she thought her husband was a victim. After hearing of his arrest, she said, "We're just very glad he's alive."

According to Lieutenant Landwehr, Butterworth told the police that he went to the house to continue the construction work, and discovered the father's body. He went on to say that he had heard some noise in the house and fled in the family's car. Butterworth claimed he had a total blank of the events that had occurred.

"I lost track of what was going on," he reportedly said.

He had no idea why he had fled to Florida, since he had no personal ties in that state. Investigation verified that there was no obvious reason for Butterworth to flee to that state.

The semen found in the Fagers' hot tub did not match Butterworth's DNA.

A check discovered that Butterworth did not have a police record, and initial reaction was that Butterworth was "not a likely" murder suspect. Friends said they had never known him to lose his temper.

Others said that he was the sort of person who would always go out of his way to do a favor for somebody.

Butterworth grew up in southern California and served in the military in Colorado after graduation from high school. He moved to Wichita about ten years before the Fager murders and had been in the construction business ever since. He was the father of six-month-old twins and a three-year-old.

Until 1986 Butterworth had been an employee of Sunshine Rooms of Kansas, a Wichita firm specializing in add-on sunrooms for businesses. When the firm stopped distributing solariums and switched to manufacturing them, Butterworth opened a firm called Sunshine Rooms of Wichita to distribute and install the solariums. Reports were that, in the weeks before the murders, Butterworth had been experiencing financial problems.

In January 1988, only days after the Fager killings, a man claiming to be BTK wrote a letter to Mary Fager. It read, in part: "I did not kill your family, but I admire the work."

The FBI would not publicly verify that the letter came from BTK, but sources within the Wichita Police Department said they were certain it was from him. One policeman said, "It made the hair stand up on the back of my neck."

It had been nine years since BTK had last been heard from, when he sent letters and packages following the 1979 break-in at Anna Williams' house.

In 2004 interviews with me, retired interim chief Kerry Crisp, retired BTK lead detective Mike McKenna, and retired BTK lead detective Bernie Drowatzky each said that they had concluded the letter was authentic. One said it was typed on the same typewriter as BTK's other letters. Other sources also verify that the letter was believed to be from BTK.

The state's case against Butterworth focused on witnesses who had seen Butterworth's van at the Fager home on the day of the killings and on the fact that Butterworth drove to Florida in the Fagers' car.

Prosecutors hit on inconsistencies in Butterworth's account and pointed to items missing when he was arrested in Florida—his watch, wallet, and wedding ring, and parking stickers from the Fager vehicle—as evidence of an attempt to cover up the crimes.

At the trial, Butterworth repeated his story that he had stumbled on the bodies of Sherri and Phillip Fager in their home, where he was building a sun room, on December 30. He testified that he heard a noise, possibly a stifled scream, from the basement before he fled in terror and shame. He swore that four days later he snapped back to reality in Stuart, Florida, after hearing a broadcast on the Fagers' car radio.

Butterworth's defense attorney Richard Ney asked to see the letter BTK had written to Mary Fager. After arguments from prosecution and defense, Judge Monte Deer examined the letter *in camera* (alone), then announced in open court that he was sealing the letter. He ruled that the letter had nothing to do with the case being tried, but it was important to an ongoing investigation in a separate case.

All available witnesses in the BTK case had been hypnotized to facilitate recall. Most had been witnesses to the December 9, 1977, telephone call and included the firefighter and bus passengers. Kevin Bright was another hypnotized witness. Hypnosis was still admissible evidence in Kansas state courts provided certain steps were taken. They have ruled that "hypnotically refreshed" memories are admissible if the trial court determines that "substantial safeguards" have been utilized to prove an adequate record for evaluating the procedure.

Dr. Robert Pace, a psychologist experienced in hypnosis, was asked by Richard Ney if he would attempt to help Bill Butterworth more fully recover his memory of the events and aftermath of the Fager family murders. Butterworth participated in twenty hypnosis sessions with Dr. Pace over a period of four months.

His "hypnotically refreshed" memory story is as follows:

The morning the Fagers were murdered Butterworth worked at their home, then went to lunch. When he returned he thought that Kelli Fager and her boyfriend—reportedly a young man who had worked with Kelli at McDonald's—were in the solarium, possibly in the hot tub. He felt uncomfortable and decided to leave until they departed. He did not see them, he said, but he saw and felt movement in the solarium and saw the glass was covered with condensation.

He went to the Wichita Mall, where Nancy Fox had worked, and at Montgomery Ward bought some new short-sleeve shirts. While there, he had a conversation with an acquaintance, a retired Wichita police captain, William Dotts, who verified the conversation and approximate time. The captain verified that he did not notice anything unusual about Bill Butterworth at that time and said that Butterworth did not appear shaken or nervous.

Butterworth reports that he returned to the Fagers' residence at about 4:30 p.m. He said the lights were off. He used the key he had been provided to open the door to the solarium. He said he saw Sherri Fager floating face-up in the spa hot tub. He felt her, and she was dead. He went into the house and found Phillip Fager lying dead on the floor near the front door. He said he saw Mr. Fager's keys lying next to him and he picked them up.

He then heard a noise and went to the door that led to the basement. He realized that someone was in there. This frightened him terribly.

He went outside to his van and tried to start it but the keys did not work. He realized he was trying to use the Fagers' keys. He went to his van and retrieved his new clothes, then used the keys to drive away in the Fagers' car.

He thought that Kelli and a murderer were in the basement. He felt cowardice and shame for running away. He thought that if he had been braver he might have been able to save Kelli.

The prosecution hammered away at Butterworth's story. They argued that the evidence supported a different interpretation of events. They believed that Bill Butterworth was lying. They accused Bill Butterworth of murdering the Fagers. They never overtly accused Butterworth of attempting or having sexual touching with Kelli Fager, but the foreman of the jury, Ron Blasi, said that was the message the jury received.

The prosecution's version of events was this: That morning, December 30, 1987, Bill Butterworth kissed his wife goodbye on his way to work at the Fagers' house. On his way there he stopped at his bank and at a Winchell's Donut shop, where he leisurely drank coffee. Sometime before 10:00 a.m. he bound Sherri Fager and drowned her in the hot tub. When Mr. Fager returned he shot him in the back, killing him around 12:30 p.m. Later in the afternoon Butterworth went to Montgomery Ward, bought some clothes, and had a casual conversation with a retired police captain. Then he returned to the Fager house and murdered Kelli Fager, leaving her in the hot tub. He drove to a nearby apartment complex and left his van there. He walked back to the

Fagers' house, got their Volkswagen Rabbit, went to his bank again, got $100 in cash, and drove to Florida. While there he called his wife and was arrested by the police. He was interrogated by three different Florida officers over a four-hour period before he asked for an attorney.

During Butterworth's trial, on May 27, 1988, *The Wichita Eagle* ran a story that reported, "Fingerprints taken from the Phillip Fager home did not match prints taken from William Butterworth and Charles Dearing, another possible suspect in the Fager deaths. . . . Dearing was one of five suspects investigated or interviewed in connection with the Fager deaths, according to a pretrial defense motion filed to seek evidence gathered by police."

Butterworth was acquitted by a Sedgwick County District Court jury on June 7, 1988. The jury apparently believed Butterworth's story, a story that prosecutors had called "a transparent lie." Many of the jurors later stated they had serious doubts about the prosecution's case from the first. Jury foreman Ron Blasi told the press that the jury thought that prosecutors simply did not have a convincing case. Prosecutors were "twisting and stretching" evidence to fit their scenario.

Police were so certain that Butterworth was actually the killer that they closed the case.

A final murder with possible links to the BTK Strangler occurred several years later. On January 19, 1991, sixty-two-year-old Dolores E. "Dee" Davis was abducted from her home a half-mile east of Park City. Dee was reported missing just after noon on Saturday, January 19. The phone call to the police came from a concerned friend. She was last seen wearing pants and a sweater at 7:30 p.m. on Friday at her home at 6226 North Hillside.

The house stood on a major thoroughfare, with noisy traffic rushing by, next to a boat-repair shop. Someone had cut Dee's outside telephone lines, then threw a brick through a large glass patio door at the rear of her home.

Dee—described as five-foot-five, 130 pounds, with salt-and-pepper colored hair—lived alone with her cats in a rented house. Most of her family lived outside Kansas. She had been living at the North Hillside address for two years. She had retired the year before after working for more than twenty years as a corporate secretary at Lario Oil and Gas Co., 301 South Market.

Sheriff's Captain James Elvins said, "It appears that small personal items were taken. It does not appear that a struggle took place. There is a lot of suspicious circumstances surrounding the disappearance of this lady." The missing items were the woman's purse and some pieces of costume jewelry.

The house and yard were cordoned off with yellow police tape. Police talked to friends and relatives. Seven detectives were assigned to the case. That's a lot for a missing person case. Foul play was definitely suspected.

Dee's body was found thirteen days later by a fifteen-year-old boy walking with a stray dog toward a farmhouse in hopes of finding the dog's owner. Dee's body was under a bridge in northern Sedgwick County, near 117th Street North and Meridian. The site was three-quarters of a mile west of Meridian.

The discovery was made at about 9:30 a.m. Her feet, hands, and knees were bound with panty hose. The boy went home and called 911.

At the crime scene, investigators took casts of footprints and tire marks found near the body. A "porcelain-type" decorative mask was found next to her body. It was described as a "female mask, the type that might be hung on a wall." Above the crime scene, an investigator in a helicopter took aerial photographs. The FBI and KBI were consulted.

The body showed no obvious cause of death. Only after a long and complicated autopsy by Deputy County Coroner William Eckert was it determined that she had been strangled—"asphyxiation caused by ligature strangulation." The body was identified by Dr. Eckert through dental records.

The abduction angle and "dump site" under a bridge made this case very similar to the Denise Rathbun case. Dee's son, Jeff Davis, told the *Eagle* on December 7, 1991, that he believed his mother had been killed by a serial killer. "The similarities between the deaths of my mother in January and Marine Hedge in 1985 are too great to ignore," Jeff said.

Jeff told the reporter that both his mother and Marine Hedge lived in or near Park City, where murder is infrequent. Hedge's death had been the first murder ever in Park City. Both Hedge and Davis had dined with their boyfriends at the same restaurant the night before they died. In both cases, the victim's car had been wiped down, as if someone had touched the car and wanted to remove his prints. Both women were diminutive and over fifty, but still attractive. Both Davis and Hedge lived alone, less than two miles from each other. Phone lines were cut at both homes. In both cases a towel with small blood spots on it were found at the crime scene. Both women were abducted on a Friday evening, after their boyfriends left them alone in their homes. Panty hose were found on or near both bodies. There was a similarity in the dump sites: Davis under a bridge in the country, Hedge beside a dirt road. Nothing valuable was taken from either home, but some small items—souvenirs—were found to be missing. There was no chance that the women knew each other. Davis moved to the Park City area after Hedge was already dead.

In addition to the many similarities between the two cases, profound differences can also be noted: Hedge was strangled by hand—a little too hands-on for BTK perhaps—and there was no bondage. Davis was strangled with her own panty hose. She was also bound at the hands, ankles and knees, very BTK-like. Hedge was found nude, while Davis wore a blue flannel nightgown and white panties. Yet, as with the Hedge case, the police could not make a conclusive determination. The specter of the BTK strangler would continue to cast its pall over Wichita and its surrounding areas.

It was a time of change in the Wichita Police Department. Richard LaMunyon retired, and in 1989 a former national police officer of the year, Captain Rick Stone from the Dallas Police Department, became the new Wichita police chief.

The entire time he was in Wichita, Chief Stone fought unrelenting battles to change entrenched Wichita Police customs as well as budget wars with City Manager Chris Cherches. Six times in six years the city manager required the police to move all their stored evidence to a new facility because a slightly cheaper rental rate was negotiated. Chief Stone objected that the few cents in savings were more than offset by the time and cost it took to catalog and move evidence. Unfortunately, in each move something was lost. This penny-pinching and moving drove Chief Stone to distraction.

Kansas is better known for its severe storms than for its serial killers. Virtually all buildings have basements as shelters to retreat from Kansas tornados. However, under this city manager the Wichita city-construction bidding procedures may have been shortsighted.

The city parking garage adjacent to City Hall was poorly built. It started falling down almost as quickly as it was opened. Detective Arlyn Smith told me that he had to leap from his car when exiting his assigned parking place, because if he stepped from his car his leg would have fallen through the huge hole next to the driver's side door.

Unfortunately, some of the BTK records and some of the evidence was in a storage area in this garage when on June 7, 1990, a terrible storm caused part of the garage to collapse, and a wall to the records storage fell outward. The Kansas wind blew many of the BTK records away.

Chapter 19

A Former Police Officer Convicted of Homicide

Charles W. Dearing Jr., born May 18, 1944, had a brief but memorable law enforcement career, from 1969 through 1971. He was handsome and charming and likable. All the cops I interviewed said that initially everyone liked him. They also said that later they realized he was a con man. Dearing, who would be convicted of robbery and murder, would attempt fraud by faking his own death. Suspected of also participating in other crimes, he is now serving life in prison without parole for strangling a woman, and one of the woman's relatives publicly accused Dearing of being BTK.

One day in 1970 Charles Dearing's roommate was arrested and charged with several robberies. When arrested, he was using Dearing's police revolver. Dearing and his roommate both said that the roommate took it without Dearing's knowledge, but some officers speculated otherwise.

That year Dearing met St. Joseph emergency room physician Dr. Mildred Criswell. All the cops loved Doc Millie, and she took care of them. She'd give them antibiotics or a shot for whatever they needed. She'd take care of the paperwork.

Criswell was smitten with Dearing, but she considered herself plain, about as wide as she was tall, and never thought that anyone as handsome and charming as Dearing would ever notice her. But, to her delight, she and Dearing went on several dates.

However, in 1971 Dearing married a nurse, Suzanne, who was working at another hospital. In September 1971 Dearing resigned from the Wichita Police Department, and he and his wife moved to Tulsa. Dearing left the department under a cloud. Officially, he left to pursue a business opportunity, but he was accused of beating Hispanic teenagers at a church dance. The FBI investigated but no charges were filed.

In September 1973 Charles Dearing and Suzanne Dearing divorced. Charles moved to Missouri, legally changed his name to Charles Pullman, then moved to Indiana, and in 1977 he married a second time.

He faked his own death and his wife attempted to collect the life insurance policy. The company never paid and the ruse was exposed.

In Missouri the next year Dearing was arrested, charged, and convicted of robbery. From prison he appealed in the courts, and he wrote letters to Millie Criswell, who was still sweet on him. Millie wrote back and started regularly visiting him in prison. He won his appeal and was released. He moved into Millie's home in Wichita, and they married in 1980. Shortly thereafter, Charles convinced Millie to move to Las Vegas. He spent his time gambling while she supported them.

On October 25, 1982, they were scheduled to go to the airport and catch a plane to Wichita. His story was that he went to a corner gas station at the end of his block to put gasoline in his car before the trip, was gone from home only about fifteen minutes, and when he returned he found his wife strangled. Initially, the police held Dearing on suspicion of murder, but they had no hard evidence against him and released him.

He collected nearly $300,000 in insurance and Millie's assets. He returned to Wichita, eventually moving into a home at a classy address on Armour Street in east Wichita.

At 2:30 p.m. on October 10, 1989, Dearing was arrested, extradited to Las Vegas, and charged with Millie's murder. A year earlier he had bragged to Janet Lawrence, a bartender at the Grape, a local tavern, that he had gotten away with murdering his wife for the money. She contacted authorities and told them what Dearing had said, and Detective Tom Dillard of Las Vegas pursued the case.

Millie's parents, Ernest and Thelma Criswell of Humbolt, Kansas, said that they had suspected Dearing all along. They reported that

Millie said he had censored her mail and never told her when family called. They felt he was keeping her from them.

Dearing's homicide trial in Las Vegas was delayed until June 1992.

According to an AP story published in *The Wichita Eagle*, Dearing's former brother-in-law, Michael Hirsch, claimed that Charles Dearing not only murdered Millie Criswell but was Wichita's notorious BTK Strangler.

At trial, Las Vegas chief deputy district attorney Mel Harmon aggressively prosecuted Dearing with Detective Tom Dillard at his side. He brought in the owner of the gas station, who testified that Dearing was there for no more than five minutes.

Based on the evidence presented at trial, Harmon argued to the jury, Dearing had direct access to the victim, there was no evidence pointing to any other suspect, there was no evidence of a break-in, and robbery was an unlikely motive because many valuables were available but were not stolen. Dearing had a history of deception, and his story about his wife's murder was one more deception. Charles Dearing murdered his wife for money, just as he had boasted to Janet Lawrence in the Grape.

Dearing's criminal defense attorney, Gene Martin, challenged each bit of prosecution evidence and disputed ten-year-old memories. But the main thrust of Dearing's defense centered on questions of whether Charles Dearing was really on trial for the murder of Millie Criswell at all, but rather on trial for being the BTK Strangler.

Janet Lawrence came forward only after she was contacted by Michael Hirsch, who had accused Dearing of being the BTK Strangler. Martin's argument was, apparently, "If Dearing is not BTK, then he did not murder Millie Criswell."

So Martin decided to prove conclusively that Dearing was not BTK. He brought in the man who in 1992 was the lead detective on the BTK investigation, one of the Ghostbusters, and a current Wichita Police Department homicide lieutenant, Kenny Landwehr.

Lieutenant Landwehr testified that Dearing had an alibi for Nancy Fox's murder; at the time she was murdered, Dearing was in prison in another state, serving time for robbery. The Wichita police had evidence that the same man, called BTK, had murdered eight people. If a suspect was eliminated for any one murder, then he was eliminated for all eight murders. Dearing was eliminated by alibi in Nancy Fox's murder, so he was not BTK.

The jury wasn't fooled. After deliberating only two hours, in June 1992 they convicted Charles W. Dearing Jr. of the October 25, 1982, murder in Las Vegas of Dr. Mildred Criswell. The judge sentenced Dearing to life in prison without parole.

Chapter 20

Psychology of a Killer

Gary Ridgway has an IQ of 82. Ridgway was the long-sought serial killer known as the Green River Killer. For twenty years a massive task force of local, state, and federal authorities hunted in the Seattle area for the Green River Killer. Twice in their new chapter of their updated edition of *The Search for the Green River Killer*, reporters Tomas Guillen and Carlton Smith mention that Ridgway's IQ is 82, because they want to emphasize that he was not very intelligent. Their unstated inference is that a man with such a low IQ should have been caught by local lawmen and FBI agents.

Gary Ridgway's IQ of 82 is well below the average American IQ of 100. Gary Ridgway failed two years of high school and finally graduated at age twenty. His entire adult life Ridgway held one simple, undemanding job that he learned how to do on his first day: he spray-painted motor vehicles. Nine out of ten Americans have a higher IQ than Gary Ridgway, including all the police officers who searched for him. The U.S. Army used to refuse induction to anyone with an IQ of 80 or below.

Yet Gary Ridgway was canny enough to murder at least forty-eight women and elude task forces of law enforcement officers for twenty years. Until he was arrested, some thought that he must be a genius.

Is BTK a genius? Probably not. BTK may well be another Ridgway, or at best a technician of some sort—he is intelligent enough to skillfully operate a computer and a photocopy machine. Serial killer expert Dr. Eric Hickey reports that a German study of serial killers concluded that the typical serial killer "possessed minimal to average intelligence." Unfortunately, it is not the typical killer, but the rare exception, who mistakenly remains in most people's minds as the typical serial killer. People remember Ted Bundy, who earned a degree in psychology and attended law school.

The German study revealed that "the higher the intelligence level of the offender, the faster the arrest of the killer." Less intelligent serial killers took on average "twice as long to apprehend as high IQ killers because they did not fit criminal profiles utilized by investigators."

The German equivalent of Gary Ridgway was Joachim George Kroll. Despite a massive hunt, he eluded capture for twenty years while murdering his victims in laundry rooms, where they felt comfortable. The boyfriend of one of his victims was held in jail for fifteen months before being released. Before his death in 1991, serial killer Kroll confessed to strangling fourteen women. He was convicted of murdering eight women and one four-year-old, and he is suspected of committing many more murders. His IQ was 76.

BTK eluded teams of law enforcement officers for more than thirty years. He murdered women, children, and men and sent cryptic letters to police and press about his murders. After decades of investigation, the police and FBI had no solid clue to his identity. Did this killer's elusiveness sound like the work of a master criminal genius?

After IQ tests became commonplace, law enforcement agencies across the country were embarrassed to learn that of all occupational categories, police officers had the lowest average IQ. To change this, police departments were among the first employers (after the U.S. Armed Forces) to begin requiring IQ tests for job applicants. But Wichita police officers tell me that once you're in the department, there is no test of deductive reasoning skills for promotion or for becoming a detective.

Ruth Finley's September 1981 hoax letter to police while she was masquerading as the Poet contained evidence confirming for the Wichita police detectives and police chief that the Poet was BTK. Yet the letter identified the eighth and ninth victims, and to that point BTK had claimed only seven victims. Using a detective's common sense, Chief LaMunyon and Detective Drowatzky decided to put Ruth Finley under massive surveillance in order to learn whether disconfirming or confirming evidence about the Poet-BTK connection could be collected. At the time they did not know what the outcome would be.

The Poet episode should have been a clear statement to everyone involved with future BTK investigations that whenever presented with confirming evidence, disconfirming evidence should also be sought. And that they should contemplate whether the answers they "knew" to be true could be otherwise. As Will Rogers observed, "It ain't what we know that gets us into as much trouble as what we know that ain't so."

In 1994 I was the program chair for a group of potential geniuses in Kansas, the greater Kansas chapter of the American Mensa High IQ Society, Sunflower Mensa.

Mensa started after the end of World War II when a group of code breakers formerly at Bletchley Park in England continued to gather to discuss their hobby of cryptography. Cryptographers at Bletchley Park, such as Alan Turing, helped win World War II by deciphering the German Enigma Code machine and addressing other code problems. They were some of the brightest people in the world.

Two of them, lawyers Roland Berrill and Lancelot Ware, started a club called Mensa, after the Latin word for table. The idea was derived from the legend of King Arthur's Knights of the Round Table, where no knight ranked higher than any other. All persons were considered equal at the round table, and all persons would be considered equal in the Mensa club, insofar as all would have very high intelligence.

Over time the club became international, membership standards were lowered, and one qualified for membership by a flexible but reasonably clear standard: if one scored in the top two percent of any accepted intelligence test, then one could join Mensa.

After soliciting program suggestions from members, I wrote to the Wichita Police Department and told them that we understood that there were some puzzling messages from BTK. I wrote that some of our members were master puzzle solvers and we would be happy to look at anything that BTK had sent and offer opinions and, hopefully, puzzle out solutions.

Homicide lieutenant Ken Landwehr was now the acknowledged Wichita Police Department BTK expert. On Saturday, April 8, 1995, he came to the home of our Mensa chapter past-president Susan Cook and at a meeting narrated a slide show presentation. It was the best-attended meeting we had had since the 1970s. We saw crime scene photos, both interior and exterior views, autopsy photos, and family photos of all of the victims. Then we viewed slides of all of BTK's envelopes, poems, drawings, and letters. Landwehr asked us only a single question, which we were unable to answer.

Although I had intended that only Mensa members attend, virtually everyone brought a guest, so nonmembers were also present. I told Lieutenant Landwehr that I could not vouch for everyone present because I did not know everyone. He said that was not a problem.

I did not realize until 2003 that this was a proactive presentation by the WPD. They did not so much expect our help as wonder who would show up and whether there would be any sequelae. We were unable to come up with any useful information, however. Such work was better left to true professionals, such as FBI profilers.

In the mid-1990s FBI agent John Douglas retired and wrote a book about profiling titled *Mindhunter*. The climax of the book is about his work on the BTK case. On page 376 Douglas writes: "Like those of his hero, Jack the Ripper, BTK's murders stopped abruptly. In this case, though, I believe the police had interviewed him, he knew they were closing in on him, and he was intelligent and sophisticated enough to stop before sufficient evidence could be gathered."

According to Douglas, a serial killer can just stop, which is contrary to what most authorities say. Most say serial killers are like cocaine addicts. They know that they risk being caught, but they can't stop. But Douglas says that they can. I guess that we can only study serial killers who are caught, so those who are not caught are not studied. Perhaps Douglas suspects that for every serial killer caught, there are many others who elude capture.

On his Web site, John Douglas answered a question from "Jennifer" with the reply: "The BTK stopped killing for a period of time because he had the crap scared out of him."

After visiting with John Douglas at the FBI's Behavioral Science Unit, author Thomas Harris wrote two books in which pivotal characters were FBI profilers, *Red Dragon* and *The Silence of the Lambs*. In *Red Dragon* its fictional serial killer, Francis Dolarhyde, was inspired by BTK. Dolarhyde took photos of his victims like BTK, and he put mirrors in the eyes of his victims just as BTK appeared to put mirrors in the eyes of the drawing of his intended victim on Pinecrest.

On March 11, 1997, FBI profiler Robert Ressler spoke at Wichita State University's Wilner Auditorium. Among other things, he said BTK had probably "left the area, died or is in a mental institution or prison."

Ressler said that at the time of the murders BTK probably lived in the College Hill section of the city, was a graduate student or a professor in criminal justice at Wichita State University, was in his mid- to late 20s at the time of the first murders, and was an expert in the methods of famous serial killers.

I did not attend the lecture, but while writing this book I heard from those who did attend. I was told that it resembled a sting operation. Robert Ressler's conclusion was not believed because there were very few criminal justice graduate students and professors, and they had all been cleared. No one thought that BTK was a WSU criminal justice professor or graduate student. The audience was liberally infiltrated by undercover cops checking out who was attending the lecture.

One man who attended the lecture was Dan Rouser. Rouser was one of Wichita's most accomplished sophisticates and was well-known in many circles. Dan's father, Ray Rouser, died in January 1986 and was remembered as "an oilman's oilman." From 1963 to 1966 Dan was *The Wichita Eagle* crime reporter until the Murdock family sold the paper to a corporation. As part of a traditional prank, Dan had thrown a firecracker in the police squad room and startled the shift sergeant. The corporation was looking for reasons to cut staff, and Dan was fired that day.

Wichita police chief Eugene Pond heard about what happened, and told him, "I want more officers with brains. I want you to apply to the police academy."

Dan did. From 1967 to 1970 Dan served as a Wichita Police Department patrolman, radio dispatcher, and computer operator.

Although Dan's main love was journalism, he also loved art. From 1972 to 1975 Dan was a curatorial assistant at the Wichita Art Museum. From 1979 to 1997 Dan had served on the Wichita Art Museum's Board of Trustees, serving at board president in 1993. Tall and handsome, well spoken and well educated, experienced and urbane, Dan

Rouser was an art museum sophisticate. Everyone knew Dan. He had all the right connections.

And the police noticed that he attended Ressler's BTK lecture.

On Thursday, February 12, 1998, Rouser was sitting in his apartment reading when he thought he heard a helicopter hovering overhead. He went to the window and saw police cars blocking off his street. He was walking to his apartment front door to go outside and see whether he could learn what was going on when he heard a knock at that door. He opened it to see Detective Kenny Landwehr, Detective Kelly Otis, and a SWAT team.

Lieutenant Landwehr put a piece of paper on Rouser's chest and said, "We have a search warrant. Sit down."

When he told me his story, Rouser said that one never knows how one will react to an unexpected and shocking event. He said that he was so shocked and stunned that he did exactly as he was told. He sat for fully two hours before he even looked at the search warrant.

Meantime, a team of detectives entered and meticulously combed through his things. One detective complained that he had too many books, because that detective had to turn each book upside down, shake it, and thumb through the leaves of the book to see whether anything was inside.

Finally, after two hours, Rouser had the presence of mind to look at the piece of paper he had been given. It was indeed a search warrant. It had been signed by Judge Clark Owens. Then he read the document. It was addressed to his apartment number at his apartment building on South Belmont.

Then he read the list of items the police were searching for: "1. Indicia of occupancy, residency, rental, and/or ownership of the premises described herein, including, but not limited to, utility and telephone bills, canceled envelopes, rental, purchase or lease agreements, and keys. 2. Letters, documents, sketches, photographs, audio tapes and/or articles pertaining to Otero and Fox homicides. 3. Identification or other property belonging to Nancy Fox or Otero family members. 4. Photographs of the interior and exterior of the residence and storage unit. 5. Evidence of storage facility rentals and/or deposit boxes."

He looked up from reading the warrant and said, "Oh," and

pointed. "What you're looking for," Dan Rouser said, "is in that file cabinet under B."

Everyone stopped moving.

He told me that the detective going through books stopped in mid-shuffle. Only Detective Landwehr moved. He walked over to the file cabinet and opened the B file drawer.

There was a file noted "BTK." Detective Landwehr opened the file and saw a photocopy of the first BTK letter, the letter BTK left between the pages of a textbook in the Wichita Public Library.

Rouser explained that Cathy Henkel had provided him a copy of the letter. She verified this fact to me personally and said that she verified that fact to the police when they contacted her. Landwehr was stunned. He seemed to have no idea that this letter was widely distributed among journalists and scholars. Rouser and Henkel told me it appeared the police thought that anyone who had a copy of this letter must be BTK.

The truth was that many journalists in Wichita and elsewhere had copies of the secret BTK information. Every one of them had been responsible and not released the information to the public.

As best as I have been able to determine, the police acted primarily on a tip that turned out to be based on a series of conversations during which the information was sensationalized with each retelling. Dan Rouser apparently drank a lot at a party, and when the subject of BTK arose, as was still common in Wichita, he started telling details about the letter's contents. He knew a lot about the BTK case because he was collecting material to write a magazine article about the mystery. Some women at the party overheard only part of the conversation and reported Rouser to the police as suspect. The women's memories may have magnified the extent of what he actually said. In any case, this caused the police to look at him again. The geographic profiling was also influential.

Dan Rouser provided a blood sample that was tested for DNA against the BTK sample obtained from Nancy Fox's crime scene. In February 1998 Dan Rouser was excluded as being BTK.

The trial had long gone cold. Every aspect of the case had been considered, and every promise had proved false. It would take a lawyer teaching a course to flesh out, at long last, the killer.

PART FOUR

THE HUNTED EMERGES FROM HIDING JANUARY 1999–MARCH 2004

—All arrogance will reap a rich harvest in tears. God calls men to a heavy reckoning for overweening pride.

—Herodotus

Chapter 21

Manson Mania

The cold winter day of Thursday, January 21, 1999, seemed to be another ordinary day. I returned to my law office late in the afternoon and turned on my computer, and as it was booting up, I pushed the answering machine PLAY button.

The first of four messages was from Kansas's Fourth District congressman Todd Tihart's office. I was disappointed with that message. The congressman was not interested in supporting an issue I favored. Politics.

The second message began with an automated voice informing me that this was a collect call from a prisoner in a California correctional institution. The automated voice went through the litany most lawyers have heard—"This call is being recorded. . . . Push this button if you wish to accept the call, push that button if you want no more calls from this number," etc.—and eventually there is an automatic blank spot for the prisoner to say his name. I could not understand the prisoner's mumbled name. However, because a California magazine had just run an article quoting me talking about the polygraph, and because the day before I had received a call from a man in California regarding the polygraph, I suspected that this was a prisoner calling about it.

The third message was a later call apparently from the same prisoner. I still couldn't understand the name of the person who was calling.

But the fourth and final message was a third call from the prisoner, and this time the name was enunciated distinctly and clearly: "Charles Manson."

I stared blankly at the computer screen. It was slowly entering my consciousness that Charles Manson had called my law office three times this afternoon. I was contemplating this amazing fact when the telephone rang and I mechanically picked it up.

"Hello, this is Robert Beattie."

"Hello," a female voice brightly replied, "I'm calling on behalf of Charles Manson. He's been trying to reach you." She told me who she was before she continued, "Charles Manson would like to make an appointment. Is that possible? Can you schedule a time to accept a telephone call from Charles Manson?"

I paused. "O-kay."

Why was Charles Manson calling me? Because I had written to him, as I had written to O.J. Simpson and others, explaining in a one-page letter that for my class I was conducting a moot-jury exercise based on his trial. In Charles Manson's case, I was putting him on moot-trial solely for Sharon Tate's murder (in each exercise practical considerations require that I limit the scope of the exercise), and I had invited him to make a statement in his defense to my students.

After negotiations with the woman who called, Manson agreed to talk with me, as long as I recorded the call and he could speak directly to the students via the audiotape. Also, I agreed that I'd not sell the tapes, and when I was on the telephone I'd listen more than I'd talk. Charles Manson was delighted. He was finally going to have the opportunity to defend himself in court against the accusation that he was responsible for the murder of Sharon Tate. This is what he has always wanted and demanded—to defend himself in court. Remember, he was removed as his own attorney early in his trial. After that, just like Bobby Seale in the Chicago Seven trial, Manson said that the entire procedure was a sham and he behaved contumaciously in the courtroom.

Why did I agree to take Charles Manson's call? Because he was calling to make a statement to my students. It was explained to me that the call would be collect, and it could not be longer than fifteen minutes, because the automated prison telephone system terminated all calls after fifteen minutes.

On Friday, January 22, 1999, just after one o'clock p.m. central time,

Charles Manson called my law office. Between his first call taken by my answering machine on January 21, 1999, and his final conversation with me on March 8, 1999, when the California Department of Corrections put an end to Manson's calls to me, he was to call a total of twenty times.

In my conversations with Mr. Manson, I always made clear that I was not Charles Manson's attorney, that I was not in any way functioning as his attorney, and that I was functioning only as an educator. That was unambiguous in my written communications and in my recorded spoken communications with Charles Manson. Our discussions of the legal and evidentiary aspects of his case were for educational purposes.

Weeks later, after listening to the first forty-five minutes of recorded conversations, reporter Roy Wenzl said to me, "You're functioning as a journalist." Wenzl said that he had talked with convicted murderers, and that his conversations with murderers and other cons sounded pretty much like my conversations with Manson. Like a journalist, I was trying to draw information from a convicted murderer. Sometimes the inmate was circumspect and sometimes the inmate was loquacious, but I was always encouraging him to say more (which was part of my agreement to listen more than I talked, anyway).

The fact that Charles Manson and the Helter Skelter murders were on my list of moot-jury exercises was always clear and it was in both my 1995 outline and in my 1996 proposal to Friends University. Manson's telephone calls to me were never any secret. I told everyone who was interested about the calls, and probably some who were not interested. The first person I informed was the university's Dean of Liberal Arts, Alton Beaver. I had kept Dean Beaver informed at each step of this exercise. Earlier I had informed Dean Beaver when I sent Manson the initial invitation letter. I immediately informed Dean Beaver when I was scheduled to speak with Charles Manson. And I continued to inform Dean Beaver each step of the way.

When I had advised the Dean that I wrote to Charles Manson, adding that I did not expect a reply, Dean Beaver was very enthusiastic and supportive of this moot-jury project, as he had been of the entire jury course. He was delighted and "fascinated"—his word—and said that he was sure that Manson's participation would provide material to create a "fascinating" exercise for my students. After I provided Dean Beaver with a copy of the first forty-five minutes of telephone conversations with Manson, Dean Beaver was even more enthusiastic in his e-mail and telephone conversations with me about the project. He said that the tape was "fascinating." He continued to be enthusiastic about the project, repeating that this was "fascinating," until the criticism started in March 1999. Then he reversed himself.

Locally, in some quarters, word of my conversations with Manson and ripples of interest about it quickly spread. In February 1999 I was invited to conduct and did conduct a mini-moot-trial of Charles Manson for Sunflower Mensa. One of my best friends is Brenda Huntsinger Williams, a woman who has received an award as Kansas' investigative journalist of the year. She was the one who recommended that I speak with her friend Roy Wenzl, a *Wichita Eagle* reporter who shared a 1981 Pulitzer Prize for his reporting on the disastrous Kansas City "tea dance" skywalk collapse. Brenda thought it essential that I talk with a print reporter about this, because in her opinion, sooner or later my conversations with Manson were going to make the news. Otherwise, we risked having some television program broadcast an incomplete, misleading, and sensationalistic sound bite about Manson's involvement with the class.

So, I talked with Roy Wenzl. I shared everything with him and provided him a copy of the tape of my first forty-five minutes of conversations with Manson. On Wednesday, February 24, 1999, *The Wichita Eagle* asked if they could take my photograph to go along with this story. I checked for the article in the Friday, Saturday, and Sunday papers, but didn't see anything. I figured that the newspaper had decided to wait until fall, when the class started.

On Monday morning, March 1, 1999, still wearing my slippers and robe, I picked the morning paper up off the lawn and carried it back in the house. My wife, a pediatrician, turned on the small television set that we have on the end of the kitchen table. The first thing we saw on TV was local CBS affiliate morning anchor Denise Eck reporting that Charles Manson was helping local attorney Robert Beattie teach a political science course at a local university. My wife and I looked at each other in stunned surprise.

Then we looked at the newspaper. On the front page was the photo taken last Wednesday in the university library. Above the fold the headline read, "Local lawyer uses killer's input in class." Near the beginning of the story, still on the front page, a paragraph reported, "Beattie says he's not trying to be Manson's lawyer or advocate. For educational purposes alone, he plans to stage a retrial in the class, using students as jurors to decide once again whether Manson was guilty in the bloody murders August 9, 1969, of actress Sharon Tate and four other people killed in her house." Those words were almost verbatim what the news anchor had just said on television.

Then the telephone rang. It was to ring almost continuously for the next twelve days.

A full report of those two weeks would require a book of its own. A few highlights include my appearing on the *Today* show and being interviewed by Katie Couric, appearing on Court TV, being interviewed by BBC Radio and NPR Radio, being interviewed by the *New York Post*, *Newsweek*, and the *Chronicle of Higher Education*, and being interviewed via telephone by journalists in Canada, Great Britain, Japan, Germany, and Brazil, and receiving media requests from all over the United States and the rest of the world. I *declined* approximately one hundred interviews, including interviews with *Inside Edition*, *Good Morning America*, *Leeza*, *48 Hours*, and dozens of other radio, television, and print media sources. When I checked my office phone at about noon that first day, the answering machine tape had maxed out and, although calls were still coming in, it was not recording them. When I pulled into my driveway the next day I found a freelance photographer, hired by the *New York Post*, standing on my front porch and snapping photos.

Even when I was not contacted by news media, I saw or heard or it was reported to me that major media discussed or mentioned my jury course. *CNN Headline News* ran a brief piece about the jury course on their news-summary screen. My daughter's best friend called to tell me that Barbara Walters led a discussion about my jury course on her daily morning program, *The View*. As it was explained to me by a producer of the *Leeza Gibbons* show, I was "the flavor of the month."

Having fifteen minutes of fame was a wholly novel event, and one for which I was completely unprepared. Quickly I started receiving calls from cranks from both camps, pro-Manson and anti-Manson.

One man demanded that he be allowed to come into my classroom and testify to my students that Manson was possessed by a demon in 1969, but that now the demon was gone. He said that not only could he prove it, but also he could provide the name and history of the demon.

Then I started receiving outright hate mail, again from both camps.

Then I received a death threat. I contacted the proper authorities and started taking special precautions. I was soon in over my head, but I tried to maintain my equanimity as I rode the whirlwind and tried not to worry my wife and daughters.

Still, I was delighted to talk about my juror-education course, The American Jury. Reporters or producers from *The New York Times*, NBC's *Today, The London Guardian*, Brazil's Television Network, CBS's *48 Hours*, and ABC's *20/20*, and others wanted to come to class in the fall to report on how the students decided. The university was also delighted about this. It seemed that our only decision was which program was going to be allowed on campus. The administration assigned me the largest classroom on campus, a room with stadium seating that looked like it belonged in an opera house.

I kept a prior commitment to speak at an evening social psychology course at Friends University. Because of the intense public and student interest, I was asked to use the Manson story as much as possible. I also decided to use a local crime that I presumed all the students would know. I began my lecture by saying that the 1969 mass murder at Sharon Tate's household panicked Las Angeles the same way the 1974 mass murder of the Otero family by BTK panicked Wichita.

There was absolutely no look of recognition.

Puzzled, I inquired, "Oteros? BTK? The BTK Strangler? Wichita's serial killer?"

None of the younger students knew what I was talking about. Only a few of the older students, adults returning to college to complete their degrees, knew of the BTK Strangler.

Because BTK had not been in the news for years, the story was unknown to the younger generation. I felt that this was too fascinating a story, worked on too hard by my law enforcement friends, and had caused this community too much grief for this to be completely unknown to a new generation. I decided that someday I would have to do a lecture on BTK.

Afterward, intermittently, I began collecting information for the BTK classroom exercise I would someday conduct.

During the fall of 1999, convicted mass murderer Charles Manson was the defendant in my American Jury class's mock trial. Manson's contribution to the class was a forty-five-minute phone interview he did with me on January 22, 1999, which was played for my student jurors months later.

Manson was probably the most notorious prisoner on the planet. Manson prosecutor Stephen Kay told Court TV that Manson received more mail than any other prisoner in history. I had not expected him to reply to my letter, but I had wanted to be able to tell my students that I had offered to let him tell his side of the story.

"I admit that I'm an outlaw, like a devil sometimes, a rebel forever, and that I'm nasty as all outdoors," Manson wrote to me in a February 8, 1999, letter. "But what does that mean? I never told anyone to kill those people."

In addition to Charles Manson defending himself in his own words—he sent me two letters and we spoke on the phone approximately twenty times—my student jurors also heard expert testimony. Among the others to testify were Dr. James Mesa, who discussed the Catholic view of the death penalty; Robert Jacobs, a crime analyst from the Kansas Bureau of Investigation; and Dr. Tom Rochat, Ph.D., a forensic psychologist.

My wife, understandably enough, was having trouble dealing with the fact that I was in communication with Manson. One day as I was walking out of the house, I said to her, being flip, "If Charles Manson calls, take a message."

In fact, Manson tried to reach me at my home number, and Mary Ann took the call. She exploded in anger when I came home. She did not want Charles Manson calling us. It was bad enough he was calling at my office. I tried to calm Mary Ann and assured her that I would take measures to see that his calls to our home number would be blocked, which I did.

At one point during the height of Manson mania when our home phone was constantly ringing, my fax machine was constantly running, reporters were knocking on our door, I was hearing myself on television and radio taped interviews, I put my arm around my wife and said, "Well, dear, we'll never see anything like this again." I couldn't have been more wrong.

Chapter 22

Events Prompt My BTK Research

In February 2002, Hurst Laviana at *The Wichita Eagle*, Dana Hertneky, a reporter with Wichita's NBC affiliate KSN, and other Wichita journalists were contacted by a California researcher named Ken Mosbaugh. He provided hundreds of pages of notes that he claimed proved that the murders of California's Zodiac killer, Wichita's BTK Strangler, and New York's Son of Sam were committed by the same group of people, members of a vast satanic cult. Their mastermind was Ted Kaczynski, the Unabomber. It was a comically ridiculous proposal.

But Dana Hertneky reported it as straight news. I thought that she would ridicule it and bring on some experts to ridicule it. The police, however, only made some vague comments and did not articulate any detailed refutation. The story was presented as legitimate: an unspecified but sinister cross-country traveling group was responsible for the murders attributed to the BTK Strangler. I was stunned.

By this time I had read John Douglas' *Mindhunter*, with its climax telling of his involvement with the BTK Strangler case. Over the years I had heard a great deal about the case from many detectives and beat officers who had worked on some aspect of the case. Pete Dubovich had been obsessed with the BTK case. Al Stewart died with his notes about the BTK case next to him on his bed. I thought of all the investment of time and effort and emotion that had gone into this case. I knew that for the majority of the young people viewing this report, this would be their only exposure to the BTK case. I became upset that they were going to think that this silly story explained everything.

On February 27, 2002, I sent an e-mail to Dana Hertneky, introduced myself, and told her that my students would be doing a mock grand jury investigation of BTK next year, and I did not think that Mr. Mosbaugh's theory was sound. She invited me to the television studio and interviewed me. My remarks were broadcast in the final portion of a four-evening series. The Kansas Association of Broadcasters would award Dana Hertneky and KSN the 2002 first place award for best news reporting in a series for her "BTK—A New Theory" reports.

I started making a lot of telephone calls. I collected what I could find in books, magazines, and online and made notes from my memories of conversations with officers, and then I called Kaw City, Oklahoma, police chief Bernie Drowatzky. He said that he thought he had some notes and old newspaper clippings in a cardboard box in a closet.

Then I called retired WPD Lieutenant Charles Liles. He was active with the Wichita Retired Police Officers Association, and he knew a lot of officers who had worked directly on the BTK investigation. I started contacting other officers, reporters, psychologists, medical doctors, and family and friends of the victims.

In March 2003 I read that former president Bill Clinton had been called for jury duty, so I decided to write to him and tell him about my course. I included basic information about the students' fall semester BTK mock investigative grand jury and asked him to send an encouraging note to my students. He did.

In May 2003 I spoke with a retired detective who wishes to remain anonymous. During our third conversation he said, "You can't tell this story in a chapter; you have to write a book." I had no intention of writing a book. A book was a lot more work than I wanted to do. I thought this would be a chapter in another book I was writing, but that was all.

Many of my early telephone calls resulted in suspicion. I received hangups, innuendo, responses that were patently false, and wild speculation. A good part of my first eight months as a BTK researcher was spent in building and renewing relationships.

I also spent considerable time investigating myths surrounding the case: rumors that had long been accepted as fact. Typically, women would tell me a litany of "facts": "They know who it is and they are following him all the time." "They know he attended a folklore class at WSU." "He is someone important they are protecting." "He is a former Wichita police officer they are protecting."

Detective Garrison had attended the folklore course, as had a lot of other WPD officers because it was an easy A, but two major investigations, the Hot Dog Squad investigation of the 1970s and the Ghostbusters investigation of the 1980s, had not found any student, staff, or faculty member at WSU, including those who had taken P.J. Wyatt's folklore course, whom they could pursue as BTK.

They had followed a number of suspects, but none had panned out, and they had not followed anyone in almost two decades.

The police were not protecting anyone, but Lieutenant Landwehr's testimony clearing former Wichita officer Charles Dearing of being BTK may have been interpreted as "protecting someone." That may also have been the source of the rumor that BTK was a police officer.

So many stories were hard to fully refute because they held a kernel of truth.

By 2003, the Wichita police had put more than 100,000 man-hours into solving the BTK case. The once massive task force working the case had shrunk to one lone investigator: Lieutenant Ken Landwehr.

It was in the fall of 2003 that I became recognized as the local BTK expert, when my students investigated BTK's crimes. The project I designed was similar in many respects to Professor David Protess' investigative journalism class at Northwestern. In that course, students investigate inmate claims of wrongful convictions. The investigation of one group of students led to the release of a man on death row.

Professor Protess and I exchanged several messages about the exercise. Protess' students tried to find information to free those wrongly convicted of crime, and my students were to investigate an unsolved crime.

I finished my chapter in July 2003. I titled it "Justice Delayed Is Justice Denied: Why Not Hold a Grand Jury Investigation on the Three-Decade-Old BTK Murders?"

"*Justitia non est neganda, non differenda*. Justice delayed is justice denied. Justice has been denied for thirty years and I think that means

BTK has gotten away with murder. I ask what is there to risk by having new minds take a fresh look at the evidence?"

In that next month, between the time I provided my course materials to the university and started teaching the class, I talked the matter over with my wife and decided to write a book about BTK. I sent an e-mail query to a literary agent, and the same day he asked for a book proposal. I was on my way to flushing out a killer.

My class featuring the mock BTK grand jury began on August 26, 2003. In my first night lecture on the BTK homicides, I turned off the classroom lights and narrated the story in the dark from the back of the classroom.

After describing BTK hiding in Nancy Fox's and Anna Williams' bedroom closets, I told the class that I believed BTK was still out there. I turned the lights back on, and the first thing I saw was many of the women students shuddering at the horrifying tale. They all looked frightened.

Oh no, I thought, I went too far. I feared that many of the students would drop the class. I worried that my class would be canceled.

But none of that happened. A couple of students did drop the class, but those who remained became completely absorbed in the material. I gave the students a copy of the letter President Clinton wrote, encouraging them in the class.

My students would be the fresh eyes looking at the evidence in this case.

On Wednesday evening, October 8, 2003, my class was held in Chief Judge Richard Ballinger's Sedgwick County, Kansas (Wichita), courtroom. Judge Ballinger, with Nancy Jo Fox's mother, father, sister, best friend, and other family and friends—a group totaling fourteen people—participated in a BTK mock investigative grand jury exercise.

I began the mock jury proceedings by telling those present about my class. I explained that each of my mock grand jurors had been assigned to investigate a different aspect of the case.

One student grand juror's assignment was to interview former Police Chief LaMunyon. That juror reported that LaMunyon had told her that he was "pretty sure" he knew who BTK was but would not give her details. They also spoke about the Poet, and the murders of the Fagers, and the Butterworth trial.

Another student grand juror, a biology major, researched the DNA angle. Invented by Dr. Kary Mullis, the PCR technique requires only a tiny, microscopic amount of DNA for a valid result. (Coincidentally, Dr. Mullis, who received the Nobel Prize in Chemistry for his work, worked at the University of Kansas medical center in the 1970s.)

According to another student grand juror, Detective Ken Landwehr of the WPD was, at that very moment, attempting to obtain BTK DNA from an envelope via PCR technique.

A student grand juror studied the effect of the media on the investigation and discovered that much of the evidence that had been acquired by an investigative press had been confiscated by law enforcement.

One student grand juror made a vain attempt to learn the title of the Wichita Public Library mechanical engineering book chosen by BTK as the hiding spot for his first communication with authorities.

That same juror studied the yearbooks from Wichita State University from the 1970s, during the time of the murders. Some of the composites put together from perhaps dubious eyewitness accounts showed BTK to have long hair, hippie hair, not just falling over the tops of the ears as was the norm even for conservative businessmen during the latter part of the 1970s. By examining the yearbooks, this student found that one could tell the difference between a student and a teacher by the haircut—and that students were much more apt to have long hair than teachers.

Judge Ballinger then explained that he wasn't there just because it was his courtroom. He was there because he had been a friend of Nancy Jo Fox.

"We grew up together. We went to church together. We were together in a youth group from, golly, from grade school all the way through high school.

"The dear lady sitting next to me," Judge Ballinger said, referring to Nancy Jo's mother, "was just about half my mom, too. She was never shy about scolding us when we did something wrong. I can't count the number of times I was over to her house, going places, causing her grief."

Judge Ballinger explained that he had been working for the district attorney's office at the time of Nancy's death. When there was a homicide, a representative of the D.A.'s office usually went to make sure nothing was done that might hamper a future prosecution.

"A homicide trial I was prosecuting, the first homicide trial I had prosecuted, was just starting," Judge Ballinger said. "I had just made my opening statement, when I got a call to report to the scene of a homicide. I explained the situation and asked that someone cover for me, which they did. If I hadn't been so busy I would have had to report to the scene of the murder of my dear friend Nancy Jo Fox."

Ballinger then told the courtroom about the atmosphere among the police during the Poet investigation: "There were cops who thought that the Poet was BTK and there were those who didn't. And those two groups did not speak to one another."

He explained that the Wichita Police Department did not believe in allowing the same detective to be in charge of the same cold case for too long. The belief is that fresh eyes are regularly needed when seeking a breakthrough in a cold case. The new detectives assigned the BTK case were allowed to read all of the old reports—those that had survived the parking garage collapse—but they weren't allowed to discuss the case with the previous detectives. That would prevent, it was believed, erroneous prejudices from being passed on from generation to generation of detectives.

Other than the killer himself, who knows the most about BTK? Judge Ballinger was asked.

"Bernie Drowatzky knows more about this individual than anyone ever could," Ballinger replied. "He put a lot of hours into this and he did a real good job of communicating with the family members as well. He didn't pass on a whole lot of information, but he would just let the family know that they were still working on it from time to time. He didn't always tell the family what they wanted to hear."

It was Nancy's mother's turn to speak. She managed to say, "I'm Nancy's mother. I really don't know what to say. It's just that . . ." She began to cry and was unable to continue. There was a long moment of silence before anyone said anything.

Then Beverly, Nancy's only sister, told the court that she lived in Kansas City at the time of Nancy's death.

"My recollections are all . . ." she said. "I knew something was wrong when I came home from work and my husband told me I needed to sit down. My mother had called. It was a horrible time for my family. I don't remember a lot of things. I remember I took a leave of absence. I took a couple of weeks off from work. Being in Kansas City felt wrong. I needed to be here in Wichita."

Nancy's friend Gloria Patterson then spoke: "I was one of Nancy's best friends. Nancy and my other girlfriend Sandra were like the Three Musketeers. We hung around together all the time, and spent a lot of time together on the weekend. If we didn't see each other, we talked to each other on the phone.

"One thing I learned [after the murder] from Nancy's mother is that you should not keep a routine in your life. Nancy and Sandra and I did have a routine at that time. On Friday and Saturday night, there was a club called Scene Seventies where we went. I was dating my husband now and Nancy was dating the door manager. And another of my girlfriends was dating one of the guys, so we were down there on Friday and Saturday nights. On Sundays Nancy would usually clean house, especially if she was mad about something. And the Sunday before she was killed she was mad. I had talked to her and she was cleaning the house. She was an immaculate cleaner."

She went on to describe that fateful day:

"At that time I worked at Pizza Hut, at the corporate office, and my sister-in-law called me. It was probably about ten o'clock and she told me that she needed to come over and talk to me. She also worked for Pizza Hut, but in another office. She told me there was a police officer there and he was asking her if I knew Nancy. So the police came out and told me that they had found Nancy. Back then there were two Nancy Foxes in Wichita, and I told them maybe it was the other one. But they gave me the address and I knew it was her. The police came and got me. Then they picked up my friend Sandra and told her. And they took both of us to the police department. When they got us there they wanted to separate us and keep us from talking to each other. Sandra and I did not want to be separated at that time. We were just in shock. We didn't believe what we were hearing, anyway. They had my husband and another fellow that Nancy used to date in another area and they were questioning them.

"They also played the tape [of the killer calling the police dispatcher] for us at that time and they asked us if we recognized the voice. He [BTK] had such a monotone. I mean, from what I remember, and I may be totally wrong, he had such a monotone voice. And I think what struck me, and it struck my husband too, was that he used the word *homicide*. That was just not a normal word for a person to use.

"We were questioned for four or five hours, and then they asked Sandra and I if they could take us over to the house and have Sandra and I go over the house with them. At that time they told us that the house had been ransacked. The phone lines had been cut and the thermostat had been turned up to ninety degrees. So we had no idea what we were going to walk in to.

"We got there and it was clear what Nancy had done. From knowing her, it was obvious from the way things were what Nancy had done. She walked in the front door. She laid her jacket and her purse down on the kitchen table. She'd gone into the living room and lit a cigarette. I think she went to the bathroom, came back out, and then took her slacks off. Like I said, she was a very tidy person. She folded her slacks up and put them over the door. And the man must have been in her closet—either in her closet or behind the curtains, Nancy had these huge velvet curtains on these windows. The plants were knocked down and there was dirt all over the floor. My first thought was that she didn't notice the dirt on the floor, but then I thought, if anything was out of place, Nancy would notice. Maybe she didn't look down or something like that. I just figured that they got her from the direction of the closet. I think the only thing missing was her billfold, her driver's license. It was fairly obvious that when he [BTK] called in, he was reading from her driver's license. Another thing we couldn't find afterward was a necklace that a friend had given Nancy. She kept it in the jewelry box, next to the photo of our bowling team, on top of her dresser, but it wasn't there when we looked.

"At first they thought it was one of the boys that Nancy had been dating, Cue Quilty. Then they found that he had an alibi. He, bless his heart, he kind of went to pure hell on that deal. They thought it was somebody she knew—and then they thought it might be somebody who worked at the Wichita Mall, where Helzberg's was."

At the time of Nancy's murder, Cue Quilty attended WSU during the day and worked at Helzberg's Jewelers in the evenings. The morning they learned of Nancy's murder, the police came and took Cue out of a class at WSU. It was Gloria who told the police where he probably was. Larry, Gloria's husband, said that when they were all down at the police station, Quilty was seen but never talked with by anyone. He was segregated from the others. Larry said that Quilty looked pale and scared to death.

Gloria said, "It was possible that one or more of Nancy's collectible tiny jewelry boxes was missing. Nancy collected little porcelain, pewter, and cedar chests. Some of them were in animal shapes. After Nancy's murder, Nancy's mother told me and Sandra to take some as mementos, if we wished. I took a tiny jewel encrusted turtle-shaped jewelry box, which she showed me. It's about the size of a man's thumb."

Gloria then summed up her feelings about Nancy: "There is one image of Nancy that I wish I could get out of my head. I keep thinking of her as a butterfly. I guess we were all butterflies. After all, we were only twenty-five years old. We went out to our clubs, and it wasn't like we did anything wrong. We partied and we danced—but we weren't floozies or something like that."

The conversation then turned to Nancy's neighbors. Judge Ballinger recalled that the other apartment in Nancy's duplex was vacant. A couple named Allen and Kathy, Nancy's former neighbors, had recently moved out.

"They had known Nancy, gone to the same church. I remember them telling me that they wondered, if they hadn't moved out, maybe it would never have happened," Judge Ballinger said.

Gloria Patterson added, "There were times when Nancy was worried about going home alone at night because there was no one living in the other side of the duplex. To this day I believe that the people to the south heard something but they were too scared to talk about it. I know that fear can take over your voice, but Nancy was such a fighter and everything, I would have thought that she would have cried out. But maybe she was so afraid that she couldn't get out a scream.

"How do any of us know how we would react to a situation like that? Nancy was a fighter, but she may have froze. I don't know. I don't know what she did. I don't know what I would do. I was told that there was no sign of a struggle. Nancy did not fight. There must be a reason."

Gloria told the court class that the day after the murder, at the funeral home, Nancy's head was so swollen that her features were unrecognizable. She was told the reason for this had to do with the position in which the body was found. Nancy's head had dangled over the side of the bed for hours, causing this swelling. The mortician had done the best he could. That was the story Gloria was told, or what she has chosen to remember.

I kept silent. Nancy's head, I knew, was not swollen because it hung over the side of the bed at all. But I was not going to say the real reason for the swelling of Nancy's head—not in front of Nancy's parents and siblings. The killer tightened the panty hose noose just enough to restrict veinous flow, so that her head began to congest and swell. I also keep mum on the police's best theory as to why Nancy cooperated with her killer and did not fight. She never believed she was in danger. She must have believed the guy was going to tie her up, then depart. Maybe he promised he would call and be sure that someone came to untie her.

Maybe that is why BTK called the operator at 8:18 a.m. Maybe he felt he was keeping his promise. Some serial killers are perverted that way.

This had started out a classroom project, then a possible armchair detective book, but tonight I was seeing more clearly how it altered the lives of those who survived, the friends and families, the haunted members of the press, and the law enforcement officers who had experienced decades of frustration over the BTK investigation.

Gloria remembered that, on the Saturday after Nancy's murder, a crank caller had phoned Helzberg's and said that "the little blonde was next." Gloria said that the police told her about the call because Gloria is a little blonde, and was the only other little blonde anyone knew.

"The only little blonde that Nancy hung out with was me," Gloria said.

Driving home from the courthouse late the night of October 8, 2003, I noticed the streets were flooded by a terrible rainstorm—but my mind was not on what was in front of me. I was thinking about the evening and how it changed my perception of what I was doing. I had studied enough about BTK that I believed I knew how to provoke him. If he was alive, he would come forward. But there was a terrible risk.

Dr. Eric Hickey, researcher and author of the standard work in the field, *Serial Murderers and Their Victims*—the book that Wichita homicide Lieutenant Kenny Landwehr used to teach his course on serial killers—concluded that one is very unlikely to be targeted by a serial killer. But if one is targeted by a serial killer, one is very unlikely to survive.

If I provoked BTK, would my family become his target? And if so, would the police identify BTK before he made his move against my family? Was this worth what it might cost? On the surface, the immediate conclusion was no. It was for the best that I drop the BTK thing and move on to a less risky project.

But my wife had been a pediatrician for more than thirty years. She had bravely walked into the hot zone. And I served as a firefighter for nine years. Three times I was injured in the line of duty, twice in arson fires, once in a trap set by the arsonist to delay the fire suppression specifically by injuring a firefighter. Long ago I decided I was willing to put my life at risk for the benefit of the good people of the community.

Our two daughters were both married and out of the house. Only the two of us were now at home.

That night I watched my wife sleep for a long time. This could end up a waste of time, or fostering only more suspicion, but I knew that when I told her of Nancy's mother's tears, and I told her that there would be no peace for so many in this case unless the story was resolved, I knew she would support me.

And she did.

Chapter 23

An Odyssey Through the Past

Fourteen years earlier, during the early morning hours of Wednesday, June 7, 1989, in east Wichita near Twenty-first Street North and Edgemoor, Terri Maness was found murdered in her home. As written in former FBI agent Dan Mitrione's careful and thoroughly researched book, when homicide Lieutenant Ken Landwehr "first saw the Maness crime scene, he wondered whether the gruesome murder might be another in the BTK series."

My reading and rereading that assertion was keeping me awake. I knew that credible officers had concluded that BTK had written to Mary Fager in January 1988. Now I read this FBI agent's book and he reports that Landwehr thought Terri Maness might have been murdered by BTK—*in 1989*!

Most people thought that BTK was dead. They would all say it almost the same way, with the flat assertion, "He's dead." Then they'd add, "These guys don't stop killing because they might get caught any more than heroin addicts stop because they might get caught. He's dead." Then, they'd qualify their statement, "If he's not dead, he's in custody, either in prison or a mental hospital."

A few cops told me of specific suspects, but when I asked why they didn't DNA test these suspects, they'd answer: It's a cold case, so it is a low priority. The cold cases are the lowest priority that there is in processing DNA. One current officer told me of a minor theft in an overnight grocery store burglary that they are running DNA tests on, and that is a higher priority than cold cases.

But if the police thought that BTK was alive and still living in Wichita, that explained their presentation to Mensa in 1995, having Robert Ressler speak at WSU in 1997, their raid on Dan Rouser's home in 1998.

I had hoped to be able to provoke a renewed investigation. I hoped a book would interest readers and some would check to see whether they had inherited BTK's souvenirs. Now I had to consider the very real possibility that BTK was alive and living nearby.

The research into the book would lead me down many strange avenues. I would conduct interviews with all the policemen on the case that were still alive or would talk to me. I would talk to judges, psychologists—and relatives of the victims.

One of the most traumatic occurred early on. I learned that Nancy's mother called all over town asking about me when I started teaching the BTK project. Then she invited me to her home to talk. We had a very good interview, but I had to ask the painful question we both wanted to avoid. I asked her to tell me how she learned of her daughter's death.

On the morning of December 9, 1977, she had been employed as a cashier and plate preparation worker in the cafeteria at the St. Joseph Medical Center, located only a couple of blocks from the Wichita Mall, where Nancy worked evenings. Nancy lived less than a mile away.

She said it was an abnormal morning. She did something she had never done before; she knocked over a cart and broke dozens of dishes. She was embarrassed and cleaning them up took time away from normal preparations. She was hurrying to have the cafeteria prepared for the lunch rush when her boss said that he needed to see her. She said that she did not have time, she was about to open the cash register. Her boss said that another employee would take care of it. This was unusual and annoying.

She went to his office thinking this was about the broken dishes or something else that was a bother.

When she entered, she saw the head of security and her husband. She and Dale Fox had divorced, and this was her second husband. Because he was here with the head of security she knew immediately that something was terribly wrong. She started crying. Her husband told her that Nancy had been murdered.

She doesn't remember much after that. She did go to the police station and listen to the audiotape of the telephone call. She did not recognize the voice.

I asked her about suspects. She had never eliminated Cue Quilty from her mind as a suspect.

She then showed me all of her remaining photos of Nancy. There were not many. She said that decades ago, at police request, she had taken most of Nancy's photos, and all the photo albums that had photos of Nancy, and turned them over. The police have since refused to return them.

Charles Liles told me they may no longer have them; they may have been destroyed. After Chris Cherches took over as city manager, the police budget was cut to its essentials. This was in agreement with what Chief Rick Stone had told me. Records of old cases were routinely destroyed to save storage space.

She looked so forlorn, holding her daughter's picture, not having many to show me. Her family and friends later collected all available photos of Nancy Jo Fox and showed them to me. There were only thirteen photos.

Shortly after Nancy's funeral, Nancy's mother's parents both died in a car accident. Then she learned that her daughter's murder was by a serial killer. It was too much.

As I was about to depart, Nancy's mother was seated at her dining room table in front of her photos, but she was not looking at them. She started wringing her hands. She started very softly repeating, "I can't remember. I just can't remember. I can't remember." At first I thought that she was grieving, saying that she was unable to remember how Nancy looked. But she kept repeating the phrase over and over—"I can't remember." She was wringing her hands with such strength that I thought her frail skin might tear. She was in a trance.

I leaned over and as softly as I could, asked, "What can't you remember?"

She looked up at me and said, "I can't remember where my husband was that night. I think he was out. I have tried so hard to remember, but I just can't remember. I can't remember." She looked away again and became lost in her reverie, wringing her hands, whispering slowly, forlornly, "I can't remember. I can't remember. I can't remember."

I almost wept.

Richard Ballinger, Nancy's sister Bev, and Gloria Patterson had each told me that Nancy's mother had coped with Nancy's death and its aftermath as well as she could, but she had been irrevocably changed. Nancy's murder killed a part of her mother, too. She was now suspicious of men whom she had no reason to suspect. Her late husband was one of them.

Nancy's mother was another BTK victim.

During the course of writing I added up facts about the different suspects in the BTK case. In order to protect their privacy, these BTK suspects are disguised composite characters. Each description contains facts I learned. I have ordered them according to my own opinion as to the likelihood of their guilt prior to the events of March 2004.

1. Suspect Baroko. Vietnam veteran, a USAF officer, who reportedly had a "nervous breakdown" after returning to the United States because his fiancée rejected him. He was a suspect in the Otero murders. He patronized Dillons. He was tall—six-foot-two—and well tanned. He rarely if ever spoke and had been seen photocopying illustrations of guns out of magazines, and purchasing gallon-sized Baggies. He lived in a house with the windows boarded up. His neighbors told me that he did not let grass grow around his home and that he raked the dirt each night. A neighbor finally asked him why he did that, and he answered that he raked the soft dirt so that the the next morning he could see whether there were any footprints around his home. He told a neighbor that he would like to kill someone.

I discussed Suspect Baroko with *Wichita Eagle* reporters Fred Mann and Hurst Laviana. *The Wichita Eagle* had previously obtained a restraining order against Baroko because he had tried to assault Hurst Laviana. The suspect lives near two unsolved murders, of Linda Shawn Casey and Sherry D. Baker.

He was the only suspect who started showing up around me and my wife after it became generally known that I was writing a book. I saw him bicycle past my home. I saw him in the grocery store where my wife and I shop. I saw him at two bookstores where my wife and I were shopping.

Fred Mann and I discussed this guy in January 2004, but Mann said that they had looked at him and knew that he haunts those same places. Fred's opinion was that it could just be a coincidence that the suspect started showing up in the same places where my wife and I were.

I looked him up on Lexis Nexis, an online legal research service, and learned that he had been arrested by WPD Officer Okoye.

I discussed this with Charles Liles and he repeatedly told me to report the guy to Landwehr. But there was a problem. In checking my records I found that, technically, he had been my client. While I was working for a law firm, some paperwork involving him had crossed my desk. I checked with two senior judges about the ethics of talking about him any further. I am following the limits required by the code of professional responsibility.

2. Suspect Barbara. A former Coleman employee and part-time postal carrier who had been treated for psychiatric illness. He lived near the Oteros when they were murdered, and his sister was Nancy Fox's neighbor when she was murdered. At one time this suspect was under police surveillance. This man was the police's favorite "short suspect." Kevin Bright picked him out of a police photo array as the man who attacked him and murdered his sister.

3. Suspect Bokardo. Career military soldier stationed in Wichita, reportedly a practitioner of bondage. Now retired, he is reportedly working as a security guard in Wichita.

4. Suspect Camenes. Former Wichita police officer who had left the department before the Otero murders under less than ideal circumstances. At one time this suspect was under police surveillance.

5. Suspect Calarent. Business executive who moved from Wichita some years ago. He became explosively angry when asked about being a BTK suspect.

6. Suspect Cesare. A man who had made a purchase at Helzberg's Jewelers while Nancy Fox worked there and who was seen patronizing Scene Seventies, which Nancy Fox frequented.

7. Suspect Festino. A man who made deliveries to Dillons grocery stores. There are Dillons links to the Otero (car was left in Dillons parking lot), Vian (lived four houses from a Dillons), and Wegerle (lived a few blocks from Dillons) murders. This suspect's family reportedly provided DNA samples.

8. Suspect Dimaris. A Wichita journalist who is reportedly a prac-

titioner of bondage. This man was the favorite "tall suspect" of many police officers.

9. Suspect Ferison. A former firefighter who served fifteen years in custody for aggravated assault, reportedly for binding and torturing a prostitute. Apparently, part of the time that he was in custody he was in a state mental hospital, not prison, and was permitted occasional outside travel.

10. Suspect Disamis. A laborer who had reportedly worked at Coleman and a foundry near Coleman. He was described as very intelligent and capable but not well educated. He reportedly did not spell well. He has vanished.

11. Suspect Datisi. A man who served prison time for assault, described as "obnoxious," and who lived near the Oteros. For a short time this man was under police surveillance. He has worked at odd jobs in Wichita his entire life. He is a local "character."

12. Suspect Camestres. A former Wichita police officer currently serving life in prison for homicide. This officer was arrested in 1989, after the 1988 letter to Mary Fager, and reportedly knew the Fager family. The suspect is serving a life sentence in prison for strangling his wife.

Fred Mann was the inside man on the Poet story, acknowledged as the best writer on the *Wichita Eagle*. He consented to several interviews with me about BTK and BTK-related events, the first on Tuesday, December 16, 2003. A lot of my information about the Poet case came from Fred Mann. He said, "Drowatzky became much too close to Ruth during this early time, often dining at her home, and he shared BTK information with her. When the Poet case finally ended, Drowatzky was blamed by others in the department as the source for Ruth's knowledge about BTK."

The differences among the police officers reminded me of the differences in the astronaut corps that Tom Wolfe wrote about in *The Right Stuff*. The astronauts did not all like each other, but they did work together to get the job done. The cops did not all like each other, but they were bound in a common cause, and they all wanted to see BTK caught and punished.

Time changes idiom, and I could not help but notice that the cops almost never referred to BTK as "BTK." They generally referred to him as "this guy." The most common word each cop used to describe him was, "This guy is mean." They did not use psychological jargon. They did not use profanity. They said he was "mean."

In the fall of 2003 Randy Brown and I had lunch at the Black Canyon Grill on North Rock Road in Wichita. Randy told me his life story and his views on the BTK investigation.

During the late 1970s and early 1980s Randy Brown was the best-known face in Wichita. An anchorman at KAKE TV, he emceed all the important local television specials, panel discussions, and events such as the local Gridiron gala. Randy told me of his years at *The Wichita Eagle*, KAKE TV, *The Wichita Sun*, and now teaching at Wichita State University. He has had as rich a career as any journalist in this community. He thought that the BTK story was Wichita's one great untold story. He was glad that I was writing this book.

We had a very enlightening lunch. He started asking me about BTK suspects, which he and every other journalist in Wichita knew as well or better than I did. But I told Randy that I was not trying to solve the case, just chronicle what happened. Randy paused as if that was a new idea. "Bob, you may get further along toward solving the case by not trying to solve it than we did being investigative reporters."

After lunch we went to a nearby Kinko's copy center. Randy had brought copies of Cathy Henkel's 1974 BTK articles in *The Sun*. They were newspapers bound in large volumes and were too large for the small copy machines up front. Randy asked the young clerk if he would make the copies on the machine behind the counter that would copy oversized pages. The young clerk said that he could not because these newspapers were copyrighted.

Of course, the newspaper had been defunct for twenty-seven years and its owner was dead. Randy and I looked at each other, and Randy said, "Well, since I was the editor of this paper, I guess I can authorize copying, can't I?"

Sometimes my answers came from unexpected sources. On a day in early January 2004, I called Dr. Robert Daniels, the former district coroner. Doc Eckert had died but I heard that Doc Daniels was still around. I left a detailed message on the answering machine about why I was calling.

That evening the phone rang, and when I answered, the caller said that I had left a message on his answering machine calling for Doc Daniels. I said that I had. The caller said that he was not Doc Daniels and I had the wrong number. Then he said, "But I know a lot about the BTK case. I dated Kathy Bright."

He told me his name and I looked at the phone book. I immediately understood what I had done. I had entered the Valley Center prefix (Valley Center is a Wichita satellite city west of Park City, known to its natives as "God's Country"), the correct first three numbers, then mistakenly entered the numbers on the line adjacent to Dr. Daniels.

We had a long talk and he explained what Kevin Bright had told him as soon as he was out of the hospital. Kevin had said that the killer could have been "Mexican or Oriental."

Kathy Bright's old boyfriend said, "If you ever get a line on him [BTK], there are a lot of pissed-off people up here that would come and visit him." I said that I'd let him know.

When Hurst Laviana, a crime reporter for *The Wichita Eagle*, called me on Wednesday, January 14, 2004, I had conducted at least sixty interviews. Hurst had not wanted to do a thirtieth anniversary story, but his editor wanted him to write one. Hurst said that he didn't have a hook, but Roy Wenzl said Bob Beattie was writing a book about BTK, so why didn't Hurst contact Bob?

Hurst called me and we spoke for an hour. At the end, after hearing everything I had done and planned to do, he said, "You really are writing a book." He then asked if a photographer could come over, and I consented. When Fernando Salazar came over, he knew what he wanted. He asked me to sit in front of my computer and hold up my notebook of the press clippings. I had the book's title on my computer screen, but he said that did not photograph well. So I printed it out, taped it to the computer monitor, and he photographed that. He said he thought they were going to run the story on Sunday.

With respect to the Wichita press, the BTK story has been unique and controversial. It has been investigated off and on for thirty years. People want this guy caught, but he has eluded capture by police or press. Reasonable minds may differ, but I think an easily overlooked aspect of this story is the relationship of the Wichita press and police.

In January 1974 *The Wichita Eagle* started its Secret Witness program after the Otero murders. The *Eagle* agreed not to run stories it obtained but instead to turn the information over to the police. That is why Detective Bernie Drowatzky picked up the BTK letter on October 22, 1974, instead of *Eagle* columnist Don Granger. Did a defender of the First Amendment become an agent of the police?

What role would the press play in reporting the BTK story now?

During the morning of Thursday, January 15, 2004, I separately interviewed Mark Chamberlin of KAKE-TV and former KAKE-TV anchor Rose Stanley. Mark told me about standing out in the cold thirty years earlier, waiting with his camera to get the shots of the police removing the Oteros' bodies. He said it was probably around 2:30 a.m. He was freezing and was thinking that maybe this was not the line of work he should do. This was his first assignment.

Rose Stanley told me about the discussion not to feature her when the BTK story broke February 10, 1978, because they didn't want BTK to focus on her and make her a potential target. She told me about the later threat and that she had round-the-clock police protection for several weeks. She said that Richard LaMunyon had assured her that BTK was now an older man and was either dead or in custody and was no longer a threat.

Charles Liles told me that our brain chemistry changes as we age. Statistics show that very few men are arrested for violence after they are age thirty-five, and even fewer after age fifty. The reason we hear about it on the news when someone over age fifty is arrested for violence is because it is so unusual. Dozen of young men are put in jail for violent offenses each day, but that is not newsworthy. It is the rarity that makes the news. Charles thought that BTK was certainly still capable of violence, but was probably not inclined toward it. Still, he warned me to be alert.

Hurst Laviana's article was published in *The Wichita Eagle* January 17, 2004, Saturday rather than Sunday, on the front page, accompanied by the photo for which Fernando Salazar had asked me to pose, where I am holding my scrapbook of clippings and the book's title is taped to the computer monitor. Beneath my photo was the caption: "Wichita lawyer Robert Beattie sits at his desk with a scrapbook containing newspaper clippings on some of the BTK murders. Beattie has conducted sixty interviews and is writing a book about the case."

The story was continued inside. Accompanying the article on the inner page of the front section was a photo of authorities removing the body of one of the Oteros from their house. In the article I was quoted as saying about the book, "It's a people story. It's also a little mini-history of the last thirty years—not only of Wichita but many of its institutions."

I told Laviana that I hoped my book would have a positive effect on the BTK investigation: "I'm hoping someone will read the book and come forward with some information—a driver's license, a watch, some car keys." That quote is also in big bold print offset in a sidebar.

"If he [BTK] has died, maybe some family member who has those items will realize that significance," I continued.

During the telephone interview, I told Hurst, "I told my wife I didn't think we'd hear from BTK—but I did warn her to expect to hear from crackpots and well-meaning people with little to contribute." Mary Ann was sitting next to me when I said that and she nodded her head. I mention this because, as published, the article concludes, "Beattie said he expects his book to draw the attention of a lot of people who remember the killings. 'I'm sure we will be contacted by both crackpots and well-meaning people who have little to contribute,' he said. 'But I do not think we'll be contacted by BTK.' "

What I told Hurst was that I did not think that Mary Ann and I would hear from BTK. I had said that to reassure my wife. But I imagine that Hurst wrote down the quote as it was printed, and it appeared to be saying that everyone, not just Mary Ann and I, would not be contacted by BTK.

James Preston Girard, a former *Eagle* editor and novelist I had interviewed earlier, contacted me by e-mail and asked me about that quote. To him, it sounded like I was trying to provoke BTK into making contact. I told Girard what happened but decided not to say anything to the *Eagle* or to Hurst. This way it worked out better than I intended. Obviously, if Girard thought the sentence was trying to provoke BTK, then maybe it would.

In some ways the response was more dramatic than the March 1, 1999, article that started Manson Mania, except the response was not at all from the press but entirely from individuals. The Saturday edition of *The Wichita Eagle* virtually sold out. That evening I went out to purchase another copy for my parents, who are living in Oklahoma, and I had to go to eight convenience stores until I found a copy.

At a Quik Trip convenience store, the clerk and I started talking about the article. It was the hot topic of the day. When I held up the picture and he realized that I was the guy writing the book, he looked at me like I was stupid and he had to explain this to a slow child. He said, "I'm a graduate of the criminal justice program at WSU. They taught me that BTK was dead. You do know that he's dead, don't you?" He nodded his head, hoping that I was smart enough to understand.

I said, "Yeah, that's what everyone tells me."

Almost everyone who expressed an opinion said that BTK was dead, even convenience store clerks.

But I did receive calls from those who had other opinions.

The first call I received the morning of January 17, 2004, was from a man who told me of a suspect who had worked machine tools and welding at a foundry but disappeared when the police wanted to talk with him about the BTK murders. He said he was the foundry manager and that the last time he spoke with Lieutenant Landwehr about this suspect, Landwehr had said that they still couldn't find him. He said that he didn't know what race the former employee/suspect was; he might have been Negro, Mexican, or Oriental. He said that he would get in touch with Landwehr again.

The next call was from Darrell Barton. Darrell was sixty years old, a former U.S. Marine Vietnam combat veteran, had lived at 1311 South Hydraulic (the house where Shirley Vian would be murdered), was a good friend of Ron Loewen, and had been a KAKE-TV cameraman. He told me several stories, and we discussed suspects.

Until the 1980s, local reporters were commissioned by the sheriff as deputies, permitting them to enter crime scenes and take photographs, interview witnesses, etc. Darrell Barton may have been the only member of the Wichita press to refuse the commission card. He thought that was an improper mingling of the police-press relationship.

He said that for years he had tried to interest various producers in doing a show on BTK but had always been unsuccessful. He wanted to meet and talk with me about doing a documentary for the Discovery Channel. He was now an independent producer and cameraman. I agreed to meet him.

Next, Heidi Hunt called. She was the first of the women who contacted me because they were serial killer aficionados. Over the next several weeks we spoke over the phone and exchanged several telephone messages. She was fascinated with the BTK story. She was so fascinated, she went to 803 North Edgemoor, the Oteros' former home, and told the residents that she was a college student writing a paper about the BTK Strangler. She said that they let her in, she went through the entire house, and had a long talk with them. I told her not to do that anymore, but I agreed that she could call me again.

On Thursday, February 12, I had lunch with Charles Liles and a former drug dealer. The dealer said that neither he nor anyone he spoke with in the underworld community knew BTK's identity, unlike many other sensational criminals in Wichita. They were as scared of BTK as the straight community. This would be like the Mafia members in *The Godfather* being afraid of BTK. He boarded up his back windows the same way Al Stewart did.

On Tuesday, February 24, I had a long lunch meeting with Dr. Delores Craig-Moreland, a psychologist. Before earning her doctorate she had been a federal law enforcement agent for six years. For her doctoral dissertation she went to prisons and interviewed felons. She spent hours and sometimes weeks hearing their stories of how they became felons. Then she obtained permission from them to read their files and legal records to confirm as much of their stories as possible.

In essence, all of them had the same story: they became felons incrementally. They started with minor offenses for which they were not caught. That emboldened them and they committed worse offenses. They were sometimes questioned but they smooth-talked their way out of being suspects with plausible stories. They took greater and greater risks until they were caught. Very few felt bad about their crimes, but they all regretted getting caught. Most focused an inordinate amount of time on some minor "mistake" in deviousness that they had made that led to their arrest and conviction. In prison they discussed their errors with other prisoners and resolved to learn from their own mistakes.

Did BTK start with small crimes, then build up to murder? Because all the victims were murdered in their own homes, it is likely that BTK felt comfortable breaking into homes and smooth-talking his way into homes. He had probably been doing that his entire adult life. While a teenager he may have started his career of break-ins and fraudulent entry. He may have started by surreptitiously taking small available things off of tables and dressers and out of purses, then quickly pocketing the items. He got away with these misdemeanor crimes and later built up to bigger crimes.

Dr. Craig-Moreland said that she thought that BTK probably selected his victims in this sequence: First, he selected the neighborhood. Second, he selected the list of candidate houses. Third, he selected the victim by watching the candidate houses. He wanted to be able to escape. He wanted to be able to enjoy his kill. Before he struck he would know the victim's routine, the neighborhood's routine, the type of vehicle the victim drove, etc. He may have targeted a dozen victims before rejecting them due to some factor that soured him on the target, finally selecting one to act on. He may have acted on several before withdrawing prior to attacking. He may have talked his way into homes, then withdrawn. He may have broken into homes, or simply walked into homes where a door was unlocked, but had not attacked the residents.

He was sexually motivated, but his actions fulfilled a very specific fantasy that evolved over time. Whatever it was, it was different now than it was in 1974. Because he had been successful in not being caught, he was probably like all the prisoners she had interviewed insofar as he studied how to continue committing crimes and avoid capture.

These ideas fascinated me. What she said made sense. I thanked Dr. Craig-Moreland and hoped that we would talk again.

Dr. Lonnie Athens' concept of "violentization," discussed in detail in Richard Rhodes' book *Why They Kill: The Discoveries of a Maverick Criminologist*, seemed to tie in with what Dr. Craig-Moreland told me. Dr. Athens compiled in-depth case studies and statistics to prove that most people do not become violent because they are mentally ill. While a minority do, most go through a long "education" where they learn that violence solves their problem, so they become violent. They go through four stages: (1) *brutalization*, often in childhood, when they suffer violence and learn that violence resolves disputes; (2) *belligerency*, where they see that their threat of violence often resolves disputes; (3) *violent performances*, where they are violent and they feel that this violent behavior satisfactorily resolved their problem, though they may be taken into custody; and (4) *virulency*, where they quickly look to extreme violence rather than negotiation as a means of addressing disputes or conflict.

Dr. Athens did significant research while teaching at Kansas State University and studying offenders at the greatest collection of prisoners in the world, nearby Leavenworth, Kansas, with its four major prisons.

Based on everything I had learned from the psychologists and profilers, it appeared that BTK likely went through the violentization stages Dr. Athens described, and went through the felon creation stages that Dr. Craig-Moreland described, and went through stages where he evolved a specific sex fantasy involving bondage.

These clinical studies led to another question: What if it was two people?

In BTK's February 1978 letter he mentioned "Ted of the West Coast" and "The Pantyhose Strangler of Florida." Those two proved to be the same man, Ted Bundy. BTK also mentioned the Hillside Strangler, which proved to be two people, Kenneth Bianchi and Angelo Buono. More than one quarter of all serial killers and mass murderers, whether they are killing for conventional or unconventional motives, prove to be murdering with one or more partners. Sometimes a dual personality develops and one or more of a team become killers when together although they would not kill alone.

As described in Truman Capote's *In Cold Blood*, the Clutter family of Holcomb, Kansas, was murdered by Perry Smith and Richard Hickock, but neither Hickock nor Smith would have been likely to have murdered the Clutters had either been burglarizing the home alone.

In late 2000 Kansas brothers Reginald and Jonathan Carr murdered five people and attempted to murder a sixth. *Wichita Eagle* crime reporter Ron Sylvester is writing a book about the Carr case, and I have discussed this case with him. Both of the Carr brothers had minor criminal backgrounds, but knowledgeable people think that if the brothers had not been united there would have been no murders. There can be no clearer agreement on this point than the fact that on October 13, 2004, in response to a lawsuit filed by the victims' families, the State of Kansas approved a $1.7 million settlement with the victims' families. Reginald Carr was mistakenly given early release by a Ford County, Kansas, parole officer. It is believed that if Reginald Carr had not been released, the murderous dual personality of the two brothers would not have formed, and the brothers would not have committed the murders.

Beyond Kansas there are much more widely known killer teams. Leonard Lake and Charles Ng partnered to create a sex torture and murder enterprise on the West Coast. The married team of Paul Bernardo and Karla Homolka sex tortured and murdered young women in Canada, including Karla's sister.

Perhaps the most horrifying team ever apprehended was that of Lawrence Bittaker and Roy Norris. They met in prison and decided when they were released they would form a team to sexually torture and murder young women. They worked hard at their "job," rehearsing by picking up women and giving them rides without attacking them. They bought a 1977 cargo van and equipped it to hold their victims while they raped and tortured them. They began their crimes on June 24, 1979. At first they tried strangling women with their hands but they found that very difficult. They learned that the easiest way was to wrap a metal clothes hanger around the woman's neck, then twist it with pliers to strangle the woman. They used a hammer and pliers to torture women. And they audiotaped their crimes and they kept other "trophies." The audiotapes are horrifying. The men were arrested in late November 1979, having had a five-month torture and murder spree.

Captain Al Stewart and FBI profiler Roy Hazelwood apparently had several heated discussions about whether BTK was one or two or more people. "Prove it to me. Prove that BTK is one man." Hazelwood believed BTK was one man. Stewart thought BTK was probably one man, but with all the duos out there committing murders, Stewart thought it should surprise no one if BTK turned out to have been two people, where only one left semen at the crime scenes.

After all, BTK went out of his way in his first letter to insist he did it all himself. Perhaps he was deliberately being misleading. That's what these killers do.

In researching this book—especially after talking with psychologists such as Dr. Samuel Harrell, who are convinced that BTK participates in bondage—I did some Internet research.

In his book *Anyone You Want Me to Be*, John Douglas describes some of the webpages on bondage. I did some research on that topic, but my online search caused me to find a bulletin board project called Crime & Justice board: http://p216.ezboard.com/bcrimeandjustice13552. This is a nonprofit website that exists to help try to solve crimes.

I was astonished to learn that only fifty-six hours after my class ended the previous fall, a "thread" topic was started on the BTK Strangler. The thread was started by "TheGoldenBoy37" on October 17, 2003. I first learned of the BTK Strangler bulletin board thread on the evening of Thursday, January 22, 2004. I began a correspondence with Bill Peterson, known online as Runes1.

Bill is a co-founder and system administrator for the Crime & Justice Board. He earned a master's degree from Georgetown in National Security Studies and had been a lieutenant colonel in the U.S. Air Force and served in Vietnam.

Crime & Justice originated in February 2002 and has been working virtually 24/7 since. They had over 2 million visits in their first twenty-two months of operation, averaging better than one person a minute in February 2004. At this point they have about 800 registered members.

The website administrators and participants have been thanked for their service in the Martha Moxley case, the Baton Rouge Serial Killer Task Force, the Valery Percy murder reinvestigation, and a JonBenet case book has been published by one of the Crime & Justice moderators.

The website is entirely pro bono and without support of any kind. According to Bill, "Our staff includes Sisu (owner and manager of CJ sites) and myself (Head Visionary—lol), and a wonderful staff of five truly dedicated 'soccer moms.'" Bill believes, "We have become the only truly proactive crime investigation website on the Internet."

The website is intended as an information exchange and forum for those with relevant information or commentary on unsolved crimes. At the time I write it is the single best online source for information on the BTK Strangler crimes.

In late February several people on the Crime & Justice website BTK Strangler thread posted messages that variously said that BTK was dead, BTK was alive, and that talking/writing about BTK would bring him back. I did not know whether BTK or anyone who might have his souvenirs might be reading these online messages, but I thought the exchanges were perfect for my comments.

On February 28 I submitted a statement to Bill, who posted it on the Crime & Justice website at 9:05 p.m. I wrote about the pathological suspicion this case has spawned and concluded by writing:

"I decided to share this excerpt from my book's foreword because of recent postings on this thread. I have met with family or friends of most of the victims, with many of the law enforcement officers who investigated this case, and with broadcast and print reporters who covered this story. Everyone suffered from these events, both the obvious bereaved and the forgotten grievers. Those who have offered me their cooperation welcome this book's examination. Reasonable minds may differ, but in my opinion this is a story that deserves to be discussed about people who deserve to be remembered."

My working title was *American Mystery: The Epic Thirty-Year Hunt for B.T.K.—The "Bind Torture Kill" Serial Killer.*

The post led to several appreciative messages.

I was honored when John Garrison, the president of the Wichita Retired Police Officers Association and editor of the association's quarterly newsletter, featured in the latest issue of "The Re Tired Copper," Jan/Mar 2004, two stories on page one on Robert Beattie. He reported that I was speaking about my BTK book at the annual membership meeting at Spears Restaurant West on Saturday, March 20. The other was an article that I wrote about writing this book. This "Re Tired Copper" issue is mailed to the address of every former police officer. Sometimes widows want to keep up with what the others are doing and will attend functions or pay for a subscription to the newsletter. I was proud to be able to address all of these officers who had worked so hard on the case.

In one of the strangest turns during my research, I met a woman who was convinced her father was the BTK strangler.

While doing research, reading John Douglas's Internet bulletin board, I became interested in the postings of a woman who described herself as a profiler. I sent an e-mail message to her, and she replied that she was Rhonda Johnson of Minnesota and described herself as a forty-seven-year-old "housewife." We began exchanging occasional e-mail messages and occasionally talking on the telephone.

Rhonda put me in touch with Alice.

Julie Ladd, murdered in 1977, had been Alice's Sunday school teacher. Alice knew that someone had confessed to murdering Julie Ladd, but she rejected that conclusion. She was convinced that BTK murdered her. I began a correspondence with Alice. Alice had been posting messages on a BTK discussion thread on the John Douglas website at least since April 11, 2003. She had been looking into the BTK crimes for months.

After reading the January article in the *Eagle* where I said that I hoped a family member might look and find some items BTK took from his victims, Alice told me that she went to her mother's in Oklahoma City and looked in her late father's stored-away stuff. The first thing she found was a "military" wristwatch with the initials "J.O." on its back. Her father had died seven years earlier, in 1997.

Alice's father lived in Oklahoma City during BTK's known activities but was a traveling salesman and spent approximately a week a month in Wichita. He stayed here with his sisters, so there was no hotel record of his being here. They lived near Adams Elementary School, and anyone staying there could have seen Josie Otero at school.

Alice told me of finding the wristwatch with the initials "J.O." and I asked why her father would have had that. She said that she thought her dad was BTK. There was a quiet moment. "Why do you think that?" I asked.

She answered, "Because on his deathbed seven years ago he confessed to being BTK. I never believed him because he was a mean old man, he was always abusive, and I never believed him. I thought it was just one last effort at hurting me. But after finding this watch, I don't know." She asked me what I thought she should do.

I told her that she had to contact Detective Landwehr.

She refused. She said that she didn't trust Detective Landwehr.

I asked, "Why?"

She was vague, but she insisted that she didn't trust him.

Over a period of weeks we talked about this issue. Technically, I was only communicating with her as a writer, not as a lawyer, but I kept our conversations confidential while she made up her mind about what to do.

Alice and I met in person for the first time on March 10, 2004, at the Village Inn Restaurant. Alice brought family photos and some photocopies of old *Wichita Eagle* newspaper clippings. She had a photo of her father wearing a cap and jacket that matched the drawing. Her dad looked exactly like the drawing of the Bright suspect. The resemblance was uncanny.

Alice said that during BTK's known activities her father lived one week a month in the target neighborhood. He was a glib salesman and could talk his way out of anything. Her uncle had served time for sex crimes. She said that her father sexually abused her when she was Josie Otero's age, and it was horrible. I began to feel uncomfortable sitting there at a table in a busy restaurant while she described what happened. She said he would begin by bringing her down into their basement. Then he would put her legs over a pipe and she would swing upside down. She said that she has thought a thousand times about little Josie Otero swinging from a pipe in her basement. Alice became so emotional, I told her she did not have to tell me any more.

She said, "There is one more thing. His nickname was 'Billy the Kid,' B-T-K."

We sat for a time without speaking while she wiped away her tears. She apologized, but I told her there was no need to apologize to me. After a while she became composed and we talked about options. If she told anyone at the Wichita Police Department, Landwehr would be the person appointed to investigate this, so she might as well contact him in the first place. She insisted that Landwehr could not be trusted.

We talked about the attention to her family if her late father turned out to be BTK. Was there any way to keep the family name out of it? I said possibly, but I doubted it. If her father turned out to be BTK, there was no reason to tar her family with that brush. They were innocent of wrongdoing; they were victims. But undoubtedly some people would blame them or not believe them. Some people would accuse them of knowing all along.

I told her that I had become acquainted with many of the victims' family and friends, especially Nancy Fox's family and friends, and they would rather know who it was than not know. I would report this story in the book, but would not identify her. The decision would be hers.

Later, she told me that she thought that a woman would be more understanding and discreet, so she contacted the deputy chief of investigations, Terri Moses. The first woman to rise to the rank of deputy chief on the Wichita Police Department, she had a good reputation. Of course, what she did was forward Alice's message to Lieutenant Landwehr.

Landwehr contacted her and took the watch. Landwehr then contacted Charlie Otero, who was serving time in a New Mexico prison, and Charlie provided a description of his father's watch.

Meanwhile, Alice told me that Landwehr contacted her and asked for a DNA sample. If the DNA markers were close to the sample they had, then the case might be closed. She consented.

Landwehr also asked if she could find a lock of her father's hair for DNA testing. She found her father's old electric razor and it was filled with his whiskers, which she said she turned over to Landwehr.

When I told Floyd Hannon about this—just because of the concurrency of my meeting with Alice and talking with Floyd—he was very interested. He thought the case might be solved.

Alice asked me to be her family's attorney should her late father prove to be the long-sought BTK. I told her that we didn't need to make that decision yet.

On Thursday, March 11, I attended a Continuing Legal Education seminar at the Wichita Corporate Hills Marriott. While there I talked about BTK with former judge David Calvert. I asked him to compare the police drawings made after the Otero murders and the Bright murders and asked if they looked like the same guy.

Judge Calvert said, "Yes. Absolutely."

I was now thinking that Alice's late father might be BTK. Alice's father looked exactly like the Bright drawing, and that drawing did resemble the Otero drawing.

I didn't know how long it took to obtain DNA results, but I was looking forward to hearing what Landwehr had to say.

Interviews with several more former police officers shed some further light on the case. Friday, March 19, 2004, I interviewed Mike

McKenna by telephone. His younger brother and I went to West High together, but I don't recall whether Mike and I ever met. I asked why he became a cop.

When Mike McKenna was seventeen years old, he worked in a grocery store. The store was robbed by men armed with guns, and he and others were forced into a frozen food freezer. When put in the freezer he asked if he could turn on the light, but a bandit said, "You won't need any light." He thought that meant they were all going to be killed. He was only slightly relieved when the robbers jammed the door shut.

Mike McKenna said that he was never happier in his life than when he saw Wichita police officers come in to free him and the others. He admired the officers' calm professionalism and decided then that he wanted to become a policeman.

Mike McKenna worked as a Wichita police officer from 1974 to 1996. He first became involved with the BTK case when Al Thimmesch assigned him to do some investigation on Nancy Fox's murder. He spent hours and hours going through tickets at Helzberg's. McKenna said that he started asking about the similarities between the Vian and Fox murders before the BTK letter to KAKE-TV in February 1978. He said that he and Bob Cocking were chastised for linking Fox and Vian.

He became a detective and followed Bernie Drowatzky as lead detective on the BTK case. He was the lead detective from 1981 to 1984 and, because the Ghostbuster investigation initially was secret, technically was not removed as lead detective in 1984. McKenna said that the 1988 letter to Mary Fager was from BTK. He insisted that was a fact.

Former deputy chief Kerry Crisp also believed the letter to Mary Fager was from BTK. Plus, he said that he might have been DNA tested back when. He was certainly tissue tested. He said that one day while he was a major on the WPD, two of his detectives came into his office and brought him a can of pop. The three of them sat and shot the breeze, and he wondered why because these guys were not people who wasted time. At the conclusion of their meandering conversation they departed, and he noticed that they took his pop can. He figured maybe they were on a recycling kick.

A few weeks later, Al Thimmesch came in to Kerry's office unannounced, sat down, and they looked eye-to-eye. Thimmesch said, "Well, it's not you."

The detectives had Kerry's saliva from the pop can tested. It did not match BTK's. Kerry was the right age and description and had attended WSU when BTK was known to have been on campus, and they decided they had to check him. "Damn!" they were thinking. "What if BTK was a cop?"

I received another call, initially anonymous, that led to a series of calls and a personal meeting. The feedback I received from my sources made me believe the story was authentic. Had I uncovered an unknown attack by BTK?

On Tuesday, May 23, 1978, near midnight at 1043 North Dellrose, across the street from Adams Elementary, Lynn Maize, a young female Wichita State University student, woke when she heard noises: breaking glass and the sound of an animal growling.

Wearing only a teddy nightgown, Lynn rose and saw a man breaking in her back glass door. The glass was broken and he was fumbling with the deadbolt lock. She screamed and the man again growled. She continued to scream as she ran to the front door.

In her panic she alternately locked and unlocked the door and deadbolt, so she couldn't get out. The more she screamed, the more the man growled. Finally Lynn got the door open and ran into the street. A woman driving by immediately let her in the car and they drove away.

Police found the man's blood on broken glass. He took nothing of monetary value, only photographs of the woman in her bikini.

Unfortunately, the break-in occurred near the beginning of serious labor disputes between the city of Wichita and the police union. Wichita police were so understaffed that only emergency work was done. The intruder took the time to look through all the woman's drawers in her home and through the glovebox in her car, and took her purse, but the only other items she was certain were missing were the photos of her in her bikini that had been taken at a pool party held at a police officer's home.

BTK indicated that he made audiotapes of his crimes. After hearing Lynn's story I wondered whether the growling was to add terror to the audiotape.

At the time this happened she thought it might have been BTK, and a police officer told her they suspected it was BTK.

This location was very close to where Alice's father stayed, only a couple of blocks away. I again wondered how soon Lieutenant Landwehr would report the news on whether her father was BTK.

On Tuesday, March 23, I had breakfast at Spears Restaurant with a large number of retired Wichita police officers. Jack Bruce and Charles Liles were both at the breakfast.

Bruce noted, "Joseph Otero was tied differently from all the others."

Liles replied, "Jack, that was so the killer could control him, move him from room to room, make him watch the others."

Bruce said, "The ropes on Joseph were the only ones that he could have tied himself."

"If there was one killer, then he held a gun on them while Joseph Otero tied his family, then the killer directed Joseph on how to tie himself."

Bruce responded, "Prove that Joseph Otero didn't murder his family then kill himself, either accidentally or on purpose."

"Jack," Charles said, "these were sexually motivated killings."

"How is masturbating on or near a dead body sex? Intercourse is sex. That's not sex."

Liles refused to argue the point.

As we departed, Bruce told me that he agreed with Floyd Hannon. He didn't think that there was a BTK. If the person who wrote the letter was the killer—and he was not certain of that—then he took good notes. He was not convinced the killer took photographs.

I did not tell Jack what I had learned from other sources.

On March 24, before 8:00 a.m. the phone rang. It was Alice. She told me two things. First, she said someone posted on the Crime & Justice board on John Douglas's website that BTK had sent another letter.

Second, she said that Detective Landwehr had just told her that her father was not BTK. Then she asked me, "Do you think by telling me that my dad was not BTK that he means my dad was BTK?"

I asked her to repeat and she did. She knew what she was asking. I began to wonder whether Alice was suffering from emotional trauma in the same sense that Nancy Fox's mother was—*almost* always coping with things well, but maybe not so well on some things. Alice apparently did suffer abuse from her father, but if Landwehr told her that her father was not BTK, then Landwehr knew for a fact that he was not. I thought Alice would be relieved by the news, but she did not want to accept it.

"If Landwehr said your dad is not BTK, then he means that your dad is not BTK," I told Alice. She remained skeptical. I told her that I had an appointment—I did—and that I had to go.

Among my errands that morning I stopped at both Wichita universities where I had been teaching to check my mailboxes and talk to several people. When I arrived back home it was almost noon. My wife said that Hurst Laviana called. I told her I'd call him back after I'd checked my e-mail.

At 11:02 a.m. Hurst had e-mailed me: "Bob, Are you going to be around this afternoon? There may be a big development in the BTK case today. If it pans out, I may want to run something by you. Hurst."

I went to our living room and told Mary Ann that I had an e-mail from Hurst as well, about a development in the BTK case. I thought of the overnight message on the Crime & Justice site claiming they had received a new letter from BTK. I doubted that, but I wondered if someone had found his things. I thought that there might be news of a development, but until this morning I thought it might be that Alice's father was BTK.

The phone rang and I answered it. It was Hurst Laviana. BTK was back.

Chapter 24

Porkchop Is Back

Hurst Laviana earned a degree in mathematics in college. Like Mr. Spock, he is tall, handsome, composed, and logical. No one had ever seen him rattled.

"Bob!" he said when I answered the phone. He sounded out of breath. "Bob, I've got to ask you for a quote. But first, I have to tell you what has happened." The *Eagle*'s Crime and Safety reporting team leader, L. Kelly, would later tell me that I might have been the only person to ever hear Hurst Laviana breathless with excitement. Under the circumstances it is understandable.

On Wednesday, March 17, 2004, Saint Patrick's Day, BTK sent a message to the *Wichita Eagle*.

The letter arrived in the newspaper's mailroom on Friday morning, March 19. A clerk opened the letter, looked at it, and placed it in a plastic bin headed for the newsroom.

Eagle editor Rick Thames said: "It might well have been tossed. At first glance, it could have been a prank."

In the newsroom, Glenda Elliott, who was in charge of routing general newsroom mail, again read it. After seeing what the envelope contained, she gave the letter to the *Eagle*'s assistant managing editor Tim Rogers.

Rogers gave the letter to reporter Hurst. He instructed Laviana to photocopy the letter and give the original to the Wichita Police Department. Hurst was on his way to the police station to attend the Friday 10:00 a.m. briefing.

"We get letters like this all the time, letters that are not news. We all thought it was a hoax at first," Laviana said.

But then he recognized Vicki Wegerle's name. "I kept thinking, this isn't the typical crank letter."

Hurst hand-delivered the letter to Captain Darrell Haynes and police spokeswoman Janet Johnson. Haynes thought the letter was probably nothing and left it on his desk.

On Monday, at the 10:00 a.m. briefing, Hurst asked Captain Haynes about it. He forwarded it to the homicide division.

Detective Kelly Otis asked for two days. Otis and Rogers reached an agreement where the *Eagle* would hold the story for two days, then on Wednesday morning the police would talk exclusively with them.

The letter contained no words. It consisted of a single sheet of paper. On the paper was a photocopy of Vicki Wegerle's driver's license and three fuzzy photocopied photos taken of Wegerle, each with the body posed in a different position.

The postmark indicated the letter had been posted in Wichita. Police said they knew where the letter had been mailed, but were not disclosing that information. It was unknown if the letter had been mailed at a mailbox or at a post office.

On the envelope containing the new BTK letter was a return address. It read:

Bill Thomas Killman
1684 S. Oldmanor
Wichita KS 67202

The name had the initials BTK. It was presumed to be a takeoff on the name Bill Thomas Butterworth, the man who had been tried and acquitted for the murders of the Fager family. About that crime, many believed BTK had once written that he was not the guy in that crime but he was a big fan of whoever was.

It was assumed that Oldmanor was a misspelling of S. Old Manor. The address was determined to be a vacant unit in a yellow brick fourplex that was part of the Parkwood Village apartments. The unit was recessed away from the street and fronted by a large lawn. Police searched the empty apartment and the surrounding area.

"Landwehr told me that he is one hundred percent certain it is BTK," Hurst said.

I said, "If Landwehr is one hundred percent certain, then he has more than just the photocopy. Wegerle was whisked away by EMS before there were any photographs, so undoubtedly her killer took the photos, but the only way to be one hundred percent certain it is BTK is to have BTK DNA, so he must have DNA. Maybe the guy licked the envelope. With just the envelope and photocopy you can't be certain that someone else didn't find BTK's box of stuff and send the copy."

Hurst and I talked about Landwehr's certainty for a little while. I agreed not to talk with other press until the following day, and I gave Hurst some quotes. Then we concluded our call.

Now I had to tell my wife and the Fox family.

I walked into our living room, where my wife was sitting in her favorite chair. "Dear, I have some disturbing news. The call from Hurst was to tell me that they have received a new letter from BTK. They received it last week and this morning the police authenticated it. Kenny Landwehr told Hurst that he is one hundred percent certain it is from BTK."

Mary Ann knew who Kenny Landwehr was because she had just sat behind him in an eight-week oceanography course she audited at WSU. She knew who BTK was because her husband was writing a book and she was sick of hearing about BTK. Now it looked like she would be hearing more about BTK.

Then I called Nancy's sister Beverly on her cell phone. "I have some disturbing news." Then I told her the basic information, the information that would be in the newspaper. She was stunned. She said, "We hoped that something would happen from the book. Maybe it has."

I went online and checked my e-mail. I had quite a few messages. Because the story had been posted on the *Eagle* online webpage, the story had been picked up and was on the Internet and wire services. The Crime & Justice ezboard.com website was abuzz.

Alice posted:

"I do wonder if this is a hoax letter from someone who has seen the crime photos, and seen the previous letters. Former investigators, media people."

It must have been a lot for Alice to handle. She went to bed thinking that her father was BTK. She woke up to learn both that BTK just sent another letter and that Lieutenant Landwehr thought her father is not BTK.

I sent her a brief e-mail. This was not a hoax. The letter was from BTK.

After the shocking events of the day, I created a passcode to prevent anyone from easily accessing my notes. The code was "porkchop." Over the next few weeks I would mention the word "porkchop" to a few friends in ways they were sure to remember without telling them what it meant. They'd figure it out if I had a stroke and they tried to access my computer.

The next morning, Thursday, March 25, 2004, at 6:00, my bedside phone woke me up and I automatically answered it. It was an AM drive-time radio station live wanting an interview. I talked with them for a few minutes. I hung up and immediately my phone rang again. It was another radio station wanting another interview. I gave them a few quotes, and after I hung up the second time, I stopped answering the phone. I let the answering machine pick up. The media onslaught had started again.

After breakfast and reading the newspaper, I did return a call from B-98 Radio's Tracy Cassidy. Tracy and I had been acquainted for several years. She promoted my jury course on her show in 1997 and one of my students told me she enrolled because Tracy Cassidy said it sounded like an interesting course.

She told me about the 10:00 a.m. police briefing. She presumed that I was going, but I had not planned to attend. It was only during the course of our conversation that I decided to go. I told her that I'd see her there.

John Garrison and I then talked on the phone. John also asked me to attend the police press conference and write an article for "The Re-Tired Copper." After all, I just wrote an article for the previous issue. I'll be a correspondent. I said, "Sure."

I put on my suit, grabbed a notebook, and, at the last moment, tossed my clipping scrapbook in my car. Maybe Tracy Cassidy or some of the other press people would want to look at it.

I drove downtown to City Hall and asked where the police briefing room was. After I arrived at the police briefing room I visited with Tracy Cassidy and Hurst Laviana. Dan Rouser was there, too.

Police spokeswoman Janet Johnson said that she didn't know everyone and she wanted those she didn't know to introduce ourselves. I introduced myself and told her that I'm writing a book about BTK. She went on to others in the room.

A few minutes later she returned and said that I had to leave.

I asked, "Why?"

"Because we are only allowing journalists, not authors, to attend the press conference."

There was no problem with not being enough room. Everyone was already seated. I whipped the issue of "The ReTired Copper" out of my suitcoat pocket. It had my byline on the front page. "This morning John Garrison, editor of 'The ReTired Copper', the periodical of the Wichita Retired Police Officers Association, asked me to attend the press briefing and later write a report about it for this newsletter."

After a prepared statement, Lieutenant Landwehr answered some questions. Most of the reporters were not knowledgeable enough about the case to ask informed questions. Some gave commentary monologues that did not ask a concrete question.

Landwehr said, "We do believe that BTK is in Wichita. The letter did originate from the Wichita area, but I don't have any idea where in the city. . . . As in any cold case, we'll be re-interviewing certain key witnesses, possibly family members, for any new information. . . . Plus, now looking at another case, we'll see if there's any link between the cases prior to this and the new case tied to BTK."

A reporter asked, "How unusual is it for a case like this to go so long, for a serial killer to go so long, without contacting you . . . with little contact, and what do you think, why do you think he waited so long?"

Landwehr answered, "I have no idea why they would wait so long. It is the most unusual case that we've ever had in Wichita. I wouldn't ever want to comment on any other cases around the nation, but it is without a doubt the most unusual case we've ever had in Wichita."

A different reporter asked, "If memory serves, there was some biological evidence at one of the crime scenes prior . . . when BTK was in his prime, if you will . . . Are you going to be pursuing that, with whether it's DNA testing or . . . is there a way you can make connections that would help you find . . . ?"

Landwehr replied, "If there is scientific testing that can link possible cases together, that scientific testing does take some time usually to do. In any case, we will look at all those to see if there's any evidence that links those cases together, possibly forensically."

I asked my only question. "Do you deny the 1988 letter to Mary Fager was from BTK?" It was a lawyerly question, requiring only a yes or no answer.

Landwehr shook his head emphatically, "No sir, I do not deny that."

A reporter asked, "How was Vicki killed? Was she home alone at that time? Do any of the others you'll look at fit that same profile? Do you already know that there's something else that looks like this, smells like this?"

Landwehr answered, "Vicki Wegerle was the mother of two children. Her two-year-old child was at home with her at the time of her death. Her husband was at work. Her other child was at elementary school at the time. We'll of course look at victimology, reference any other linkage possibilities and any other M.O. that would have been used by the perpetrator to link, again, any case, as well as forensic. Again, those are hypothetical . . . We'll probably need something more substantial, such as forensic evidence."

The renewed hunt was on.

Chris Frank of KAKE-TV asked if I could come by their studio for an interview, and I agreed. He also asked me if I had something I could show. He remembered that I was holding a scrapbook in the photo that Fernando Salazar took last January. I told him I tossed the book in my car and I'd bring it in a couple of hours.

Then a representative of KWCH-TV asked me the same and I agreed.

While I was outside walking to my car a KSN reporter asked me if I could stop by their studio for an interview. I agreed.

Then I went to see Roger Stewart, Al Stewart's son, owner of Wholesale Neon. He was beside himself. "Holy shit, Bob," he said. "Wegerle was the last homicide case that Dad looked at. It happened the day of his retirement."

Roger took me into his office and showed me the photos of his father's retirement party. One showed a smiling Al and Leyola Stewart with a retirement cake in front of them. Another photo showed a large group that included Ghostbusters detectives Paul Dotson, Paul Holmes, and a young Kenny Landwehr. No gray hair on smiling Landwehr in this photo.

"Do you think BTK knew Dad was retiring that day? Do you think this was some kind of going-away message from him? That would be awful."

"I don't know, Roger. If this happened on a special day for your dad that happens once a year, the odds would be 365 to 1 against random chance, but your dad only has one retirement party in a lifetime. If this is just a coincidence, it is an amazing coincidence. It could be a coincidence. This story is filled with amazing coincidences"—I thought of dialing the wrong number and calling Kathryn Bright's boyfriend—"but it could have been just what you are thinking," I said. Al Stewart's retirement party occurred only about three hours after Vicki Wegerle's body was found. It was plausible to think that it was no coincidence. BTK might have been more amused than annoyed if he knew that the Ghostbusters unanimously thought that the husband did it.

"Dad always hated it that BTK could recognize him, but he couldn't recognize BTK. All the Ghostbusters thought that they may have seen him, but who the hell knows." Roger was upset. He shook his head back and forth in worry. "I bought Dad's old house when he and Mom moved to Colorado. If he knew where Dad lived, then he knows where I live."

Roger and I talked for an hour, then I went to KAKE-TV.

While Chris Frank interviewed me, he asked if I would flip the pages of the newspaper article notebook while they filmed.

Then he introduced me to Sandy. She and I would later talk several times by phone. I was at KAKE TV an hour or more.

Then I went to KSN for an interview of an hour or more.

Then I went to KWCH for an interview. When that was concluded, a man introduced himself. He was from *CBS Evening News with Dan Rather*. He lived in Dallas, and this morning a phone call from CBS Evening News woke him. He was instructed, "Fly to Wichita, find this author, and get him on camera." He ordered a satellite truck and camera crew to drive up from Oklahoma City. They had all just arrived at the local CBS affiliate station to try to track me down.

By the time I went home, it was late afternoon and I was exhausted. When I walked in the phone was ringing. Mary Ann walked up to me, annoyed. "I did not retire from medicine to become your secretary." She plopped an 8½-by-11-inch notepad in front of me. "You have fifty-five telephone messages."

People had been calling or coming to the door since I left. The phone hadn't stopped ringing. Each time a call was completed another call came in. The phone continued to ring and the answering machine was full. It was no longer taking messages and Mary Ann was no longer taking messages.

I received messages from a television program in Japan, a magazine in Germany, a radio station in Australia, and from print and broadcast programs from all over the United States, including a movie production company.

The first call that I returned was to Detective Kelly Otis. He asked if I could come to the police station "so that we can pick your brain." KBI agent Robert Jacobs, who spoke to my students during the Manson mock trial in 1999, was there too. I told him I'd call him tomorrow and we'd set a time.

I then called Nancy Fox's mother. We had a good talk. The news was unsettling, but we both hoped that this new letter would lead to a breakthrough. She said that Detective Landwehr had called her and apologized for not calling sooner.

Shelly Hansel, representing the *CBS Early Show*, appeared at my door. Mary Ann answered the door and let her in because she knew Shelly Hansel. Mary Ann was the pediatrician for Shelly's children. The *CBS Early Show* wanted me to appear on camera in the morning. She would pick me up around 5:00 a.m. My wife told me privately that Shelly was one of the more courteous and professional television people she had ever dealt with, and she thought it would be okay if I went with Shelly. I agreed.

I returned a number of telephone calls. When I was not on the phone, the phone continued to ring until after 9:00 p.m.

At 6:00 Wichita time I was in a rented meeting room, seated in front of a camera, and my microphone was working. I would be interviewed by Renee Syler. One of the technicians told the New York center, "The talent is ready." I laughed and said, "No one's ever called me 'the talent' before."

Friday morning was even more hectic than the morning before. I received constant calls from local and national print and broadcast press and from local people. Although I had calls from several FOX network programs, including Geraldo Rivera, I agreed to appear on the Greta Van Susteren program and on the Rita Cosby program. I agreed to meet with a representative from CBS *48 Hours* and to an interview with *People* magazine. Six publishers or literary agents called me. Cathy Singer from *Dateline NBC* called and wanted me on their show. Three different ABC national shows and ABC radio wanted me on their programs. *Dateline NBC*, CBS *48 Hours*, and an ABC news magazine wanted exclusives. They told me that I could only be interviewed by one of them.

I would later meet with associate producer Steve McCain of CBS *48 Hours*. We talked for a long time and I agreed to go with his program. They were doing a full hour, not just a segment as part of an hour, and he said, "We are staying with this story all the way through the trial."

Steve did not know how much that statement affected me. This had been an absolutely unsolvable case; now he was thinking the guy would be arrested soon and the case would go to trial. One of their correspondents would be the narrator, but I would be the "go to" guy for facts. I agreed and we shook hands on the deal. There was no money involved, but at least I could be sure that the story is not distorted.

Then I went to lunch with private investigator Emery Goad, "true believer" journalist Dan Rouser, and the rest of the crowd at the old journalists' Final Friday lunch in the basement of Watermark Books at Douglas and Oliver. Naturally, we spent the hour talking about BTK.

When Vern Miller was Kansas Attorney General, Emery Goad was one of his four investigators. Miller said that Emery Goad was "tops."

Goad was a *Wichita Eagle* newspaper reporter in 1969–1970. In 1976 he started his private eye business, Kansas Investigative Services, which he still runs. He has seven employees. Much of the business is routine, but every now and then he is hired for more interesting cases, or apparently routine cases turn interesting.

With his ever present Royal Jamaica cigar he went to serve some routine papers to an older woman. While he was waiting at the door he heard sirens approaching, lots of sirens. Then he saw police cars come from every direction. He was wondering what was going on, still calmly chewing on his cigar.

Then the police came for him.

Turns out the home was that of Terri Moses's mother. Terri Moses is the current head of Wichita Police investigations. Terri Moses's mother had called 911 and screamed into the phone that BTK was trying to break down her door.

Enough cops knew who Emery was that he avoided arrest.

In 1986 Emery Goad was the private investigator Bill Wegerle hired to find his wife's murderer. Goad told me that after he worked on the case for a week, he was convinced—as was Steve Robison—that Bill Wegerle was innocent, but he was unable to pick up any leads on the killer. Goad did not rule out the possibility that Wegerle was murdered by BTK.

Then in 2000 one of Emery Goad's clients said that a relative of hers was BTK. He claimed to have murdered Vicki Wegerle. Goad did some investigation and wrote a report. He shared the report with Kenny Landwehr. Landwehr interviewed the family and then went to the suspect and asked for a DNA sample. The suspect let Landwehr take a blood sample. The DNA sample eliminated the suspect.

When I finally arrived home, I made a few quick calls asking about Detective Kelly Otis. On December 7, 2000, four people in a house in northeast Wichita were shot to death. On December 15, 2000, there was another quadruple homicide in northeast Wichita. Detective Otis worked the December 15 murders and talked with Jonathon Carr, one of the brothers later convicted and sentenced to death.

I was told that Kelly Otis was a good guy, a straight shooter, and his only agenda would be solving the case. He was working on cold case homicides. One of the people I talked with was Levato Velo.

I called Detective Kelly Otis and agreed to meet him at the police department sixth-floor homicide section. I would see him, then go to the Greta Van Susteren Fox News interview. The Fox News satellite truck was set up right outside the police station.

That afternoon I met with WPD homicide detectives. I gave them two copies of my 17-page single-spaced timeline, one for the WPD and one for the KBI. I also provided the suspect names that had come up in my research and we discussed each man.

At the conclusion of our meeting I was asked, "What about the prime suspect?" I shrugged, not sure who they were talking about. Of course, they were no longer talking about suspects, they were talking about me.

The detective, raising an eyebrow, said, "Robert Beattie."

I knew what they were doing. The FBI profilers told them that when BTK was confronted, he would say something like, "I can see why you think I'm a suspect." He would provide a plausible explanation. This is a disjunctive logic interrogation test: If you indicate that you understand why they think you are a suspect, then you genuinely become a suspect.

My voice remained even. "I am not a suspect," I said. The detective was relieved by my calmness. He nodded his head and said, "You are not a suspect."

Anticipating the request, to save time I volunteered, "Hey, I'll give you a cheek swab or whatever you want." They didn't need to waste time on me, but I didn't know whether they would take a cheek swab. DNA testing cost $5,000 apiece in the Ghostbusters era. I don't know what it costs now. Detective Kelly Otis said, "We're having a swab-a-thon. Since you offered a sample, we'll take it."

A detective put on gloves, took out a DNA swab test kit with two Q-tips, swabbed one cheek with one, then the other cheek with the other, put it back in the test tube and labeled it. Later, of course, the DNA testing excluded me as a BTK suspect.

Later, from Levato Velo, I learned how they verified that BTK murdered Vicki Wegerle. The photocopy with Vicki's driver's license and the Polaroid photos of the murder in progress (Vicki was alive in the first photo, her eyes filled with terror) was convincing, but there was more. Six months earlier cold case detective Kelly Otis had investigated Vicki's murder. He first made a timeline using all available witness reports. He concluded that Bill Wegerle could not possibly have murdered his wife. Independent witnesses placed Bill Wegerle away from home all morning, and others had spoken with Vicki Wegerle during the morning, so the killer had to be someone else. All those detectives who thought Bill Wegerle had murdered his wife were wrong. Kelly Otis did not use any new information, just the information in the files. Bill Wegerle should have been eliminated as a suspect shortly after the murders.

Looking through the file, Detective Otis had learned Vicki Wegerle had tissue under her fingernails. She had fought and scratched her murderer. That tissue had been preserved. Six months earlier, in October 2003, Detective Otis had the tissue sent for DNA testing. But because it was a cold case, it was low priority. On March 22, 2004, it became number one on the test list. In less than a day they verified that it matched the DNA from Nancy Fox's crime scene and the envelope that Kenny Landwehr had tested in 2003. BTK had murdered Vicki Wegerle.

They were going to cheek-swab as many men as it took to find BTK. When Detective Landwehr assembled all the detectives working on this case, he said that this time they were not going to stop until they get him.

Overnight I received several more messages about my name being bantered about on the Internet as a BTK suspect. In the morning I receive several telephone calls. I send an e-mail to Bill Peterson and he posted excerpts on the Crime and Justice website—

> RUNES1, ADMINISTRATOR; 3/27/04 1:36PM
>
> Robert and I have been loosely collaborating on BTK for several months. The thrust of his work is historical and social commentary, ours at Crime & Justice is aimed at crime-solving. On a few occasions we shared private sources and we protected them. We have our separate sources in LE too.
>
> Late on March 25th he sent this:
>
> "I am a bit overwhelmed. Will offer another contribution once I catch my breath. This will soon be "yesterday's news" to virtually everyone else, but you were there first and I won't forget. According to my sources, the message is unquestionably from BTK. Robert"
>
> This morning he wrote:
>
> "By the way, I gave a cheek swab for DNA analysis. As you believe, and the authorities know, I am not BTK. Even so, the cops are too busy trying to catch this guy to issue a particular denial clearing any one suspect. Many many in-

dividuals have been tested. We can't ALL be BTK. The detectives were joking that they have been conducting a "Swab-a-thon," which will be the title of a new chapter in my book.

"This suspicion is unfair, but I've already said that suspicion is the theme of my book. You remember that such unwarranted suspicion is the theme of Rod Serling's *Twilight Zone* episode, 'The Monsters Are Due on Maple Street.' The monsters were us, taken over by the mob mentality.

"I and some others will just have to tolerate some public suspicion until law enforcement either identifies the guy or the attention dies-down and LE does say something clearing us.

"Events have unfolded in such a rapid and shocking manner that I am operating on high tension and little sleep, as are many of the police.

"The e-mails and PM's are flowing and among the many points being articulated on an increasingly wider basis is that BTK has been reading Crime & Justice. More on this in another post 'pride of authorship' I'll post as soon as time permits."

Chapter 25

Swab-a-thon

The police almost immediately began cheek-swabbing old suspects. According to the *Eagle* on April 2, "One local resident, who asked not to be named, confirmed Thursday that he had been asked to provide a DNA sample. He said he was approached by plainclothes police officers Tuesday while speaking with a county employee in the lobby area of the Sedgwick County Courthouse. He said the officers led him out onto Elm Street, where they had a mobile DNA lab set up in the back of an unmarked car. The officers took swab samples from the inside of his mouth. He said they told him they were performing similar testing on a large group of men, including current and former police officers who have worked on the case. The man said he had been questioned in the 1970s during the initial BTK investigation. He said the detectives who interviewed him and his girlfriend then didn't ask much about the case. Most of the questions, he said, centered on their sex life. He said BTK's recent resurfacing clears him. He said that when Wegerle was killed in August 1986, he was in the county jail serving time on assault charges related to a domestic dispute."

The man has since given me permission to identify him. He is John Polson, long an activist in unpopular causes, and long described as "obnoxious." He was one of the guys followed for a time back in the 1970s. John was quickly eliminated as a suspect by DNA testing.

Not everyone who was asked for a DNA sample complied with the police request. And, without a search warrant issued by a judge and based on probable cause, police could not force someone to give a DNA sample. Taking a sample without a court order and without permission would constitute illegal search and seizure.

On April 6, 2004, Kim Wilhelm of KWCH 12 Eyewitness News reported that at least one man on the BTK suspect list had refused to give police a sample of his DNA. The man refused to be identified because he did not want to have his name associated with the BTK investigation, but he did appear on-camera in shadow. He told the reporter that his intention was not to be difficult or hinder the investigation, but he was interested in protecting his "personal information."

"I understand what's going on, though," the man said. "The community is in panic, and everybody who apparently has a grudge is also adding to this tip list and is making worse work for the the detectives."

Police told the man that he was on the suspect list because of an anonymous tip. The tipster, the man explained, was apparently someone who had an ax to grind and was reporting him as a suspect as a way to harass him.

The man told detectives that before he gave them a DNA sample, he would have to be certain that his DNA profile would not be used for anything else. "I'd like to know that it's going to be destroyed when they notice I'm not BTK," said the man. "I also want a guarantee that no reference to what was discovered in the swab will be kept in any kind of database."

This man called me to tell me about his experience. When he was swabbed, the police told him he was the 600th they had done. This was good news and bad news. It was good that many samples were being taken, but he was also no indication that they had narrowed down the list of suspects.

In June he gave me permission to use his real name in this book. He is Jeff Garrett, a local radio personality. Probably someone who did not like his radio patter called him in as a suspect. It is ridiculous to consider Jeff a suspect. He was 16 years old when the Oteros were killed. Jeff and I attended West High School together. Jeff produced the school's underground newspaper, *The Worst Word*, a parody of our official school paper, *The West Word*.

Police even DNA checked former Wichita mayor Bob Knight

because someone called in and said that his first and last initials are B and K and he is the right age and at one time was the right build.

Businessman John Pieratt called and told me about his experience being swabbed. He gave me permission to use his name. He consented to the police request for a DNA sample, but he thought it was ridiculous. He was in Vietnam in 1973–1974 when the Oteros were murdered. He suspected that he was called in by someone he was having a business conflict with, or it might have been the fact that he was murder victim Shannon Olson's neighbor.

The police checked Dr. Jim Erickson, a retired Wichita State University English professor who for a time shared an office with Professor P.J. Wyatt. He told me the story and gave me permission to use his name.

Dr. Erickson was at one time in the 1970s arguably the best known face in Wichita. In the years before cable television, as "Ole Flick" he hosted the KAKE TV all-night movie program. He would deliver witty monologues about the movies before and after and during some commercials. If you stayed up late or rose early, the only thing on television was "Ole Flick," Dr. Jim Erickson.

Dr. Erickson told me that two detectives came to his home, said that his name had come up in the BTK investigation, and they would like to obtain a cheek-swab for DNA testing. Dr. Erickson invited them in and asked them to wait a moment because he was frying a hamburger and it was time to flip it over. They followed him into the kitchen, he flipped his hamburger, they did the cheek-swab, and they departed. He said it was no problem at all.

When I told this story to Dr. Erickson's good friend, WSU anthropologist Dr. Dorothy Billings, she said she did not believe that story.

"Why not?" I asked.

"Because everyone knows that Jim Erickson can't fry a hamburger."

Wichita criminal defense attorney Les Hulnick said he believed police can keep DNA information forever. "There are no limitations to when, if ever, they have to give up your DNA sample."

Wichita police assured those submitting to the swab-a-thon, however, that their samples would not be entered into the National DNA Database. That database keeps DNA profiles of over 1.5 million convicted offenders. According to FBI officials, federal law states that only convicted felons—not possible suspects—can be run through the database.

"I don't have anything to hide," said one man. "If it comes to that [a search warrant], I'll give the swab. But not without asking what my rights are and knowing what they are."

Many people thought suspicious volunteered to submit their DNA so that their names could be crossed off the BTK suspect list. If a person were to voluntarily allow a DNA sample to be collected from his person to eliminate him as a BTK suspect, it would be an "actionable invasion of privacy" to use that sample in an attempt to link that person with a non-BTK crime.

Regarding the civil liberties of those asked to give DNA samples, Hulnick said in late July that he was worried about the people who could be "innocently caught up" in the investigation through police requests for DNA samples.

Hulnick told reporters, "I've heard that literally hundreds of people have been asked to give the police department DNA samples. Well, if they're asking hundreds of people, then I just have to assume they don't have a clue who they're looking for and so I think it's a very dangerous situation."

The danger, Hulnick explained, came if DNA samples were stored in the same database as convicted felons'. Hulnick said, "It is conceivable that DNA could be used for an untoward purpose and that being framing somebody without equivocation. That's one of the reasons I would prefer not to have my bodily fluids on file with the government. If they don't have my DNA there can be no monkey business."

According to the KBI, DNA samples given voluntarily in connection with the BTK case were not put on any national DNA databases, but instead placed exclusively into the BTK evidence file.

On April 6, investigators warned those who were in a hurry for a DNA-based solution to the case to be patient. Tim Rohrig, director of the Sedgwick County Regional Forensic Science Center, said taking DNA samples was a quick process, but conducting the DNA test was time-consuming. More than a thousand DNA samples had been taken since BTK reemerged, and it was going to take weeks to get through them all.

Rohrig said, "Because cases vary so widely, it is hard to come up with an estimate for the amount of time involved in processing a typical sample."

Rohrig added that some time could be saved by processing batches of evidence instead of individual samples. His center told law enforcement that they could expect a six-to-eight-week delay between submitting a sample and getting test results, and that this estimate did not include the glut of samples that had been coming into the lab because of the re-emergence of BTK.

Each DNA sample, once processed, is compared to the DNA profiles of more than a million people in a nationwide DNA database. Most of those profiles are gathered from people who are entering the prison system.

Recent advances in DNA technology can now match two samples with almost a hundred percent certainty. DNA is a genetic indicator every bit as specific to an individual as his or her fingerprints.

Great strides were made in DNA technology during the 1990s. Police can now extract usable DNA from the sweat on the inside of a glove. According to the *Kansas City Star*, "It's a technology that wasn't perfected in the days of OJ Simpson. Today the technique, called PCR/STR (polymerase chain reaction/short tandem repeat) has brought the odds of identifying suspects from one in twenty in the old blood grouping days to one in eighteen quadrillion.

"Of course, like all sciences, DNA 'fingerprinting' has evolved. In the late 1980s and early 1990s, crime investigators used a DNA technology called RFLP—for restriction fragment length polymorphism. With this technique, scientists used radioactive 'probes' to hook on to pieces of DNA. Just like an individual's DNA, the pattern of radioactive decay is unique. The technology was extremely accurate in identifying suspects but cumbersome. Also, the tests took weeks. If the DNA wasn't present in enough quantity, or if it was old or damaged, a good test couldn't be done. PCR, meantime, is easier, less expensive and more reliable. It also does not require lots of DNA. That's because scientists can make as many copies as they want of whatever DNA they find. This gives them an unlimited supply to do unlimited tests. From a tiny speck of DNA from fifty years back, scientists can use the new technology to make a fresh copy. Then they analyze it, mapping specific spots on as many as thirteen chromosomes. The chances that these spots on the thirteen chromosomes will be the same in any two people (other than clones or identical twins) are one in eighteen quadrillion."

The new test takes as little as two days to complete. The time-consuming part comes when that information is fed into the FBI's DNA database, which holds the DNA information for tens of thousands of convicted felons.

Would BTK give his DNA? Surprisingly, the answer is likely to be yes. Gary Ridgway, the Green River Killer, gave a DNA sample on April 8, 1987. The problem was, it was not tested until 2001. Ridgway did not want to be caught, yet he gave the DNA sample that led to his arrest. Ridgway murdered many more women while his DNA awaited testing. During the fourteen years after he gave the sample he must have thought that the DNA testing did not identify him as the killer. He must have thought that some quirk of fate intervened.

What intervened in the Green River Killer investigation was unbelievable police stupidity that has not been seen in the BTK investigation. In his own book *Chasing the Devil* Sheriff Reichert says that they did not test Ridgway's DNA sample because under the method available in 1987, if they did the test then they would not have enough to use for a second test. The reasoning is unsound. If the test excluded Ridgway, then there was no need for a second test. If the test identified Ridgway, then there was probable cause for arrest. A court order could be obtained for a second test. The women murdered by Gary Ridgway after April 1987 need not have died.

BTK eluded police for over thirty years and must have felt that he had the same protection of fate that Gary Ridgway thought he had. BTK might give a DNA sample. After all, he had eluded capture with the help of luck.

Near the end of April, Levato Velo called me and in so many words said, "It's not Suspect Barbara, it's not any of the suspects. DNA has cleared all of them. They don't know what to think." Nor did I. It had been taken as a given that with all serial killer investigations somewhere in the files is the killer's name. Bob Keppel had criticized the West Coast Ted Bundy investigators for not realizing that Ted Bundy should have been near the top of the list of suspects. Ted's name was developed by three avenues of the investigation and was on three different lists of suspects.

But that is not what happened here. All of the top suspects were cleared. The results puzzled everyone.

Soon, WPD, FBI, and KBI teams were obtaining DNA cheek-swabs from six different clusters of men. (1) They were checking all their old suspects, including Suspect Barbara and the men that I discussed with the detectives. (2) They were checking men who were age 20 to 50 when they worked at Wichita's Coleman Company factory in the era that Kathryn Bright and Julie Otero worked there. (3) They were checking former Wichita State University students who had enrolled in the folklore course taught by Professor P.J. Wyatt. (4) They were checking former U.S. postal employees who worked in Wichita in the 1970s. (5) They were checking everyone called in to the BTK tipline, no matter how ridiculous. (6) And they were checking old cops.

John Garrison called me. "Bob," he asked, "is there a cheek-swab support group?" He was joking, but the cheek swab he had just had terribly upset his wife. She said, "How can they suspect you? You devoted years of your life to trying to solve this case. You tailed suspects. It was your idea to ask P.J. Wyatt to look at the 'Oh Death to Nancy' poem. It's insulting," Sharon said.

John said he was not nearly as upset as his wife and family. That seemed to be the common reaction among the hundreds of police officers who were swabbed. Virtually all the old detectives told me the same thing: "Thirty years of detective work has failed, so they are putting everything into DNA testing."

The speculation that I might be a suspect came from the question "Why has BTK surfaced now?" Bill Peterson posted the following on that thread on the Crime & Justice website:

"Crime & Justice has been deeply involved in murder cases before. We have played an active role in the investigation of the Michael Skakel murder of Martha Moxley which led to his conviction and sentence of 20 years to life after Skakel and his family managed to keep ahead of the law for over 27 years. Crime & Justice played a supportive role in the Baton Rouge Serial killer Task Force. We are actively investigating the death of Valerie Percy in 1960's Chicago. And our most recent case is Marilee Burt in Littleton (Denver), CO in February 1970.

"Of BTK and Wichita this past week, Robert Beattie said to us:

'I am a bit overwhelmed. Will offer another contribution once I catch my breath. This will soon be "yesterday's news" to virtually everyone else, but you were there first and I won't forget. According to my sources, the message is unquestionably from BTK.'

"Robert explains the historical BTK:

> Finally, I mention that there is a vast misunderstanding about BTK, including among many profilers and police, as well as the press.
>
> When BTK first contacted the police via the press on October 22, 1974, he did NOT contact the police looking for public attention. He was looking for attention and acknowledgment from the police.
>
> BTK contacted the police via our newspaper's SECRET WITNESS program because on October 18, 1974, others had been arrested for the Otero murders. The police, not the press, arrested the men. BTK was provoked to contact the police because SOMEONE ELSE was believed by THE POLICE to have committed the murders. BTK planned and executed these murders. He wanted the police to know that. The SECRET WITNESS program was advertised as a way to anonymously contact the police. BTK took the easiest available avenue to anonymously contact the police. The press did not see the letter until it was leaked. Then the police were angry because a Wichita weekly newspaper, THE SUN, leaked the subject's code name. The police would rather that THE SUN had leaked other information and withheld the code name BTK."

Runes 1, Administrator, 3/28/04 10:43am

To my disappointment, the people who repeatedly confronted me were journalists with major press organizations, including *The Wichita Eagle*, Fox News, CNN, and *The Washington Post*. I always thought they were joking until they insisted that they were serious. Then I'd stare at them in silence before saying, "If you have any evidence to support your conclusion you must provide it to the police at once." Because they had no evidence this would cause most of them to stop. But then they would still try to defend their conclusion. "You can't deny that BTK appearing now is good for your book."

I'd reply, "Well, it hasn't been good yet. So far this has only cost me time and money. But presuming it will help my book become profitable, to think that the chain of reasoning runs from BTK's sending a letter to *The Wichita Eagle*, to interest in my book, then concluding that I'm BTK, is like concluding that Geraldo Rivera murdered Nicole Brown Simpson and Ronald Goldman because it was good for Geraldo's career."

That generally concluded this aspect of our conversation, though some parted by wistfully saying, "It would make a good story, though."

Writing about the BTK case in his book *Obsession*, FBI profiler John Douglas discussed one of BTK's letters in which he described the Otero crime scene: "The detail was incredible; I'd never seen anything quite like it. He even noted where [Josephine's] glasses were left lying. How'd he do this? Was he compulsive enough to go through the entire house taking meticulous notes? He sure as hell wasn't doing it from memory eight months later. Of course not! He was looking at crime-scene photographs, just as I was. Only he'd made his own. He'd brought a camera to the scene, or, more likely, taken one from the [Oteros]."

If BTK was taking his own crime scene photos, he either had to be a photography buff with his own darkroom or he was using a Polaroid camera that produced instantly developed photos. No photo lab would develop photos such as those that BTK took without reporting it to the police,

Discussing the fractured syntax in BTK's letters, Ken Stephens—a *Wichita Eagle* reporter who covered the BTK case for many years—commented: "It was almost like English wasn't his first language. But I suspect nearly every clue he's ever given involves misdirection."

Eagle editor Rick Thames described the paper's strategy regarding the newly revived BTK story: "We tried very hard to define the potential for danger through our interviews with police, but they were pretty tight-lipped. So we just tried to lay out the story as dispassionately as we could, offering people everything that we knew. And then as the story developed, I felt like it was very important that the *Eagle* report on it with as much depth as possible, not just because people were interested in it, but because there was an active search. And the possibility that the BTK could still be caught."

The global interest in the story soon caused problems at the *Eagle*.

"People were trying to get their work done and couldn't get it done," said Thames. "We also had people trying to walk into the building without being invited, that sort of thing."

It was clear that the newspaper was working with the police on the case. They reported, for example, that the new letter contained the key characteristic that verified to police that it was from the real BTK, but the paper agreed not to disclose what that feature was.

Did Thames worry that covering BTK would stimulate the killer's urges?

"Just the opposite has been the history," the editor said. "We just have to report the news going forward regardless of what may be going on in someone's mind. And what we try to do is provide our readers with what they need to know and what they want to know about the case."

Hurst Laviana said, "One theory is that he's just seeking publicity and likes to scare people and this is one way to do it. I think most people thought he was dead or in prison. I don't think anyone who's been investigating this case thought he was walking the streets of Wichita. I think every police officer who has worked on this case, every reporter who's reported on it has always wondered what ever came of BTK. This in a small way answers part of that. He's still here."

All *Eagle* employees who touched the March letter from BTK gave police finger and palm prints for comparison purposes.

Just as the killer used distinctive knots when binding his victims, all of BTK's letters bore a distinguishing mark since his 1979 packages to Anna Williams and KAKE TV. Only the police and the killer knew what it was—except for maybe a thousand journalists, professors, and others who had seen the drawing and poem. I thought people had been remarkably responsible containing the information.

Retired police official Mike McKenna told the *New York Times*, "He has a special way of signing his letters."

The Wegerle killing had been the talk of the Indian Hills neighborhood for several years after the murder, but most residents had never heard of it in 2004. Still, with the news that the serial killer was still in Wichita, or had returned, most Indian Hills residents did not want to give their names to newspaper reporters.

And the "oldmanor" address was the talk of its neighborhood. The apartment complex's manager, Abby Tietsort, told reporter Tim Potter, "I'm just dumbfounded on why he used that address. It's got everybody around here shooken up."

The return address raised the question of why the killer picked it. Did he at one time live there? Did someone he knew or was stalking live there? Did it have a symbolic significance? Did he still live in the area?

Ms. Tietsort distributed a letter to the residents of the apartment complex informing them of what had happened and asking them to report anything suspicious.

The weekend before the new BTK letter, WPD received one suspicious person call. The weekend after the letter became public knowledge they received eighty-one such calls. Calls ranged from someone's porch light bulb being unscrewed to someone hearing a knocking on the side of their home. Weather caused some problems with phone service, resulting in panicky customers who believed their phone lines had been cut.

Vandals were exploiting the BTK fear. "BTK" was spray painted on a work van in the northwest part of Wichita. Two blocks away, a garage door was vandalized with the same thing.

The *Eagle*'s website, kansas.com, set up a discussion board on the case, and it quickly revealed that Wichita was filled with amateur sleuths, all with their own opinions regarding the search for BTK.

According to website manager Alice Sky: "The corporate counsel basically said don't treat it any differently than you treat any other bulletin board you have. Our policy is if somebody calls and complains about something, we'll look at it, we'll take it down if it's offensive."

Only one message was deleted, a message that gave the address of someone with Bill Butterworth's last name. A member of the family, no relation, called and asked that the address be removed from the website, and it was.

The message board's disclaimer read: "Although we do not have any obligation to monitor this board, we reserve the right at all times to check this board and to remove any information or materials that are . . . objectionable to us in our sole discretion and to disclose any information necessary to satisfy the law, regulation, or government request."

In June 2004 I asked that a post be taken down. The poster referred to him or herself as RBeattieJr. This was not a friendly, chatty poster either, but a somewhat creepy one—no one I wanted being even slightly confused with me.

The news that BTK was still around rekindled sorrow, and hope, in the families of the victims.

Nancy Fox's father broke down when he saw on TV, for the first time in years, film footage of his daughter's home.

Dale Fox told reporter Stan Finger, "I hope he has made a real bad mistake on his part, and that he'll get caught this time. He's a clever guy. A smart guy. To evade everyone all this time, he has to be. I don't know why he does all of this, but I hope this will be his fatal mistake by resurfacing this way."

About learning of his daughter's murder and being taken by police to identify her body, Fox told Cindy Klose of KWCH 12 Eyewitness News, "It's something you'll never forget. You try to block it out of your mind, but get to talking about it, it all comes back."

Nancy's stepmother, Ruth Fox, added, "If they could catch him, that would be our prayer. To get him and make sure that justice is served him in the most cruel way. When a life was taken so drastically like that and so brutal, it's really hard to deal with. It's just almost unbearable. To brutally murder someone like BTK has done to his victims, I have no mercy for him at all."

The latest news also gave hope to Kevin Bright, who said, "That's what I want: Catch him so we can all be at ease."

"I pray for that person," Kevin Bright told the Associated Press in March 2004. "I pray that he'll see he's lost and he needs a savior and that he needs to be right for God and be right for mankind and give himself up. He many not get caught here, but one day he'll be standing in front of the Lord for judgment."

Bright has moved several times since the murder. It must be hard to rest easy when you are the only adult survivor of a BTK attack. After the March 2004 BTK letter was received, Kevin—as might be expected—

contacted Wichita police. An assistant to the lead investigator told him police would talk to Bright, but only if he came to investigators.

"I was surprised by that," Bright said. "I'd just like to know where they're going with the investigation. It wouldn't hurt to talk to somebody. But I can't second guess what they're doing."

Of his sister, Kevin recalled to KAKE-TV in May 2004: "I always remember her smile, always had a great smile. She was kind to people. She liked to be with people and she was just a good person. I miss her."

Kathryn's father, Charles Bright, said, "I guess what gets me the most is, she had her whole life ahead of her. Folks are not supposed to have to bury their daughters and sons."

Vicki Wegerle's brother-in-law, Ron Wegerle, told the Denver *Post*, "We were just kind of shocked that it's coming back to life again." He said the family had long suspected that Vicki had been killed by BTK, but had no proof until the recent letter.

Just as had been the case the first time BTK terrorized Wichita, the sale of security devices skyrocketed during the last days of March 2004. Locksmiths, security system installers, and gun shop owners all reported increased business.

Baysinger Police Supplies, which sold pepper spray, stun guns, personal alarms and other security devices, reported doing three weeks' worth of business on March 25 alone. The public relations director for SecureNet Alarm Systems said that calls to that company increased ninefold in the days after the new letter surfaced.

Many of the people seeking new security systems in their homes were the same ones who had had systems installed during the 1970s, during the first wave of BTK fear. Now they wanted those systems updated.

John Daily, the store manager of a gun store/firing range called The Bullet Stop, told a reporter, "We've sold out of mace twice already, and inquiries about our personal safety and basic gun courses are way up."

Schoolchildren in Wichita were suffering from anxiety about BTK as well. At the end of March school leaders sent information to all teachers and others who dealt directly with students. The district advised not to initiate BTK discussions with students, but if students brought it up on their own, teachers should be prepared to dispel rumors and discourage "Halloween-style" discussions. Teachers were advised to review with their kids the stranger-danger safety tips.

In response to Wichita parents who were afraid that their children were being traumatized by BTK stories, the *Eagle* interviewed Liz McGinness, head of the mental health and crisis counseling team for Wichita schools. She suggested that parents respond truthfully to their children's questions, but not to get into excessive detail.

She suggested parents say, "There was a series of unsolved crimes in the '70s and '80s, and the person people think is responsible for those crimes has written a letter to the newspaper. Police have new clues about who he might be, and they're doing everything they can to find him." Leave it at that, if possible, she said.

Terri Brown—a clinical social worker with Adult, Child and Family Counseling in Wichita—agreed. "Kids don't need to know all the gory details about how many people he killed and how he did it. There is something to be said about filtering information."

Brown added that, since children "feel bulletproof," it was equally important that parents warn their children to be careful.

Especially vigilant were Wichita's neighborhood watch groups—such as Citizens on Patrol, the South Central Progressive Neighborhood Association, the Mead Neighborhood Association, and the North Riverside Neighborhood Association. Leaders of these groups agreed that keeping an eye on neighbors' houses was very important.

"You're not going to see much unless you occasionally look out," said Jerry E. Miller of the Mead Neighborhood Association. "Since BTK apparently stalked or scouted his victims, somebody had to see him at least once before he did anything."

Miller suggested that people in Wichita keep their lights on, speak frequently with their neighbors, keep windows and doorways free of debris, and be quick to report to the authorities anyone behaving suspiciously, such as loitering in their neighborhood.

Along with the increased anxiety in Wichita came an increase in self-defense courses, particularly those aimed at teaching women how to fend off an attacker. One such course was taught by Kathy Wright, a staff instructor with Rape Aggression Defense Systems in Virginia, which offers the course in colleges and universities all over the United

States. The program was begun in 1989 by a campus police officer at Old Dominion University, where there had been a rash of attacks. The course doesn't just teach women how to fight back, but how to be aware they are in danger in the first place. The best way to be safe from an attack, it was taught, was to make sure the attack never occurs in the first place.

The class was held at Wichita State University's Heskett Center. The women could take the course for free thanks to a $9,000 grant from WSU's Student Government Association (SGA). BTK had Wichita so panicked that even the notoriously tight-fisted SGA would cough up thousands of dollars.

On March 25, 2004, the day after the new letter became public knowledge, former FBI profiler Gregg McCrary said that BTK couldn't resist flaunting his crimes. McCrary said the letter was a way of saying, "Look what I've done."

According to McCrary, terrorizing an entire city is like "playing God. It's a heady, intoxicating experience. They're not afraid to make contact with the media or police. That's all part of the game for a guy like this. He's outwitted law enforcement and everybody else all these years."

What separated BTK from all other known serial killers was the huge gaps in his chronology. "I can't think of another case like that," McCrary said. "Where has he been?"

McCrary's best guess was that he had been in prison. When the new letter was received, police looked through lists of inmates who had been recently released, just in case the reason they had not heard from BTK since 1979 was that he was in prison.

On March 25, Delaina Renfro of KWCH, Channel 12 Eyewitness News did a feature story about BTK and the book I was writing about him. I told her: "The officers had been telling me since I started BTK was dead. The vast majority of officers say he must be dead or he would still be killing because some said they had a specific suspect in mind that had died." I explained that I wasn't nervous about my own safety: "He wants publicity, and if I'm not around to write the book he's not going to get that."

Wichita was swarmed by media from around the world. Everyone had an opinion about who the killer was and why he was "back." One thing was for sure. No one was enjoying the media's feeding frenzy as much as BTK himself.

John Philpin, a retired forensic psychologist in Vermont, agreed that something must have taken BTK out of commission. Speaking the day after the letter with the Wegerle photos was made public, Philpin said, "It would be hard to believe that he would be sitting right there in Wichita all that time."

Philpin, who has written seven books about serial killers, asked, "What was satisfying him between 1986 and 2004?" Philpin opined, "He will contact [the press] again. I don't think he'll wait too long. I think he'll savor the next few days . . . he's got the pot stirred." Philpin noticed that BTK's crimes showed "elaborate forethought," and added, "Everything he does has a purpose."

On March 25, BTK was a topic of discussion on the *Deborah Norville Tonight* show on MSNBC, which was guest-hosted that night by Dan Abrams. Dan's guests were Wichita *Eagle* reporter Hurst Laviana and Harold Schechter, who is a professor at Queens College in New York City and the author of several books about serial killers including *The Serial Killer Files*.

Dr. Schechter pointed out that BTK was unlike any other serial killer that had come before. "It's a much more common pattern for serial killers to increase the pace of their murders. It's very, very rare, almost unheard of, for a serial killer to murder seven people and then basically stop for a period of years. And apparently if this last—if this is the BTK Killer, then he committed this series of very, very savage murders in the early 1970's, stopped for nine years, until 1986, and then disappeared again for another whatever it is, you know, eighteen years. Serial murder to some extent is a sex crime. The early BTK killings were very sexually sadistic. Serial murder seems to be a crime of younger men. So, it could be the case of this person's, you know, very, very sick libido has decreased somewhat with age, and so he doesn't feel quite as compelled to commit murders," Dr. Schechter said.

On March 26, 2004, KSNW featured an interview with a woman they showed only in silhouette and referred to only as "Sandy." She claimed that she had almost become a BTK victim in 1979.

One day that year, Sandy came home from work early. She usually didn't get home from work until after 5:00, but on this day she came home early, arriving around 3:30. She saw a light in her basement. That was unusual, so she went to investigate. She found broken glass on the floor and semen all over her walls.

She was soon convinced that BTK was the man who entered her home. "The police, they told me he has a thing for lingerie, so he went through all my drawers and with the semen on my walls in my basement it was a repeated type of problem that he would do," said Sandy, who lived in the 300 block of Old Manor, just three blocks from the Oteros' house.

Old Manor Road had another importance to the BTK case. It was the street name—although spelled "Oldmanor"—used in the return address of the March 2004 BTK letter.

But after her possible visit from BTK, "Sandy" never went back. She moved, changed her name and bought a gun.

"I refuse to be his victim," she said to reporter Dana Hertneky. "He's a scary man. There's something definitely wrong with him."

In my talks with a number of people who have worked on this case for a long time, one theme kept being sounded over and over again. Former deputy D.A. and former U.S. attorney Jackie Williams told me that BTK came back because of my book, specifically because of my quote about someone producing a victim's driver's license. His reasoning was that I was quoted in the *Eagle* talking about someone producing a victim's driver's license and then a copy of a victim's driver's license was sent to the Eagle. After so many years of the killer's silence, Jackie did not think that was a coincidence.

The psychologist who had worked on this case the longest, Dr. John Allen, the Ghostbusters' consultant, met with me. He had me rest on his therapy couch. He could see that I was under stress. When I asked him why BTK came out of hiding, he pointed his finger at me and said, "Your book."

Mike McKenna, a former lead detective, told me that he told both ABC News and Rick Thames, editor of *The Wichita Eagle*, that Beattie's book "is what caused BTK to send the letter in March." McKenna told me, "He [BTK] found out you were writing a book and he's thrilled to death about it. He wants to get all that's due to him. He gets off on the excitement of the book."

Pat Taylor, the detective who tailed suspects with Pete Dubovich, told me that he met with two FBI agents. They had a long talk and swabbed his cheek for a DNA sample. Their final question was, "Why do you think this guy came out of hiding now?" Pat said he looked at them like it was a stupid question. "Beattie's book."

Chapter 26

A City Under Siege

On the night of March 30 the Wichita killings were again featured on *Deborah Norville Tonight* on MSNBC. Deborah's guest was former FBI profiler Clint Van Zandt, a retired FBI agent who had accurately profiled Ted Kaczynski, the Unabomber.

Attempting to explain the gaps in the BTK chronology, Van Zandt said, "So then you go to, well, was he incarcerated, in jail for some other offense that was never linked to this? Was he in a mental institution? Did he perhaps marry or have some contact with someone else who allowed him to play out his fantasies in that relationship and now the relationship has changed? Has he moved? And I think the scary thing for this community, Deborah, is that the off chance he may have stayed within that community, perhaps may even have been interviewed by either the media, someone writing a book, law enforcement. And he's stayed there, he's worn this mask over himself these twenty-five years and now he's raised his hand and said, I'm still here. This is like some terrible *Silence of the Lambs* revisited movie again and for this small community in the western part of the United States, now they have to relive a nightmare they thought was over with twenty-five years ago."

The nervousness had spread across the city. By Friday, April 2, 2004, the number of tips received by the Wichita Police Department had risen to 1,043 phone tips, 575 e-mail tips and twenty-five letters.

On April 3, investigators announced that they felt the Otero killings, the first to be attributed to BTK, were the most important when it came to solving the case. "Since this was the first in a string of homicides related to BTK, we believe that it has special significance, and we want to hear from anyone who may remember anything related to the Otero homicides," said Lieutenant Landwehr. "We want to hear specifically from anyone who may have seen someone around the Otero residence or around their vehicle at the Dillons parking lot.

"We are using all available resources, and we continue to work closely with the FBI, the KBI, the Sedgwick County Sheriff's Department, the Sedgwick County Forensic Science Center and the Sedgwick County District Attorney's Office," he said. "We are very grateful for the assistance that we have received from those agencies.

"We also appreciate all the tips and leads we have received from the public," he added. "The overwhelming response we have received from citizens is reflective of our city's community policing philosophy, and we could not effectively pursue this investigation without their help."

The new communication from BTK rekindled bad memories for those who had been part of the original investigation in the 1970s.

"I wish I could wipe the memory clean," said Keith Sanborn, who had been the Sedgwick County district attorney in 1974. Describing the Otero crime scene, he said, "It looked depraved. There was a disrespecting of the dead people. I don't think we wanted some of the details of that disclosed, to head off false confessions, but there were several things done. It was bad. It hurt everyone involved emotionally. I'll never be able to shake the memory of it."

Former Wichita sheriff Vern Miller said that BTK was a "yellow-bellied snake of a coward of a creature." On Thursday, March 25, Miller said, "I went to a gathering this morning, a board meeting of the Parallax Drug Treatment Center. Every woman there felt terrified; every man was furious and wanted to hunt the yellow coward down. Now everyone feels frightened again. I talked to an old friend last night, and I'm sure he said what a lot of people think. He said, 'Vern, tonight the gun lies beside the bed.'"

Those in charge of projecting a positive image of Wichita to the world were obviously concerned about the damage BTK's re-emergence would cause, from a public-relations standpoint. John Rolfe, the president of the Greater Wichita Convention and Visitors Bureau, said, "One of the great draws of Wichita is that it really is a very safe and friendly city. One individual doesn't change that."

I didn't feel comfortable myself. Arlyn Smith had a chilling thought. He told me that it was possible I had spoken with the killer. It might not have been an interview, but at some point since I started talking about BTK, possibly beginning as early as February 2002, when I was interviewed by Dana Hertneky on KSN, this guy might have arranged to talk with me.

My days during the end of March and the beginning of April 2004 reminded me of "Manson mania," and like that phase of my life, the world's sudden interest in BTK brought constant contacts from strangers.

Mary Ann and I had one of our few arguments when a strange man came to the door and knocked. I had already answered the door a few times and had always regretted it. When Mary Ann started to answer the door I asked her not to. She asked, "Why?"

"Do you know who he is?"

"No."

"I don't know who he is, but every single person who has come to our door since March 24 has wanted to talk with me about BTK. I don't want to talk with him," I said. "I am trying to work on responding to some of these hundreds of other messages. If he wants me to contact him, then he can leave a note on the door."

"But it is impolite not to answer the door," she protested.

The guy continued to knock on the door. Mary Ann was getting angry. When she tried to pass me, however, I put my hands on her shoulders, stopping her. "I'm asking you not to answer the door to strangers until this thing passes over. It's not purely a matter of my convenience; I don't want you to be confronted with some crazy guy."

The strange phone calls had started and Mary Ann had stopped answering the phone. After a time we were not even screening calls because the calls were constant. At intervals we would go listen to messages. We would call back the ones we wanted to talk to, and ignore those we didn't. Some calls made us feel uncomfortable but were too vague to be called menacing. One fellow called repeatedly and always said, "I'm bored, Robert. I'm bored. Give me something to do."

Mary Ann was miffed, but she agreed not to answer the door to strangers until this thing blew over.

The strange man left and did not leave a message.

The barrage was constant. In April, when I went out to mow my front lawn, I thought that one of our neighbors must be having a garage sale because there was so much traffic on our little-used street. Several cars slowed in front of our house and several stopped just adjacent to our home. I continued mowing the lawn, but as I went back and forth, I did not see anyone having a garage sale. I was puzzled by the parade of cars.

Then I paused and looked at the people in the vans and cars and trucks that were stopping or driving slowly past my home.

There was no garage sale. They were looking at me.

Coincidentally, that evening I received an e-mail from a friend, an elected official, who wrote, "Bob, in Wichita your name is on everybody's lips today. You're part of the BTK mystique now."

Sometimes the attention became disturbing. On a Saturday afternoon Mary Ann and I went to a nursing home to visit Mary Ann's 97-year-old mother. Her memory and hearing were going, but she was always cheerful and happy to see us, as we were happy to see her.

The previous year our youngest daughter traveled through Amsterdam, in the Netherlands, and brought Mary Ann a bag of tulip bulbs. When we departed to visit Mom, the tulips planted across our front yard garden were in full bloom. They were glorious. When we returned, half of the tulips had been pulled out of the ground, stomped on, and thrown around the walk, drive, and yard.

Mary Ann started weeping. "Why?" she asked me. "Why?"

As I held her, she went on, "Tulips just give us beauty. Why would anyone do this?" This was a mean thing to do, like kicking someone's dog. I presumed this was done by one of the strange men who came to our door.

On April 12, Jeanene Kiesling of KAKE-TV reported that Wichita police had raided the home of Nathan Thomason and his mother at 1505 South Bleckley. Police were investigating the theory that Thomason's deceased father was BTK. When police knocked on the door, Thomason answered and recognized the caller from television as "one of the lead investigators on the BTK case."

Police took Nathan and his mother to the police station at City Hall, where they were interrogated for seven hours. In the meantime, police went over their house with a fine-tooth comb. According to Nathan, the police put "everything all out in the middle of the floor. They went through my closet."

Nathan's mother, Shirley Thomason, had met her husband in Texas in 1976, and they moved back to Wichita later that year. They stayed in Wichita until 1993, when Nathan Senior was sent to prison for sexual assault. He was released six years later and committed suicide in 2001.

Nathan junior gave police a DNA sample. He says police later told him he was no longer a suspect and neither was his father.

On April 15, Kansas Attorney General Phil Kline met privately with Wichita mayor Carlos Mayans and police officials to pledge his commitment to finding the BTK Strangler. Mayor Mayans said that he arranged the meeting "to make sure that we have everything we need from the attorney general and the KBI for now."

In a press conference after the meeting Kline said, "Anything they need, we will provide."

He announced that the KBI had dispatched three cold-case investigators to help Wichita police with the case. Even though almost a month had passed since the latest communication from the killer was received, investigators, according to Mayor Mayans, continued to work "24/7."

In addition to the Wichita police department, the FBI and the KBI, investigators from the Sedgwick County sheriff's office and the Kansas Highway Patrol were working on the case.

Kline said that the BTK investigative team's command center, which had been functioning out of a temporary location, was being moved to City Hall.

Mayor Mayans said, "The community wants to have this case as a priority. The public should have a level of comfort that law enforcement is on top of things, and that we are doing all we can to try to solve the case."

That assurance didn't satisfy everybody. On April 21, KSNW-TV in Wichita reported that the Wegerle family had felt haunted by the murder of Vicki for eighteen years, and were extremely skeptical about the competence of the Wichita police. Police said that Vicki was considered a possible BTK case right away. Vicki's relatives do not believe that is true. The Wegerles say the police always insisted that this was not the work of a serial killer. They believed Vicki was murdered by her husband Bill, who had discovered her body. About BTK, Glenda Wegerle, sister-in-law of Vicki, said, "He can burn in hell. My brother has not been vindicated; he has been a suspect for nearly eighteen years." Glenda said she was convinced Vicki didn't have a chance against her killer. "He watched and he waited for her—so we don't know all the details, but how could she have stopped that? How could she?"

As the police investigation pushed deeper into April, Wichita's public relations department had a problem. The Women's International Bowling Congress was scheduled to hold their United States championship tournament in Wichita beginning in the third week in April and running through July 6. During that time, the city was expecting 42,000 guests to arrive in town, many of them women traveling alone. And it was obvious that news of the BTK Strangler was making many of those prospective visitors very nervous. The convention was expected to draw $25 million for the city and $55 million for the state.

On April 8, Roseann Kuhn, the congress' executive director, told reporters: "We've had some inquiries about whether it is safe to come to Wichita, but to my knowledge no one has canceled their travel plans. We wanted them to know that, yes, we are concerned about it, and we are taking the appropriate measures to make sure they'll have a good experience in Wichita. The profile of this person [BTK] does not fit coming into hotels and coming into bowling centers and attacking people. I'm more concerned about tornadoes and bad weather than I am about a serial killer."

"These ladies come from all around the world," said John Rolfe, the president and chief executive of the Greater Wichita Convention and Visitors Bureau. "It's a big convention and we want them to feel safe about it." Wichita Police Chief Norman Williams posted a letter on the bowling congress' website, pledging that every effort would be made to assure the safety of the bowlers.

Of course, while the authorities were saying the women bowlers would be safe, I looked up the photo of Nancy Fox with her women's bowling team. Nancy was murdered the night after she bowled in a women's bowling league at Seneca Bowl. Part of this women's bowling tournament was to be held at Seneca Bowl.

On April 29 I spoke to a meeting of the Wichita Crime Commission, which was chaired by former deputy chief Bobby Stout, the Commission's executive director. The Crime Commission is composed of Wichita's financial and law enforcement movers and shakers, since both businesspeople and law enforcement personnel have a shared interest in reducing crime. The subject of BTK was the number one topic of discussion in Wichita. The place was packed with judges and oil millionaires and their spouses. The executive director told me it was their largest attendance ever. Bernie Drowatzky came up from Oklahoma, and I started with remarks about Bernie and led a round of applause for Bernie's work.

During my lecture, talking about my developing manuscript, I told another story from my interview with *America's Most Wanted*. At the end of the interview Darrell Barton asked me, "Let's imagine that this guy is arrested and he says, 'I want to talk to Beattie. I want Beattie to write my story.' What questions will you have for him?"

I told Darrell that I didn't have any questions for BTK. I won't write that book. Someone else will have to write that book. Maybe at one time I could have written that book, but I have become too close to the victims' families and friends, to the cops who have devoted so many years of their lives to this case.

Darrell was a bit flustered at my response. A typical journalist or author would love such an opportunity, but I was not approaching this from the perspective of a journalist. Darrell asked, "Well, you will attend this guy's trial, won't you?" I answered that I probably would.

Darrell said, "Let's imagine that you are seated at trial just a row behind the defendant. At a quiet moment you and he are near each other and are looking at each other. Do you have anything to say to him?"

My eyes flashed in anger visualizing that moment and I said, "The only thing I'd have to say to him is—'Goodbye.' "

Darrell threw his notes into the air and said, "Cut."

I concluded by telling the Wichita Crime Commission that while I was telling the story of these crimes, this investigation, and its consequences, my book was about the people and our community. "I am not writing 'The BTK Story.'" I received a loud round of applause.

Former BTK lead investigator Bernie Drowatzky, the old friend of my parents who had been the detective to retrieve the very first BTK letter from the textbook in the Wichita Public Library in 1974, was also making himself available to the media. As of April 30, 2004, Drowatzky had been interviewed by NBC, Fox, *People* magazine, and the John Walsh program, *America's Most Wanted*.

Susan Peters of KAKE-TV asked Drowatzky where, if he were still running the investigation, he would start looking for new clues. Drowatzky said he'd look on the Wichita State University campus, where BTK copied some of his letters. He based this on the fact that Kevin Bright said the killer asked him, "Didn't I see you at the university?"

Drowatzky revealed that Wichita police also took the Coleman Company connection very seriously and, on more than one occasion, took Kevin Bright with them to stake out the company, parking out front. They let their witness watch all of the people who came and went. Kevin never saw anybody he thought might be his sister's killer, however. During the interview Drowatzky confirmed that back then Kevin Bright was hypnotized in a search for new clues.

Drowatzky told the reporter that another clue might lie where Joseph Otero worked as an instructor at Rose Hill Airport. But Drowatzky made it clear that he believed DNA would turn out to be the key to the case. He also said that, in his opinion, it didn't make any difference how old BTK was. If he wanted to kill again he would.

"My personal opinion is he's normal, he has a job, goes about his business every day, fits in everywhere," said Drowatzky. "I don't think he's outstanding as a weird person or anything, and that's one of the reasons he's so hard to catch."

The months of March and April had been a whirlwind. I had been on live national TV and radio. I had given a half-dozen magazine interviews—for *People, Cosmopolitan, FHM*, and others. That was okay, but almost every day strange men, crackpots, with theories about aliens and demons and whatnot, continued to come to my door.

Then Heidi called back. We had not spoken in a while. This talk started off like our previous conversations. Although most Wichita women feared BTK, I soon came to learn that a few women were sexually aroused by him. When Heidi first contacted me on January 17, 2004, I thought she was another serial killer aficionado. Over the next several weeks we spoke over the phone and exchanged several telephone messages. Now she called me and started talking about having sex with BTK. She wanted to meet him. She thought that I could facilitate a meeting. BTK really turned her on.

My jaw dropped in astonishment. She had that breathy voice some women have when aroused, and at the climax of our conversation she said, "Oh! I want to meet him!" I thought she might be masturbating.

I was shocked! I told her that I did not know who BTK was, that I would not help her meet him, and I did not recommend that she try to contact BTK.

Heidi told me that she had interviewed retired *Wichita Eagle* editor Buzz Merritt by falsely telling him that she was a student writing a report about BTK, and that she had persuaded the current resident of the old Otero home at 803 N. Edgemoor to let her tour the home using the same student ruse.

This woman holds a responsible job. At first I was worried about her. Then I realized that I cannot be the counselor for every person I meet whose interests are dangerous or bizarre or personally repugnant to me. Still, after developing all my relationships with people in this community who have suffered from this case, and knowing what he did to his victims, I became sickened at the thought of a woman finding BTK sexually attractive and offering herself to him. After concluding my phone conversation with Heidi I became nauseated and vomited into the trash can next to my telephone.

That some women find a grotesque murderer attractive is not a new phenomenon. A number of women proposed relationships to serial killer Ted Bundy and one married him. This aspect of my experience reinforced my decision, though, on how to write this story. This book is not "The BTK Story." It is about the hunt for BTK and the consequences of his crimes.

Chapter 27

Contact—True or False?

On Wednesday, May 5, 2004, Jeanene Kiesling of KAKE-TV reported that, just before noon, their TV station received a suspicious letter that mentioned BTK. Typed on the label was "KAKE-TV 10" and the station's address.

When Chris Frank of KAKE-TV called me, I was at home interviewing retired WPD beat officer Lowell Hollingshead, who discovered Nancy Fox's body. Frank told me they had received a letter and that it looked suspicious. He wanted to know if I wanted to see it. I asked him to describe it. He described it in some detail. It did not have the feature BTK had included in 1979. I declined and finished my interview with Lowell.

Later, Frank called back and offered to bring the letter over. Again, I said no thanks. The police took the KAKE letter and I heard through the grapevine that the police were leaning toward a conclusion that the letter was genuine. KAKE broadcast a scene showing news director Glen Horn turning the letter over to Detective Kelly Otis.

That day I did decline to accept the letter from KAKE, but late Wednesday night I started receiving copies. Personnel at KAKE with copies had started faxing copies to others. The others started sending their copies to me. I started studying the document.

I wrote the following lightly censored report about the material that KAKE received. I evaluated the KAKE material using some of the same techniques as are used when a new sonnet is found and suspected of being from Shakespeare. I concluded that the person who sent the new material was not the same one who had written the earlier BTK letters:

> A rough naïve Bayesian analysis indicates to me that this is probably not from BTK. [section omitted] . . . However, different analysts may legitimately choose different factors. I am sure that WPD or KBI crime analysts must have already done this analysis in detail.
>
> The factors I attributed to previous BTK exemplars include:
>
> 1. Unique feature.
> 2. Mention of specific victim (Anna etc.)
> 3. Mention of specific position victim was left or was to be left.
> 4. Mention of unnecessary information. ("Runs good.")
> 5. Deliberately misspelled words.
> 6. Deliberately odd punctuation.
> 7. Photocopied multiple times.
> 8. Photocopied on public machine.
> 9. BTK salutation.
> 10. Claim of social motivation. ("I write for sake of the taxpayer.")
> 11. Unambiguous reference to sex motive.
>
> Arguably, all of these factors are absent from this letter. Certainly, most of these factors are absent.
>
> Factors that conflict or confound comparison with previous messages include:
>
> 1. Same stamp.
> 2. Same apparent style of address and return address.
> 3. Sequence: first sent to Eagle, second to KAKE; next to victim?
> 4. Vast plausible information about MO, ID, RUSE.

5. Reader confirmation bias. Social science studies show we routinely place three times as much emphasis on confirmatory evidence as we do disconfirming evidence, if we acknowledge disconfirming evidence at all. This is how we delude ourselves into "knowing" something that isn't so. In this case, it is possible that an informed reader could read the confirming evidence but ignore the disconfirming evidence.

> On seeing this I almost immediately told KAKE that the author of this document could be any investigator, any woman who had been involved with an investigator and had heard a lot about the case, any child or close friend or relative who had heard a lot about the case, possibly some members of the press, and possibly someone not otherwise suspected such as the middle-aged woman known as "The Poet."

When I evaluated this I had just written my chapter about the police being deceived by Ruth Finley. It was fresh in my mind how that embarrassing episode sidetracked the BTK investigation. I was terribly worried that the police would think this was from BTK without legitimate confirmation. Just by looking at the letter, I did not think that one could conclude that it was from the killer. I hoped that history would not repeat itself with the police following a hoax.

On Thursday evening, May 5, Glen Horn, the young news director at KAKE, once again offered to show me the new letter. This time I accepted. I felt badly about not telling him, but due to my promises to those who had provided me copies of the letter, I did not say that I had already spent many hours evaluating the material.

The first thing I said when taking a quick look at the letter was, "This looks like it is from someone who attended one of my lectures." The use of the phrase "The BTK Story" immediately rang a bell with me and that night KAKE broadcast my apparently snap reaction. I was to broadcast a theme of caution, that it could be a hoax.

One reference in the letter was to "PJ". Police, naturally, wanted to investigate any possible meaning of PJ, and possible connections the letters PJ may have with the case. The public did not yet know of P.J. Wyatt, the folklore professor at Wichita State University.

"We are trying to determine if it is a part of a puzzle we are working on," said Wichita Police Deputy Chief Terri Moses.

The first page was typed, and included titles for a list of chapters. I share this because KAKE TV broadcast this, perhaps unintentionally, and it has been widely posted on the Internet. The table of contents read:

THE BTK STORY

1. A SERIAL KILLER IS BORN
2. DAWN
3. FETISH
4. FANTASY WORLD
5. THE SEARCH BEGINS
6. HAUNTS
7. PJ'S
8. MO-ID-RUSE
9. HITS
10. TREASURED MEMORIES
11. FINAL CURTAIN CALL
12. DUSK
13. WILL THERE MORE?

The second page of the letter to BTK had the title Chapter 8 (the chapter entitled MO-ID-RUSE) and was a puzzle filled with letters in vertical rows. Some spelled out words, some numbers were intertwined. On their 10:00 p.m. broadcast of Thursday, November 4, 2004, KAKE broadcast a clear copy of this page.

The third page had a photocopy of an open billfold, with what appeared to be two ID badges. The first of a Southwestern Bell employee. The other for a Wichita public school's special officer.

Bernie Drowatzky compared this letter to other letters sent by BTK and said, "There are indications it could very well be, or someone that's well studied on the case."

The letter showed an address of 408 Clayton, an address that does not actually exist. Clayton, located on the west side of Wichita, runs north and south. The March BTK letter had a return address of Bill

Thomas Killman at 1684 S. Oldmanor. In reality, a man named Douglas B. Killmer lived at 1682 S. Old Manor. This letter had a return address of Thomas B. King at 408 Clayton. In reality, a man named T. Jack King lived at 407 N. Clayton. BTK had done his research and was amusing himself.

On May 6, KAKE-TV's Chris Frank reported that police had said that the new letter had "valid issues" to it, and that a news briefing had been scheduled for Monday, May 10, at which time police would announce whether the letter was from BTK or if it was a cruel hoax from a copycat.

Police revealed that the names on the two business cards, photocopies of which were included with the letter, belonged to real people—both men. The ID card linked to Wichita public schools contained the name of an actual district employee who retired in 1970 and died in 1977. At the time of his 1970 retirement several articles about this man were published in the Wichita *Eagle and Beacon*.

However, in an apparent inconsistency, the copy of the school ID badge contained a logo not used by Wichita public schools until 1988, district spokeswoman Susan Arensman said. She said officials found it on only one document prior to 1986.

The other business card belonged to a man who retired twenty years ago from Southwestern Bell Telephone. Both police and KAKE-TV spoke with this man, and he said he didn't know why his card was included.

Police said that, if the new letter was done by a copycat, it was an individual who had "done his homework."

Over the weekend I heard that the police planned to announce that they did believe it was real. Saturday afternoon, May 8, Glen Horn authorized me and my fellow members of MENSA to evaluate. Brooke Erickson, a KAKE-TV reporter, brought the puzzle. At my invitation Detective Arlyn Smith joined us. We had the puzzle for one hour and KAKE TV filmed the entire time.

The grid included hidden words such as "school," "telephone" and "ID ruse," suggesting that BTK might have passed himself off as a telephone repairman or as a school district employee coming to consult with parents. Since there was no sign of forced entry at three of his victims' houses, police long had suspected that he found a way to be invited inside.

When KSN asked me to come to their studios and appear live to comment before and after the police press conference, I agreed.

Press from around the country attended. Unfortunately, the police did not seem to appreciate the effort the national press made to attend. A short statement was read and no questions were taken. All of the press people were angry. The police could have just as easily released a printed statement and saved the journalists and crews from the travel.

On that Monday morning KAKE reported: "In the KAKE suspicious letter, the sender had one page with two identification cards. One was of a Southwestern Bell employee, who's still living in Wichita. So, how could the sender randomly have an ID card more than twenty years old lying around their house, and then decide to send it to us. Beattie says even though the game and letters are impressive and many experts we've talked to believe the letter is from BTK, he's still not convinced."

Later that day, Lieutenant Ken Landwehr told reporters that the WPD was treating the letter sent to KAKE as "possibly" real. Police were turning the letter over to the FBI to do analysis using the latest technology and forensic science, and to determine the letter's authenticity. Police again asked for help from the public, based on information contained in the letter.

"We are specifically interested in talking to anyone who was approached at their residence between 1974 and 1986 by a man presenting himself as an employee of a school or a utility company," Landwehr said. "Obviously, we are not interested in legitimate encounters. We want to know about situations where a man attempted to get into your house under suspicious circumstances."

As a service to the public, the *Eagle* published on May 11 some tips regarding "What to Do if a School or Utility Official Comes to Your Door." The article advised: "The Wichita school district, SBC Communications, Westar Energy and the Wichita water department do not send employees to houses unsolicited. Question those who want access to your house if you did not request such a visit. All such employees travel in company or government vehicles with proper logos; they wear uniforms and carry proper identification. The only school officials who make house calls are teachers, principals and Wichita police resource officers, whom you would know from your child's school. If you don't know them, don't let them in. SBC employees have identification that has a holographic image of the company logo. Westar meter readers or anyone needing access to yards for repair work will not ask to enter your home. None of the utilities dispatch people to homes when the residents are not there. Any suspicious people or activities around your house should be reported to police by calling 911. If you have any doubts whether a person at your door is actually affiliated with the utility, lock the door and call the utility's customer service department to verify that someone has been dispatched to your house."

Following the police briefing, Westar—the Wichita electric company—and other utility companies wanted to make sure the public could easily identify workers. Karla Olsen of Westar told Kim Wilhelm of KWCH-TV that each Westar employee wore a company shirt or cap. Olsen said workers would come to a resident's door only if service were about to be disconnected or if crews couldn't get into the backyard.

"We will never ever ask to be in the house," said Olsen. "It's just access to the backyard for meter reading or if we need to do a repair in the backyard and we do not have access."

The Wichita telephone company had similar rules for its workers. Technicians wore company shirts and carried photo ID badges with a holographic image of the SBC logo. Customers were encouraged to ask to see a technician's ID badge before allowing him to enter the home or yard to do repair work.

Wichita City Water and Sewer workers also carried photo IDs, and wore shirts with a City of Wichita logo. All workers drove marked vehicles.

City officials told the public that its employees had been ordered never to enter a home unless they were invited in to check out a specific problem.

Former Wichita police chief Richard LaMunyon pointed out to KAKE-TV that in the Shirley Vian and Vicki Wegerle cases, police did not know how BTK got in. They only knew he was let in by the victims without using force. BTK might be trying to prove to us, LaMunyon speculated, through the KAKE letter, that he got in to commit those two murders with fake IDs.

"It's very possible someone could knock on your door, show you some ID that puts you at ease and then they move right on in," said Bernie Drowatzky.

May 10 turned out to be one of the busiest days I had ever had in terms of dealing with the media. I did six television interviews: local ABC (tape), local NBC (one live, one tape), local CBS (tape), NBC national news with Tom Brokaw (tape to be broadcast later), and Court TV Catherine Crier (live). Fox News tried to reach me but we missed each other. And I did an interview for a local magazine. In between those interviews I had nine off-the-record communications with press or police or retired police. The Catherine Crier show was my final interview; I had been doing interviews or talking for nine solid hours, and I was tired. My wife said it was my worst interview. I told Crier that I thought BTK had been more active over the years than people think. Just because he had not committed any murders didn't mean he had not been committing crimes, and that there were several breaking-and-entering cases that deserved closer looks. I reported that one retired lead detective had told me that he thought their parameters had been too narrow. BTK might never have stopped killing. Catherine Crier and her guest profiler looked stunned.

John Garrison, the past president of the Retired Wichita Police Officers Association, stopped by my home while NBC national news was there. He told the segment producer, Ted Elbert, "This man [pointing at me] is the greatest single repository of knowledge about the BTK case. Over coffee, all the cops agree with me. Bob is the only person to talk with all the cops who worked on this case. For the past 30 years, within the department the investigation has always been compartmentalized. That means once you were reassigned and no longer on the case, the new guys assigned to the case generally didn't talk with you. They read your reports, and that's all. We haven't talked with each other, but we've each talked with Bob. And Bob has not only talked with all the cops, he's also talked with all the laboratory guys, victims' families, the district attorneys, the press, and everyone with a story to tell. You're interviewing the right guy."

John would not say that on camera, though. He wouldn't go on camera at all. Still, it was a nice validation of my work.

During another of those May 10 interviews I told Michael Schwanke of KWCH-TV that if the new letter was actually from BTK, I was not surprised. I believed that BTK wanted to tell his story and he wanted the public to hear it. I told Schwanke that I expected further communications from BTK to press outlets. If BTK wrote directly to the police, he risked the letter never being publicized. If he wrote to one of the local newspapers or TV stations, he was assured that his message would, sooner or later, become public knowledge.

Also quoted in the report was former WPD Chief Richard LaMunyon, who said, "Each time he communicates I think he wants us to have this information . . . I think he wants his story told."

On May 13, an article appeared in the *L.A. Times* about the new letter. I told reporter Stephanie Simon that I was inclined to believe, but was not convinced, that the letter was authentic. I told her I was sure of one thing: If the letter was a hoax, the real BTK would write soon to set the record straight. After all, in the '70s, BTK expressed frustration at inaccurate or incomplete reporting on his assaults. At least twice he wrote to the media to ensure they got the story right.

"He wants to have his story told," I said. "One way or another, the press will hear from BTK again."

Chapter 28

The Task Force

Ghostbusters detective Paul Dotson has publicly explained that he was the WPD representative to the creation of the MAIT manual (Multi Agency Investigative Team) for serial killer task forces. In the 1980s a National Institute of Justice grant helped pay for a meeting to design aids to local law enforcement in multiple agency response to serial murder investigations. Dotson wrote:

"Our group advocated the requirement for close cooperation and collaboration between all jurisdictions (law enforcement and prosecutors) from the beginning of any possible serial murder investigation through the final prosecutions. We referred to our team concept as the Multi Agency Investigative Team approach. Our published manual addressed most components found in complex serial murder investigations." The intent was to "maximize all investigative resources" to identify and successfully prosecute "the serial killer."

I started studying task forces of the past that had investigated serial killer cases with positive outcomes. The investigation cases I studied included the Boston Strangler, the Unabomber, the Atlanta child murders, and the Green River Killer case.

The Boston Strangler task force was believed to have captured the criminal they sought, but due to DNA testing we now know that Albert DeSalvo was not the Boston Strangler. Susan Kelly's 2002 *The Boston Stranglers* reports that Albert DeSalvo's body was exhumed, and on December 7, 2001, it was announced that DNA testing had excluded him as the murderer of Mary Sullivan, the final victim attributed to the Boston Strangler. Author Kelly reveals the dynamics of the task force that led to their acceptance of Albert DeSalvo as being the Boston Strangler.

DeSalvo was never prosecuted as the Strangler. He could not have been prosecuted because there was insufficient evidence against him to bring him to trial. Not one police officer from any of the towns where the Boston Strangler's crimes were committed ever interviewed DeSalvo. DeSalvo was interrogated only by people on or obtained by the task force. DeSalvo was convicted of crimes other than those of the strangler. It was criminal defense attorney F. Lee Bailey's idea to have DeSalvo publicly confess to being the Strangler. Bailey thought that this confession would lead to DeSalvo being put in a mental institution. Instead, DeSalvo was put in prison, where he was murdered. John Douglas wrote on page 362 of his book *The Cases That Haunt Us*: "There is no evidence that Albert DeSalvo had any knowledge or insight as to the true identity of the Boston Strangler or Stranglers." Individuals and agencies on the Boston Strangler task force did not work well together, and the task force was a failure.

The Unabomber, Ted Kaczynski, was caught, but not by the task force per se. At the recommendation of Attorney General Janet Reno and FBI Director Louis Freeh, on Tuesday, September 19, 1995, exactly five months after the Oklahoma City bombing, *The Washington Post* was the first to publish the Unabomber's Manifesto. The Unabomber was number one on the FBI's Most Wanted list. He had eluded capture for 17 years. The FBI task force had not developed any leads to the Unabomber. They thought it might help.

It was the publishing of the Unabomber's manifesto by the press that was responsible for apprehending the killer. The Unabomber's brother, David Kaczynski, recognized the manifesto's content and style as that of his brother, contacted an attorney, and then the authorities were contacted. That fairly quickly led to the killer's identification and capture. This task force has a passing grade, but it required the cooperation of the press.

The Atlanta Child Murder task force was responsible for apprehending and convicting the serial killer. This task force worked well and, thanks to FBI profiling, captured someone the police had not been looking for, a black male serial killer. FBI profilers John Douglas and Roy Hazelwood had told the police that the killer was a black male, whereas the Atlanta community and press had been looking for a white racist. Among other things, the FBI pointed out that a white male would likely be remembered by the primarily black residents of the neighborhoods where the children were taken, whereas a black man would not be unusual. The killer was someone who, when seen, was not thought to be out of place.

As has been noted, the Green River Killer task force had the killer's DNA in 1987 but did not process it until 2001. This DNA collection did lead to the killer's apprehension and confession, but only after an unnecessary 14-year delay.

Of these modern era serial killer task forces, only one, that of the Atlanta Child Murders, was responsible for catching the serial killer they sought in a timely manner.

Would the 2004 BTK task force identify the killer? I thought so. They appeared to be doing everything right.

Most serial killer investigators have a steep learning curve. As is clear in the BTK investigation, it took the Wichita Police Department years before they even realized that a serial killer was preying on Wichita citizens. Then they called and consulted other investigators. John Douglas suggested that an experienced team be assembled to fly to serial killer emergencies and guide the investigation.

How can cross-department knowledge help in a serial killer investigation? There are many illustrations. Ken Duckworth had been a detective before he became emergency communications director. In the 1960s he knew that a caller-ID and voice recording system could one day help in a homicide investigation. That the system he foresaw and implemented did not catch BTK in 1977 is no indication that cross-disciplinary knowledge is a bad thing.

There are major disagreements about how to investigate serial killers. Bob Keppel's book *The Psychology of Serial Killer Investigations* says that the police should not talk with the press. He says that in 2002 Chief Moose hurt rather than helped the Beltway Sniper serial killer investigation by talking with the press.

However, Keppel's remarks on serial killer related matters are often refuted by the evidence. In a *Wichita Eagle* article bylined by Deb Gruver with Hurst Laviana contributing, published on April 3, 2004, Keppel is quoted as saying, " 'No profile is 100 percent. I've never profiled a case that's exactly correct.' He quickly answered 'none' when asked for an example of a case where the profile was right-on in matching the killer. 'Is that a short enough answer?' "

In Dr. Brussel's profile of Mad Bomber George Metesky, he even told the police what the bomber would be wearing. Clint Van Zandt's profile of Unabomber Ted Kaczynski was accurate. Robert Ressler's profile in the Elverson-Calabro case was so accurate that Lt. Joseph D'Amico told a reporter, "They [the profilers] had him [the suspect] so right that I asked the FBI why they hadn't given us his phone number, too." Others have profiled cases that are exactly correct.

The study of other cases is worthwhile. At the suggestion of retired detective John Garrison, in January 2004 I read Joseph Wambaugh's book *The Blooding* about the hunt for England's Narborough serial killer. Garrison always thought that they should be doing DNA testing on suspects but could not convince the police to do so. Only after the March 2004 letter arrived did the swab-a-thon start. The Wichita police and profilers believed that when BTK was confronted, he would either confess just as the Yorkshire Ripper did, or he would at least acknowledge that he understood why he was a suspect. The police also believed that he would try to elude DNA testing just as the Narborough killer did.

Peter Sutcliffe, England's Yorkshire Ripper serial killer, did not commit his first murder entirely for the same reasons he committed his later murders. Many police and psychologists believe that BTK murdered the Oteros for a different reason than he murdered his later victims. For example, Chief Hannon told me that he thought that the Otero murders were *not* sexually motivated, but the killer found he became sexually excited while strangling Josie Otero. Bob Keppel wrote extensively about the Yorkshire Ripper investigation in his book on serial killer investigations. He said that it took five years to catch the killer basically because the investigation was a failure.

But they caught the killer in five years.

FBI profiler John Douglas concluded that Gary Ridgway's "Call Me Fred" February 1984 letter was a hoax. *The Seattle Post-Intelligencer* newspaper of November 7, 2003 reports: "Yesterday, sources close to the task force said investigators did a slow burn after Ridgway told them the letter was from him. Sources said the FBI expert, a psychological profiler, essentially had blown off the letter, dismissing it as the work of 'someone inside the task force seeking undue attention.' On Thursday, November 27, 2003, the paper reported: "Now the profiler, John Douglas, acknowledges that he was wrong."

Profiler John Douglas's conclusion that the letter from Green River serial killer Gary Ridgway was from a cop was an error, just as my conclusion in May 2004 that the letter from BTK to KAKE TV was a hoax was an error. Laboratory forensic means proved that the letter to KAKE was from the serial killer.

Profilers from different disciplines continue to disagree about definitions and causes. In his book *Profiles in Murder: An FBI Legend Dissects Killers and Their Crimes*, Russel Vorpagel says flatly, "Profiling is based on statistics, on the odds." This is the social science model similar to the American Psychological Association's *Diagnostic and Statistical Manual* for mental disease. Seen in this context, each time a doctor evaluates you, you are being compared with a "profile" of a person known to have a specific disease or syndrome, and you are statistically matched with a diagnosis. In 1979 the APA eliminated the final diagnosis of "psychopath" as a mental illness and changed the term into two distinct words: "sociopath" and "antisocial." A psychopath is antisocial but not psychotic; the psychopath, who does not have a conscience, is not mentally ill.

However, it is debatable whether the absence of conscience should be considered mental illness. Dr. Robert Hare writes extensively of this in his recommended book *Without Conscience: The Disturbing World of the Psychopaths Among Us*.

In her book *My Life Among the Serial Killers*, psychiatrist profiler Helen Morrison, M.D., thinks that the Green River Task Force work was inferior to that of the Ted Bundy investigation, primarily because the Green River investigation was "too territorial." Unwilling to consider the help of "outsiders," they did not operate well as a task force.

Dr. Morrison's view is that a serial murderer does not have a personality structure the way the rest of us do. She attributes the absence of this structure to genetic factors. She points out that "there have not been any murders from serial killers until they have become adolescents." She believes that changes in brain chemistry beginning in adolescence trigger their murderous behavior.

An anthropologist I consulted has a different view. She believes that serial killer behavior is culturally based, not genetically based.

What are perceived as extraordinary behaviors are often culturally based. By definition, crime and insanity exist in relation to others. Behavior defined as a crime in one culture may be the norm in another. Homosexual behavior is the norm in the gay and lesbian subculture and was at one time the norm in historical Greek culture. Behavior that an anthropologist may consider "cultural diversity" a military court-martial may consider a crime.

And there are subcultures within every culture. In an American criminal subculture, such as are found in crime families and prisons, "crime" is the norm. Most subcultural norms are invisible to those participating in their rituals. For example, a large subculture of American women put dirt on their faces and glue in their hair. They don't call these items dirt and glue, they call them "makeup" and "hairspray." This is the dominant custom of the American female subculture. Men in business dress wear nooses around their necks. They call them "neckties." These behaviors are so customary that they only sound silly when spoken of in abstract terms.

The BTK serial killer identified his subculture when he made his list of serial killers—Harvey Glatman, etc. Those are members of his subculture and his behavior is "normal"—within the norm—for him. He will be devious and deceptive, though generally outwardly "normal."

And there are those, such as Sheriff Dave Reichert and investigator William Tatum, who believe that the causes of serial killers are supernatural.

The BTK investigation took the detectives into odd areas, such as consulting psychics and studying numerology. In the Unabomber investigation the detectives studied the possible meanings of the return address on the package and book the bomb was hidden in on June 10, 1980. The name on the return address was "Enoch Fisher" and the book was Sloan Wilson's novel *Ice Brothers*. They read the novel for clues and studied the name Enoch for clues. When the Unabomber was captured, both proved to be meaningless, other than to be deceptive, as was Gary Ridgway's "Call Me Fred" letter.

Shouldn't the task force consider BTK's letters to be deliberately deceptive? That is what members of BTK's subculture do.

Chapter 29

More Contacts

Throughout 2004 I continued interviews. Two women wanted to talk with me separately, and I told them I would meet them wherever they felt safe and comfortable. We met in the two most right-wing churches in a right-wing town. When I arrived home, my wife was viewing the noon news and told me that the police had issued a new statement. The FBI confirmed that the May 5 letter to KAKE TV was from the killer, and the Wichita Police Department received a letter on June 4 from the killer. This letter describes the Otero murders, and it contains chapter one from the killer's book, "A Serial Killer Is Born."

This was stunning news, though it was good news in context. Although the DNA from the Otero crime scene had degraded and could not be used to link BTK to the Otero murders, BTK had just linked himself to the Otero murders. Now, if captured, he could be prosecuted for them.

It reminded me of a 1999 KSN twenty-fifth anniversary story about the Otero murders. Mike McKenna was interviewed, and he said, "This man's still here." He had a prime suspect that he did not name, but he told me enough about his prime suspect that I confirmed he was talking about the same suspect that Dr. Harrell had. This guy had been a suspect since the Otero murders. He said two of the Ghostbusters thought this was the guy. They did get a search warrant for his safety deposit box, but when they went to the bank they were told that the guy had just been there an hour earlier. He had apparently cleaned it out.

* * *

On July 17 the police retrieved another message from BTK. It was in a standard business envelope found in the central Wichita library book return at 204 S. Main. In their two-minute twenty-five-second verbal statement, the police told the public to put deadbolt locks and peepholes on their doors, keep their windows locked, don't let strangers into their home. The police statement resulted in frightening the community. The letter apparently contained a disturbing message.

On August 20 the police released the "Oh Death" poem and publicly acknowledged the P.J. Wyatt involvement, which was first known to Detective John Garrison in early 1978 and was thoroughly investigated.

Former Detective Dan Stewart (Detective Charlie Stewart's son) told me that he took Professor's Wyatt's folklore course in 1967—the course was always considered "an easy A" and a lot of officers enrolled in it—and she sang the "Oh Death" song. She used a different textbook in 1977 when Detective John Garrison took the course.

On August 26 the police released most of the "Oh Anna, Why Didn't You Appear" poem. They announced what the Columbia University professors had concluded nearly a quarter-century before: it was an original work.

Was that all of BTK's contacts this year? In the fall I was contacted by one of the best known businesswomen in Wichita. She had a long track record of credibility. She said that she received a letter in February from Bill Thomas Killman on south Oldmanor. She remembered the letter because she thought the name must be Native American. He wanted to meet with her to talk about a job, but the appointment was never made and she threw the letter away.

But she was certain that the return address on the envelope was Bill Thomas Killman on south Oldmanor. She used to live with her aunt on north Old Manor and she wondered if Old Manor changed to Oldmanor when it was south. Wichita has quite a number of streets that change names depending on whether they are east or west; she thought maybe there were changes on street names north and south. She was very convincing and she appeared to have no motive to inject herself into this case. It could only drive clients and customers away for her name and business to be associated with this.

At a Kimmy's Café breakfast with former vice detectives Larry Samford and Bill Ammons, both told me that they had never heard of Dr. Harrell's 1974 suggestions to obtain cooperation of the local madams and prostitutes and run a bondage lure for BTK. Both said they thought the operation would have worked.

I heard from young television reporters from KWCH, KSN, and KAKE, that they were bored with the BTK story.

The majority of the younger generation do not think that they are in any danger from this "old man" BTK, who must be in his 50s or 60s. On the other hand, I am aware that serial killer Ed Gein (the inspiration for Robert Bloch's killer in *Psycho* and Thomas Harris's "Buffalo Bill" killer in *Silence of the Lambs*) was age 54. Sexual sadist David Parker Ray was a 59-year-old uniformed and very fit Park Ranger when he was arrested. And, of course, there is the model for fiction's cannibal serial killer Dr. Hannibal Lector, the 64-year-old Albert Fish, who also wrote letters to victims similar to BTK's, hid in closets while waiting for his victims, and strangled them. These killers were aged and infirm in the eyes of the young, yet they were experienced and dangerous killers. This guy BTK was still active and still out there. He had made threats against specific people. He might kill again.

Many times I was asked at public forums if I felt bad because my book "obviously" is responsible for bringing BTK back out. I told them about one of my meetings with Nancy Fox's mother after the March letter was revealed. When I was departing her home she stopped me, saying, "I want to say something to you. A lot of people are saying that your book is responsible for this guy coming out of hiding. If that is true, good. Now the police have something to work with that they did not have before. Now they are actively investigating and will not stop until they catch him. If your book is responsible for that, I'm glad." I gave her a hug.

Back on Sunday, June 6, 2004, when the police were being railed against in local and national complaints, I had written an op/ed piece that appeared in the *Eagle* under the headline "All against BTK" (not my choice). It read:

"Recently, many upset people have tried to engage me in recriminations about the police failure to put the domestic terrorist BTK in custody. But what more can be done? All of the old and new suspects have apparently been cleared by DNA testing. Is anyone coming forward with anything new? Not as far as I know.

"The BTK investigation has been thorough and exhaustive. The story is the same today as thirty years ago; it's about the incredible suffering of the victims, the almost pathological frustration of the public, and the investigators' stoic endurance when faced with their inability to solve a case that obsesses them.

"Some communities crumble when faced with such trying circumstances, while in others it becomes their finest hour.

"If at the end of this storm we have protected the many innocent while hunting the single guilty party, if we maintained our poise and decency in the face of indecent horror, then we can be proud of ourselves. That is a goal worthy of a great community."

On Wednesday evening, October 27, 2004, I had dinner at Wichita's Olive Garden restaurant on Rock Road with Nancy Fox's mother, Nancy's sister Beverly, and Nancy's best friend Gloria. That morning they had met with Detective Kelly Otis and had looked at all the photos that had been turned over to the police in 1977. They were relieved to learn that they had Nancy's baby pictures; they had not been lost.

The police would not provide copies or return the originals, but Nancy's mother, sister, and best friend were happy to relive memories of Nancy for a couple of hours.

When we finished dinner, Nancy's mother picked up her plate and looked under it, grinning at Beverly. Beverly lifted up her plate to show there was nothing under it but tablecloth. This caused the three women to break into laughter, which I did not understand.

They explained that when they were kids Nancy's mother had a well-known and inflexible rule that you had to clean your plate. If you did not clean your plate, you had to clear the table and wash, dry, and put away the dishes. When Nancy and Beverly were children Nancy hated lima beans, but her mother thought they were healthy and often put them on Nancy's plate. One day Nancy did not want to do the dishes and she stealthily slid the lima beans off her plate, shoved them under her plate, and then covered them with her plate. Beverly learned to do that too, and for a long time they managed to get out of doing the dishes by sliding the lima beans under their plates, waiting for Mom to leave, then throwing the lima beans in the trash before Mom came back. But one day Mom caught them. Thereafter Mom looked under their plates and they had to lift up their plates to show there was no food under them. Every family has such stories. They all had a big giggle over it right there in the Olive Garden.

I laughed along with them. But as I laughed I began to feel terribly sad and angry. Nancy Jo Fox, this wonderful young woman who everyone said was great with children and would have been a wonderful parent, was not here. She should have been here laughing with her mother and sister and best friend. It should have been her laughing at this convivial dinner instead of me. I am glad that I have met these wonderful people, but there should have been no reason for me to meet them.

On July 22, Michael Schwanke interviewed me at Channel 12's CBS studio. When we finished and I was preparing to depart he said, "Someone wants to talk with you."

I said, "Okay." I thought he meant the news director.

Then he said, "Charlie Otero." He gave me Charlie Otero's contact information. Schwanke said that when he met with him in that New Mexico prison where he was serving time for domestic abuse, the only person Charlie Otero mentioned was me. So I wrote to Charlie Otero and offered to correspond. If he preferred, I explained in the letter, he could call me collect.

Charlie Otero and I soon spoke by telephone. He had only wonderful things to say about his mother. She was a saint. His father was a good man who loved to play the bongos. They were a happy family.

But since the murders he had been filled with hate. He doesn't know who to hate. He's angry with his father and believes that his father knew something was wrong.

He also said that I was the first person to confirm that his family was murdered by BTK. I told Charlie that the DNA is degraded so it might not be possible to convict the killer, but Charlie said that if the killer was caught for any of the murders, that would be okay.

Charlie is scheduled to be released from prison on January 15, 2005, the thirty-first anniversary of his family's murder. He plans to come to Wichita.

* * *

I then exchanged some messages with Stephanie, Vicki Wegerle's daughter. Afterward I had several meetings and telephone calls with Glenda Wegerle, Bill Wegerle's sister.

Glenda Wegerle confirmed that on September 16, 1986, 25-month-old Brandon told her that a stranger had come in the house. She did not remember his exact words, he may not have used the word "stranger," but his message was that a strange man came in the house and hurt Mommy. This was before Bill came home after 8:00 p.m. and told her that the police accused him of murdering Vicki. Glenda told me that she never thought for a second that Bill could have murdered Vicki. She always knew he was innocent because Brandon said that a stranger hurt Mommy.

And Glenda was still angry about how the police told Bill about the events in March. They showed up at Bill's workplace and identified themselves. Bill thought they might be coming in to arrest him. Without preamble they showed him the photocopy with the photos and driver's license and asked if he could identify the woman. He, of course, identified Vicki.

The police sometimes have odd ways of delivering bad news.

In my view, Bill Wegerle has suffered as much unjust misfortune as any man in this tragedy.

After Vicki was murdered, Glenda worked hard at understanding what they were going through. She went to college and completed her degree. Then she went to graduate school. She became a doctor of psychology. Had Vicki not been murdered, she might not have chosen this path. Her story is one of prevailing over adversity. When I think of Dr. Glenda Wegerle, I think of the Kansas State motto, "Ad Astra per Aspera," to the stars through difficulties.

On Saturday morning, October 23, at Kimmy's Café, I had breakfast with eight retired detectives. Five of them had been cheek-swabbed. It was now something to joke about. With over a thousand men DNA tested it was now virtually a Wichita status symbol to have been cheek-swabbed. Congressman Todd Tiahrt had arranged for a special federal grant to help pay for more DNA testing capacity. If you hadn't been cheek-swabbed then you were a nobody. Detective Larry Samford mock-mournfully asked, "Bob, when are they going to get around to me?" He did not want to be left out. This was quite a difference from the reaction of the first cops cheek-swabbed six months earlier. It was now chic.

Before long Wichita had a BTK parody published in its alternative periodical *F5*. It was in the April 2004 issue.

And it was not long before someone on the Internet started selling BTK T-shirts.

Wichita's newspaper, *The Wichita Eagle*, had a monopoly, so they printed only the stories they wanted. They had withheld certain information that the police wanted withheld. The talk radio stations discussed BTK from time to time, but they were not actively investigating the story. Only the television stations were competing hard for viewers' attention. A witness told me that during times of intense BTK interest most people turned to KAKE TV, and KAKE TV held them by continuing to run a BTK segment until the other two stations, KSN and KWCH, stopped running theirs.

Some old-time journalists were very disappointed with the way all three of Wichita's television stations were covering the story. No one reporter stayed with the story. In my case it took months before I was interviewed by the same reporter. Each time I was interviewed I had to educate the reporter on some story basics. They were cycled through assignments, and these young reporters were not much interested in the story. None were going out at night, staking out possible BTK locations, investigating on their off hours.

In October 2004 KWCH did a quick history of all of BTK's contacts, his letters and telephone calls. I was glad that I caught the report on videotape because I reran the segment to verify what I thought—in their history they omitted the May 2004 letter to KAKE TV. I asked an experienced reporter, "If a hundred years from now someone reviews the KWCH film to report on this story, am I correct in understanding they will not know of the May 2004 letter to KAKE?" I was told yes. "That is television. It is commerce first, then journalism." KWCH omitted reporting a fact because they did not want to provide any advantage to a competitor.

What if any of the recent Wichita murders were committed by BTK?

On Wednesday, September 22, 2004, forty-three-year-old Carol Mould was found dead in her home in Butler County, near Wichita. She was believed to have died in a fire.

Yet Wichita's Lieutenant Landwehr was called to the scene. The news media speculated whether this could be a BTK-related death because Landwehr was out of his legal jurisdiction. The official statement was that Landwehr was asked to come to the scene only because of his experience.

That statement was questionable because many available fire department investigators had vastly more experience in investigating fire deaths than Kenny Landwehr. It reminded Wichita natives of the original stated reason that the Wichita library delayed opening on Saturday morning, July 17, 2004. Police investigators were present and the press was told there was a bomb threat. After an hour the press pointed out that homicide detectives working on the BTK case were present, but the bomb squad was not. Only later did the Wichita police acknowledge that a letter from BTK was found.

On Saturday Butler County Sheriff Craig Murphy announced that Carol Mould was murdered and the fire was set afterward. Little information was released.

Carol's husband was psychologist Dr. Douglas Mould, one of three area psychologists practicing in gerontology. The three often pass each other at nursing homes and it is unusual for them not to speak each working day. One of the other three is Dr. Glenda Wegele.

I do not know whether they have found any unrevealed evidence, or any other link, or merely suspected a link because of Dr. Wegerle and Dr. Mould's professional association, but Lt. Landwehr did immediately come to the crime scene on Wednesday, not on Saturday after an autopsy confirmed Carol Mould was murdered before the fire was set.

That brought us back to the same basic question: Who was BTK? How was it that there was no DNA sample from him when so many men in Wichita, and practically all of the suspicious ones, had given authorities a DNA sample.

This would seem to indicate that BTK was not a convicted felon. Convicted felons have their DNA on the federal database. The three good BTK samples of DNA would have found a match in the database by now.

In the absence of DNA, I then asked myself: What are BTK's known attributes? The best guess of what was known came from witnesses and the killer's actions.

AGE: In 1974 between ages 25–35. In 2004 between ages 55–65.

HEIGHT: approximately five foot ten (more likely taller than shorter)

BUILD: (in the 1970s): Medium. Not stocky, not thin. Probably still a medium build.

HAIR: Dark. Longish style conformed to the '70s era. Mustache. Probably gray now.

TEETH: Possible gap between two front teeth, though this was implied by an early morning letter taken by a postal worker. The postmark showed that the letter was mailed the previous evening.

CLOTHING: In 1970s, green/olive drab army jacket, sometimes jean jacket.

BAG: Carried bag of some type. At least once, bag had flower(s) on side. Other times carried a doctor's bag or bowling bag.

CIGARETTES: May have smoked Marlboros.

AUTO: Blue Chevy Caprice; also drove a truck or brown van.

HANDGUN: .22 caliber Colt Woodsman automatic.

PRESENCE: Not out of place in library. Does not call attention to self. Mild demeanor. Pleasant in conversation. Dangerous but glib and reassuring. As Dr. John Allen said, he wears "the mask of sanity."

CONFORMIST: He was invisible in the 1970s and 1980s because he conformed to the norm in appearance.

DEVIOUS: He acquired skills in being devious that permit him to elude the police and elude suspicion. He probably has eluded prosecution for crimes other than the BTK murders.

As a lawyer, I had a strong interest in what would happen if these recent contacts led to the BTK Strangler's being caught. I interviewed Bill Butterworth's old attorney, Richard Ney, who has the reputation of being Kansas's best criminal defense attorney. I spoke with him both by phone and in person about how, hypothetically, he would defend BTK. He told me, "If I took the case I would, of course, explore all possible defense avenues and put the prosecution to its proof—but with DNA evidence, there is little hope of an acquittal." Ney also confirmed for me that the 1988 letter to Mary Fager was from BTK.

I then interviewed criminal defense attorney Jay Greeno, Kansas's most dedicated opponent of the death penalty. Greeno defended one of the notorious Carr brothers, who in 2003 were convicted of raping, torturing, and murdering five people and sentenced to death. That case caused Greeno to lose his financial position and be kicked out of his own law firm. Regarding BTK, Greeno told me that, if the DNA evidence could be excluded, then BTK had a chance of acquittal. Greeno has had success in defending cold cases, especially where reliance on memory is pivotal. Greeno would fight hard to exclude DNA evidence, and if he could not, he would fight hard to question its probative value. After all, the biological samples from which the DNA was taken are decades old. Perhaps they could have been contaminated.

Of course, that covered only a possible criminal case. He could be convicted on other grounds. I told Steve McCain of CBS *48 Hours* that BTK could be defined as a "domestic terrorist" under U.S. Code Title 18, section 2331, sub-section 802 of the USA PATRIOT ACT. That act proclaims "(A) The term 'domestic terrorism' means activities that involve acts dangerous to human life that are a violation of the laws of the United States or any State; (B) appear to be intended (i) to intimidate or coerce a civilian population; (ii) to influence the policy of a government by intimidation or coercion; or (iii) to affect the conduct of a government by mass destruction, assassination, or kidnapping; and (C) occur primarily within the territorial jurisdiction of the United States."

I argue that by this legal definition BTK is a domestic terrorist and therefore the full capacities of the federal government, including the military, homeland security, and intelligence resources, were lawfully available to the Wichita Police Department investigators.

Still, the most satisfaction would be gained by a criminal prosecution. In fact, this was one of the dangers in this long-simmering case. In recent years the Kansas Supreme Court has repeatedly overturned convictions brought by the Sedgwick County District Attorney's office because of unconstitutionally overzealous prosecution. In the 1998 case of State versus Donesay, the high court used particularly pointed and harsh language in reversing a case that Sedgwick County District Attorney Nola Foulston personally prosecuted.

This BTK prosecution would be such an emotionally charged trial that dangers for the prosecution lurk everywhere. Everyone I discussed this with told me that they hoped that if a BTK prosecution occurred, the Sedgwick County District Attorney's office would proceed with a straight trial on the evidence, be unfailingly polite to everyone, not seek to provoke the public's or the jury's emotions, and take their time selecting a jury.

If BTK was arrested and charged soon, he might be charged with the Otero, Bright, Vian, Fox, and Wegerle murders, and with the attempted murder of Denise Cheryl, Laura Johnnie, and Anna Williams. My understanding was that the DNA evidence supported prosecution for the Nancy Fox and Vicki Wegerle murders. At some point there would have to be a decision made whether to prosecute BTK for all the murders or just these two. BTK implicated himself in the Otero murders with the June 4, 2004, message. If BTK was arrested while in possession of other evidence, such as Joseph Otero's watch, Anna Williams' scarves, some article of Shirley Vian's or Kathryn Bright's, then the prosecution might risk attempting to obtain convictions for those crimes as well.

That leads in turn to the question: could he receive the ultimate punishment? In 1972 the United States Supreme Court held that America's death sentencing practices needed to become uniform because they were issued inconsistently. The court's ruling effectively vacated all death sentences and required a new two-tier system: first a guilt-phase trial, then a sentencing trial, and these may be by two different juries. Later, the court ruled that only juries, not a single judge, may render a death sentence.

Kansas did not have a death penalty during the years 1974 to 1994. BTK's known murders occurred during those years. Unless he committed murders in Kansas before or after that time he could not receive the death sentence.

Regardless, all these considerations seemed moot the entire time I was writing until, only a few short weeks ago, the impossible finally happened.

The BTK Strangler was caught.

Chapter 30

BTK Contact Increases

On Thursday, October 21, 2004, I sent an e-mail to Hurst Laviana at *The Wichita Eagle* reminding him that the thirtieth anniversary of BTK's first contact was the following day. If the killer was going to make contact again, it could happen tomorrow.

On Friday, October 22, 2004, around 7:00 p.m., Wichita UPS and FedEx carriers arrived to make routine pickups at boxes in the 200 block of North Kansas Street outside the Omni Center building. A lot of traffic passes this location, and these express delivery drops are often full.

A male UPS deliveryman said "Hello" to his female FedEx colleague, and they chatted as they worked. Night had fallen and it was dark near the box. Inside, among the properly labeled material was an unsealed, unaddressed 8½-by-11-inch manila envelope. As he was walking to his truck, he removed the contents from the envelope and looked at them. The UPS driver expected to find what he finds virtually every day: paper documents to be delivered, an address that he would put on the UPS delivery bill, and a check to pay for the service.

What he finds is a plastic Baggie. It contains about ten five-by-three-inch cards. Printed on each card are either reduced-in-size photographs or words. Most of the words seem to be gibberish, but not all. On one is a poem to and about the Wichita police. It begins "Detective Ken Landwehr" and ends with threatening the detectives with death. Another is a revised version of the table of contents he sent to KAKE-

TV in May. The killer is now writing "The BTK Files" instead of "The BTK Story." He has carefully drawn lines through the first chapter, "A Serial Killer is Born," and chapter eight, "MO-ID-RUSE." These are the two chapters that the police already have. The final chapter, "Will There More?" has been changed to "Will There Be More?"

Chapter One seems to be included, but is reduced in size so much that it cannot be read without some type of magnification. This chapter includes information about BTK's life, such as when he was born, his fascination with trains, and that he had a technical education.

The most memorable card holds several photos that have been reduced in size. There are at least two photos to each card. One photo may be a driver's license. One photo is similar to Harvey Glatman's. This is of a bound woman, on her knees on the floor with a rope tied around her mouth, her hands tied behind her. She is alive and staring directly into the camera with an expression on her face of absolute terror.

Why is BTK threatening Landwehr and the others? Does he want to intimidate those who may come to ask for a DNA cheek-swab from him, or to arrest him?

On October 28, 2004, retired Detective John Garrison, past president of the Wichita Retired Police Officer's Association and current editor of the organization's bimonthly periodical, "The ReTired Copper," received a letter from Lt. Ken Landwehr, current lead investigator of the BTK investigation, that said in part, ""We feel it is necessary at this point in our investigation to request swabs from some former police personnel. We are collecting swabs to eliminate with certainty personnel who were employed during the time period in which the BTK murders occurred. It is our contention that by being as thorough as possible at this time it may counter defense strategies at a later date."

This letter was published in the October/November issue in mid-November 2004. I thought this letter told us a lot about the investigation. My reasoning is that Landwehr's request confirmed that the authorities had legally admissible DNA from BTK that they intended to use in the prosecution. This meant that the D.A.'s office was behind the request to swab retired officers. Why would they do this? There are several possibilities. What if some DNA samples were not "clean"? If

DNA was obtained that appeared to be from more than one person, then the authorities wanted to be able to identify and eliminate those who may have come into contact with the sample.

At 7:00 a.m. on Monday, November 29, 2004, Nancy Fox's mother receives a telephone call from a Wichita Police Department detective working on the BTK investigation. The detective says that tomorrow morning at 10:00 there will be a press conference where Nancy will be mentioned. The detective also says that twenty detectives are now working on the case and that they have some good leads.

Nancy's mother calls me and tells me what the detective said.

We talk for a while and I thank her for her call. Then I think about the implications. I take as a given that they would not tell this heart-broken woman that they have some good leads unless they had some good leads. There were only three detectives working on the case. I suspect that the new detectives have been assigned because of the threat against Ken Landwehr.

On Tuesday morning, November 30, 2004, at the 10:00 a.m. press briefing Lieutenant Landwehr says:

> Since March 2004, BTK has sent numerous communications to the media and the police. In these letters, he has provided certain background information about himself, which he claims is accurate.
>
> Based upon a review of that information, the following facts about BTK are being made available to the public in the hopes of identifying BTK.
>
> He claims he was born in 1939, which would make his current age 64 or 65. His father died in World War II, and his mother raised him. His mother was forced to work, so his grandparents cared for him. His mother worked during the day near the railroad. He had a cousin named Susan, who moved to Missouri. His family moved a lot, but always lived near a railroad. His grandfather played the fiddle and died of a lung disease. His mother started dating a railroad detective when BTK was around eleven years old. This relationship would have occurred during the years 1950-1955.

> In the early 1950s he built and operated a ham radio. He has participated in outdoor hobbies including hunting, fishing, and camping. As a youth he attended church and Sunday school. He had a female, Hispanic acquaintance named Petra, who had a younger sister named Tina. Around 1960, he went to tech military school. He then joined the military for active duty and was discharged in 1966. He has a basic knowledge of photography and the ability to develop and print pictures. In 1966 he moved back in with his mother, who had remarried and was renting out part of her house. His first job was as an electromechanic, requiring some travel. After attending more tech school, he worked repairing copiers and business equipment; this sometimes required travel and he was away from home for extended periods.
>
> He admits to soliciting prostitutes.
>
> He has a lifetime fascination with railroads and trains.
>
> Based upon the investigation to date, police believe that BTK: Frequented the WSU campus in the early 1970s was acquainted with P. J. Wyatt, who taught a folklore class at WSU during the 1970s; has written or still writes poetry. An example of this is the "Oh Anna, Why Didn't You Appear" poem and the "Oh! Death to Nancy" poem that were released in earlier media advisories. And he has utilized fake identification to gain access to people's homes or to conduct surveillance.
>
> Based on the information contained in the letter, police are again asking for help from the public. Police want to talk to any citizen who currently knows, or recalls anyone having a similar background to the one described above.

The press widely reports this information.

Quite a few reporters asked me, quite upset, "If they have had this information for thirty years, why are they only now releasing it?" I reply to everyone that I believe this information arrived in the June letter that the police received. After six months they have been unable to locate anyone matching this description so they are asking the public for help. The best thing they can do is see that this description is widely distributed. After checking with my sources I realize that at least some of this information arrived in the October UPS drop. The police released the information after only five weeks, not five months.

After the description is widely reported, according to my sources, at least two different people independently report the same man to the Wichita police as a BTK suspect. They claim that the man matches several points of the BTK self-description. One person says that he has long suspected this man of being BTK.

The police are intrigued and begin surveillance of the reported man.

On Wednesday morning, December 1, 2004, a BTK task force detective reached an agreement with a business to permit police surveillance detectives and a police surveillance vehicle to remain on and come and go from the business property.

Detectives came and went from the business, the van sat in the business parking lot, and other detectives drove around and around the block where the suspect lived. Meanwhile, other detectives tried to learn everything that they could about the suspect.

They concluded that the suspect was BTK. At least one detective telephoned two longtime investigators and left the message, "We got him."

The Wichita Eagle learned of a large number of police keeping a nearby residence under surveillance, and kept a reporter and photographer nearby the rest of the day.

At 8:31 p.m. the arrested man is booked and charged with misdemeanor trespass. According to a Kansas Bureau of Investigation spokesman, the man's DNA sample is sent for comparison with BTK, but the police quickly think that their optimism was misplaced. They are unsettled and uncertain, but after being sure earlier in the day that "We got him," they suspect that this is not the guy.

The local media become aware of the arrest and of the rumors that BTK has been arrested, as do retired police officers. I received my first call from the press at 9:45 p.m. and was on the telephone and exchanging e-mail messages until I went to sleep about 2:00 a.m. When I rose, showered, and read the morning paper, I saw *The Eagle* had handled the story by putting the news of the arrest under the fold in the paper's second section, never mentioning BTK, and showing only a rearview photo of the arrested man. That morning I sent an e-mail to *The Wichita Eagle* complimenting them on their responsible coverage. If the arrested man is to be charged with more, then everyone will learn soon enough. If there is no more, then the press will be proud that it behaved with restraint. Not all of the press was so restrained, and speculation flew that morning.

Later that day, the arrested man was released. The trespassing charge against him was eventually dismissed, though he later paid a $10 fine for a housing code violation for having paint peeling off his house. By 3:00 p.m. the arrested man has apparently departed, while eleven satellite trucks are in the City Hall parking lot and the world press is waiting for the 4:00 p.m. statement by Wichita Police Chief Norman Williams in anticipation of hearing that the BTK Strangler has been arrested.

Instead Chief Norman Williams said to the reporters, "We have not, and I repeat, we have not made an arrest in connection with BTK." In the context of his full statement he implied that the arrest was entirely unrelated to the BTK investigation—other than that they came across the unrelated old warrants in the course of the BTK investigation—and the police always knew that it was unrelated to the BTK investigation, which few in the press believed. The next day, Landwehr acknowledged that the arrested man was cleared by DNA testing.

Friday afternoon, December 3, 2004, I spoke by telephone for some time with Nancy Fox's mother. She was very upset. The arrested man's name was almost identical with her boys' favorite coach at Wichita South High School. She said that during the previous morning she and her adult sons David and Freddy cried for two hours while they thought that their old coach had murdered Nancy and had been laughing at them for so many years. They were so angry they pounded on the furniture and shouted. How could any man be so cruel as to pretend friendship with them after having murdered their sister? When they learned that the arrested man's name was different from that of their old coach, they were relieved from that pain, but still thought that the arrested man was BTK. Then when the news broke that the man arrested was the wrong man, they became cold and bitter.

Nancy's mother was furious about every aspect of the mess—why can't they catch this guy?

After the fiasco of arresting the wrong guy, then being unable to admit their mistake, the trust, respect, and reputation of the Wichita police and the district attorney's office plummeted. One thing I heard said was that "the Wichita Police couldn't catch a cold."

On Tuesday morning, December 7, 2004, not yet five full days after Chief Williams' statement to the assembled press, the Wichita Police released the following media advisory:

> BTK MAY CHANGE REGULAR ROUTINE
>
> Since the November 30 media release, police have received approximately 350 tips. Since BTK resurfaced in March 2004, the Wichita Police Department has received more than 4,500 tips.
>
> The Federal Bureau of Investigation Behavioral Analysis Unit told Wichita Police today, "Since the media release on November 30 outlining BTK's life story, and the subsequent community focus on the investigation, there may be observable changes in BTK's behavior."
>
> The FBI indicates these behavioral changes could include disruption in his normal habits and routines. He may have minimized his contact with others; he may have unscheduled absences from work or doctors' appointments; and he may not be interacting with people as usual.
>
> Police encourage any citizen with information to contact them.

The next day, late on Wednesday evening, December 8, 2004, the twenty-seventh anniversary of Nancy Fox's murder, BTK telephoned the Quik Trip twenty-four-hour convenience store near the corner of Hillside and Harry streets in Wichita. This is across the street from and is the closet convenience store to where Helzberg's Jewelers was located in 1977, where Nancy Fox had worked the night she was murdered. A young male clerk answered the telephone and heard BTK tell him of a package located near Ninth Street and U.S. Interstate 35, which runs north-south through the center of Wichita. BTK insisted

that the clerk write the directions down, but the clerk refused and BTK became angry and hung up. The clerk thought it was probably a prank call but he told his supervisor, who called the police. The police went to that area but neighbors later reported that the police took out their flashlights and looked on the north side of Ninth Street, around the Health Department and University of Kansas Medical School buildings, not in Murdock Park on the south side of the street.

Almost a week later, during the dark hours early on Tuesday morning, December 14, 2004, a man walking through Murdock Park on his way to visit his brother passed a white plastic trash bag that seemed to have something in it. When he walked back through the park he saw the bag again, was curious, and picked the bag up. He opened the bag and was puzzled by what he saw, which included a Kansas photo driver's license issued to Nancy J Fox.

The man took the package home and called KAKE TV. Personnel at KAKE thought that this was probably nothing, but sent a cameraman to look at it. The cameraman decided this was a package from BTK, and the authorities were summoned. The package contained Nancy Fox's driver's license, a doll, panty hose, and apparently chapter two, "Dawn," in the killer's *The BTK Files* manuscript.

On Thursday, December 30, 2004, Chief Williams again breached his own rule about Landwehr being the face of the BTK investigation and gave the local press a long interview answering questions about the BTK case. He said that more resources should be devoted to the case, and I soon learned that more Wichita Police officers were being assigned to the case. Also, the BTK Task Force had created two-member teams consisting of a WPD detective with an FBI agent, with each team investigating one crime. They were repeating what Captain Al Stewart had the Ghostbusters do twenty years ago. Maybe they would have more success this time.

On Tuesday, January 25, 2005, KAKE TV received a post card from BTK. It was self-identified as communication "#8" and had a Carlsbad Caverns, New Mexico, postage stamp. The card directed them to north Seneca Street between Sixty-ninth and Seventy-seventh streets near Valley Center, a small but growing Wichita satellite town that was home to Kathryn and Kevin Bright. When reporter Chris Frank and a cameraman arrived they found leaning on a ROAD CURVES sign a Post

Toasties cereal box weighted down by a brick. On the box was written a letter "B," the large "T" in Toasties was circled, and under the T was written the letter "K." They concluded that the post card was not a hoax and telephoned the police, who arrived very quickly.

According to the post card, the police, and my sources, the box contained jewelry. It also reportedly contained Chapter 9 of *The BTK Files*, "HITS." And the post card referred to another package, asking whether communication #7, dropped on or about January 8 at a home improvement store, had been found.

KAKE TV sent a crew to the two stores in the Wichita area but did not locate a package. My sources tell me that the police found #7. It was reportedly in a Rice Krispies cereal box and contained items similar to those in the Post Toasties box. Items of jewelry included a pin, a piece of jewelry with a fake nickel, and a double-strand necklace.

Shortly after noon the next day, Thursday the 27th, I arrived at the residence where Steve Relford, son of Shirley Vain, was staying. Relford had contacted me three days earlier, and we'd spoken on the phone a few times.

Steve is a tough, lanky, muscular man with heavily tattooed arms. His baseball style cap had the image of a death's head and two skeleton hands with their middle two fingers upraised in an "up yours" gesture. Steve acknowledged that he had spent much of his adult life in jail and said that he did not want to discuss any aspect of that.

Steve fought hard to keep back tears when he described how the man stripped his mother, tied her wrists together with tape, put a bag over her head and a rope around her neck. At one point he became so grief-stricken that I changed the subject.

Fortunately, not long after that Steve's wife came home. She held him and I could see that they loved each other very much. She told me that they had been married several years but it was only about two years ago that he was able to discuss this with her at all. At a time when Steve was upset and his wife was holding him I thought of what Dr. Jody Gyulay had said about grief and bereavement. I told Steve, "I can see how talking about this upsets you. I am not a counselor or therapist and I don't know what the right thing is to say to provide you any comfort." I was going to offer to try to find a qualified grief therapist for Steve to talk with when Steve and his wife both softened and told me they appreciated my concern. They indicated that they would find ways to cope.

At my request Steve's wife then took a photo of Steve and me. That was the only time Steve took his "Death's Head" cap off.

On Thursday morning, February 3, 2005, KAKE TV received another post card from BTK. This card referenced KAKE evening coanchors Susan Peters and Jeff Herndon's winter colds, about which they had joked on the air. BTK said, "Sorry about Susan's and Jeff's colds." He also wrote, "Thank you for your quick response on #7 & 8. Thank to the news team for their efforts." In that evening's live broadcast Larry Hatteberg talked directly to BTK, saying that the message had been received and passed on.

The people I spoke with thought that BTK was attempting to do two things with his message. First, probably in anticipation of a jury trial, he was trying to spin the story to cast him in a more personable and human light—as if he cared about the television broadcasters. Second, he wanted to become national news, encouraging on-air a local television news anchor to broadcast a message directly to a serial killer.

On Wednesday, February 16, 2005, KSAS Fox 24 business office, located at 316 North West Street, received a padded envelope from BTK. The name on the package's return address was "P J Fox."

Publicly released portions of the card included:

- Communication: #11
- Contents: C.4. [possibly refers to *The BTK Files* Chapter 4, "Fantasy World"]
- Message: If they received and can read or understand #10 . . . KAKE is a good station, but I feel they are starting to be single out, because of me, and causing problems among the people. Let's help the NEWS MEDIA and WPD by using this package as a start.

Most of the people I spoke with thought that BTK was deceiving everyone again by causing puzzlement over the number and sequence of communications. There is no acknowledgment of a BTK communication that he labeled "#10." A plausible sequence is:

#1 *The Wichita Eagle*, March 19, 2004 (photocopy)
#2 KAKE TV, May 5, 2004 (letter and photocopy)
#3 Wichita Police, early June 2004 (letter)
#4 Library, July 17, 2004 (standard #10 size envelope)
#5 UPS drop box, October 22, 2004 (large manila envelope; bag inside, contains a threat to Landwehr and Chapter 1)
#6 Murdock Park, left December 8, found December 13, 2004 (plastic bag containing bag and Chapter 2)
#7 Cereal box north Wichita area home improvement store, left January 8, 2005
#8 Cereal box near Valley Center, left week of January 17, 2005, on Seneca street
#9 KAKE TV post card, January 25, 2005 (labeled #8, but refers to "Post Tosties" & "#7")
#10 KAKE TV post card, February 3, 2005 (Susan and Jeff's colds; thanks for quick response to #7 & 8)
#11 KSAS TV Fox, February 16, 2005 (padded envelope containing jewelry, printed message(s) including Chapter 4, and photo)

At 10:00 a.m. on Thursday, February 17, 2005, Lieutenant Ken Landwehr held a press briefing where he said, "The BTK investigation is the most challenging case I have ever worked on and BTK would be very interesting to talk with. I am very pleased with the ongoing dialogue through these letters."

Epilogue:

The Hunt Ends

Friday, February 25, 2005, I attended a Final Friday lunch at Watermark Books with retired journalists and *The Wichita Eagle*'s current editor-in-chief, Sherry Chisenhall. Entering the reserved lunchroom shortly before noon, I nodded to Wichita Police Department Deputy Chief of Investigations Terry Moses. Despite the evidence that things were happening—reports that the security camera tapes at Home Depot Northeast were being examined frame-by-frame, the BTK Task Force detectives were working at 3:00 a.m., and that a suspect was under twenty-four-hour surveillance—I thought that everything must be quiet at the moment because Terry Moses was sitting here having lunch.

Shortly after 1:30 p.m. I kept an appointment to meet with Larry Hatteberg at the KAKE TV studios. Larry pulled me into a side room. "Bob," he said, "something's happening." He gave me a stare, paused, and then a nod.

"Something's happening" was code for BTK's arrest.

"Really?" I asked. "It's happening now?"

"It's happening now or it has already happened. Bob, go check your sources."

"Wow," I said. We realized that we had no time to savor the moment. Perhaps there would be time for that later. We parted.

As I strode through the KAKE TV lobby, reporter Jeff Golimowsi was exiting. He yelled back to someone that he was going to Park City, which is a working-class community north of Wichita. I thought of driving north to Park City but decided to first talk with Roger Stewart, Captain Al Stewart's son. This would be news that Roger had been waiting to hear much of his adult life.

On my way to see Roger I did something I have never before done except when I was driving an emergency vehicle with lights blazing and sirens wailing—I ran two red lights. I rushed in and Roger saw that I was excited. He jokingly asked, "What is it, Bob? Have they caught BTK?" He laughed. I stared at Roger. I paused and tried to select my next words carefully. "What would you say if I told you yes?" Roger's demeanor changed in an instant.

Then I told him what had happened and that I expected we might see something soon. Roger turned on the television in his office and moments later we saw KAKE TV interrupt a soap opera with a live shot of police outside a home in Park City that the police had blocked off. A bomb squad truck was outside the home.

"Roger," I said, "something's happening. I am on my way home to make phone calls. You might want to call your mom."

During the twenty minutes it took me to get home I was deep in thought. I had been wrong this week not to put credence in the Internet reports that the BTK Task Force had a suspect under surveillance. I turned on the radio to listen for news, but nothing yet was being broadcast.

When I arrived home I turned the television on and began making telephone calls.

Who had been arrested?

Dennis L. Rader.

Almost sixty years old, Rader was the supervisor of the Park City compliance office. Married since 1971 to the same woman, he had two grown children, was registered to vote as a Republican at his current address, and was the elected president of his Lutheran church congregation. He had no criminal record. Apparently stable and well respected, he had dog catching among his duties for the town government.

I called Nancy Fox's mother and told her the news, but she already knew. The police had told her.

By now the television stations were broadcasting views of 6220 Independence Street, the home of Dennis L. Rader since 1974. The house was two blocks east of the intersection of Sixty-first Street and U.S. 35, the interstate highway we had presumed BTK had driven up and down to make his drops at the UPS box, Murdock Park, north Seneca, and with access to Highway 96 and the Home Depot. Dennis Rader had almost immediate access to this expressway.

Saturday morning, I went to the 10:00 a.m. press conference at City Hall. Eventually, the press conference started, and when Wichita Police Chief Norman Williams said, "BTK is arrested," the auditorium broke into cheers and applause.

Sheriff Steed announced that the man in custody would be charged with the murders of Dee Davis and Marine Hedge, both of Park City, Kansas. Chief Williams announced Dennis L. Rader would be charged with the murders of Joe, Julie, Josie, and Joey Otero; Kathryn Bright; Shirley Relford Vian; Nancy Fox; and Vicki Wegerle. In total the man accused of being BTK will be charged with ten counts of first-degree murder. His bond was set at $10 million, $1 million for each victim.

After checking public records and media reports, and conducting interviews with people who had close interaction with him, I learned the following about Dennis L. Rader, the man arrested as the BTK Strangler.

Rader was born on March 9, 1945, and lived his early years in Pittsburg, Kansas. He was baptized in their Zion Lutheran Church. His family moved to Wichita while he was a child, and he graduated from Heights High School in 1964. He attended Kansas Wesleyan College in Salina, Kansas, and Butler County Community College in El Dorado, Kansas. He joined the U.S. Air Force, where he served for four years. He worked at Leeker's grocery and at Coleman. I have been told by several retired Wichita Police officers that during that time Rader's application to the Wichita Police Department was rejected.

Rader apparently started attending courses at Wichita State University in 1973. In 1979 he graduated with a bachelor's degree in Administration of Justice.

Rader has been a registered Republican at the same address, 6220 Independence in Park City, Kansas, since 1975.

Reportedly Rader was a Boy Scout and Cub Scout leader and encouraged his son to become an Eagle Scout. He is remembered as an expert at knots and had various items tied in a specific knot in items around his home and in the ropes he used to catch dogs.

Although the author is uncertain about Rader's employment from July 1973 to November 1974, it is certain that the Otero and Bright murders occurred during this interval.

From November 1974 to July 1988 Rader worked at ADT security systems. He installed and supervised the installation of home and business security systems.

The Relford, Fox, and Wegerle murders and the Anna Williams break-in occurred during the years that Dennis Rader worked for ADT.

Rader was fired from ADT in 1989, worked as a supervisor for the US Census Bureau, then, on May 10, 1991, started work as a compliance officer for Park City, Kansas.

On Wednesday evening, March 2, 2005, I interviewed a man who worked and socialized with Dennis Rader from 1976 to 1988, during Rader's years at ADT. He attended Rader's WSU graduation party in 1979. Typically, after work he'd drink a beer with Rader at the Playpen (now the Laid Back Club) at 911 E. Morris. He remembers ADT then being located at 430 Washington, only a few blocks from the payphone at Central and St. Francis (approximately 400 N. Central), where BTK reported Nancy Fox's "home-i-cide." Wichita Fire Department Captain Wayne Davis thought the man who made the phone call was wearing a uniform and drove a van, possibly with starburst advertising on it. That does describe the ADT vans.

He said that Rader was very good at electronics, had a temper and would occasionally throw things, always carried a blue gym bag, and frequently got roaring drunk.

He also said that after leaving the Playpen Club, Rader would go to "strip clubs" such as Revolution West.

Prostitutes were reportedly available at some strip clubs.

I was told that Rader was very resentful about being rejected as a candidate by the Wichita Police Department. When the labor of installing security systems became burdensome and Rader's temper frayed, Rader was reported to say, "I shouldn't have to be doing this. I should be a police officer."

The Sunday, February 27, 2005, *Wichita Eagle* included a photograph of Dennis Rader seated at a church Valentine's Day dinner. Across the table from him was a heavyset man with a beard. That man is Gene Moravec. We spoke by telephone that night, and I mention Mr. Moravec's name with his permission.

The members of Christ Lutheran Church, 5356 North Hillside in Park City, had elected Dennis L. Rader president of their congregation. Gene Moravec supported Rader's election. Mr. Moravec said that he learned of Rader's unexpected arrest while he was attending a wrestling tournament.

Mr. Moravec told me, "I found Dennis to be quiet, personable, always there to do tasks, whatever needed to be done, whatever you asked. He always kept an even temper. He was never upset with things." He said that he has known Dennis Rader for thirty years.

All the people I interviewed about Dennis Rader had varying perspectives and opinions about him, but none suspected that he was BTK. Nor, based on the evidence known to me at the time of this writing, should they have suspected him. There was no evidence leading authorities to him until Rader provided it himself.

Reliable sources tell me that if this account is inaccurate they will not correct me (they do not want to be accused at any trial that may take place of disclosing information outside of official channels), but based on the admittedly incomplete information available to me on March 1, 2005, this is a brief account of the breaks in the case and the arrest of the man the police have accused of being the BTK Strangler.

When BTK left a Rice Krispies cereal box at the Home Depot, security cameras caught a vehicle driving around and around in the parking lot. That was the only vehicle that the cameras recorded repeatedly driving around the lot. That vehicle was one routinely driven by Dennis L. Rader.

When BTK mailed a package to KSAS Fox 24 news, he included a floppy disk. That floppy disk was traced to a computer at Christ Lutheran Church, used by congregation president Dennis L. Rader.

At some point Wichita police apparently obtained a court order to secure biological material from Dennis Rader's daughter Kerri's medical records. That showed a familial link to the DNA from BTK.

With at least those three facts pointing to Dennis L. Rader, they started following him.

At 12:15 p.m. on Friday, February 25, 2005, at the intersection of Sixty-first Street North (Kechi Road) and Independence Street, just south of his home in Park City, Dennis L. Rader was arrested without incident by WPD Detective Dana E. Gouge and members of the BTK Task Force. Rader was questioned for nearly eight hours, then booked into the Sedgwick County Jail at 7:58 p.m. by Sergeant Jared O. Schechter.

The government and private individuals and institutions began proactive efforts to capture BTK in January 1974, a week after the Otero murders, with Don Granger's "Secret Witness" column. The efforts continued with the police placing classified ads in the newspaper in October 1974 and apparently also in January 2005 during a brief police "dialogue" with BTK. I believe these efforts continued throughout the course of this investigation, including April 1995, when Ken Landwehr spoke to our Mensa meeting.

Retired FBI supervisory special agent and profiler Clint Van Zandt called me and indicated—as he has said on television and in print—that he thinks publicity about my book brought BTK out of hiding.

A front-page *Wichita Eagle* article headlined "Ex-chief: Rader likely appeared on early lists," bylined by Hurst Laviana and published on Friday, March 4, 2005, reported: "LaMunyon said he thinks the latest communications from BTK, which started with a letter to *The Eagle* in March 2004, were prompted by a January 2004 *Wichita Eagle* story that marked the 30th anniversary of BTK's first killings. The story focused on Wichita lawyer Robert Beattie's efforts to write a book about the case."

A front-page *Wichita Eagle* article headlined "Pastor: Disk gave police key clue" bylined by Dion Lefler and Tim Potter and published on Wednesday, March 2, 2005, reported: "Liles said he believes that publicity surrounding a BTK book being written by Wichita lawyer Robert Beattie prompted the resumption of the taunting communications with police that had occurred around the time of the killings. 'With his ego, he couldn't stand to let anyone else tell his story,' Liles said. 'It was always my hope that he would screw up on communication, and that's exactly what happened.'"

On Saturday night, February 26, 2005, I received the following e-mail from retired Wichita Police Chief Floyd B. Hannon Jr. Chief Hannon had read the first portion of this manuscript concerning the Otero case and did not agree with all the views that were expressed. But Chief Hannon wrote: "My daughter called from Topeka and said to watch the news at 10:00 a.m. this morning. What I observed made my day. There has not been a week go by during the last thirty years that I have not thought about the Otero case. My hope has been that before I left this earth I would know the killer. This goal has been met. I am upset that you are not receiving credit. Without your interest in writing a book and bring back action to the case and also causing the person who committed the crimes to start showing off this case might still not be solved. For this I thank you."

After Dennis Rader's arrest, Nancy Fox's mother called and invited my wife and me to have lunch with her and Nancy's sister Beverly. Tears came to my eyes when Nancy's mother told me, "Without your class and your book I don't think this guy would have ever been caught. I thank you from the bottom of my heart."

We will never know for certain whether any of the proactive attempts to resolve this case were responsible for the end of the hunt for the BTK Strangler, but it is gratifying to know that some of the key people, including a couple of former police chiefs and victim Nancy Jo Fox's mother, believe that my efforts helped bring the case to resolution.

Life's other dangers remain, but the danger from the BTK Strangler appears to be at an end. This nightmare in Wichita is apparently over. I realize that the pain of the victims' families will never cease. But I am hopeful about my community. This was a test for us and tests remain, but we shall pass them. Whatever setbacks confront us, they will be met as the temporary obstacles they are.

Status as of March 2005

Mary Ann Beattie, M.D., my patient wife, is enjoying her retirement. She expects to enjoy it more after her husband completes this book.

Lieutenant Charles Liles (WPD, retired), once the commander of the Wichita Police Canine Unit, once WPD west side field commander, and once the records lieutenant, was the 2004-2005 president of the Wichita Retired Police Officers Association. He provided invaluable guidance and introductions that helped make this book possible. He and his wife Sherri have moved out of the Wichita city limits and now live near Viola, Kansas. At their new home Charles has several acres of woods, plains, and ponds to attend to and this keeps him busy and reasonably happy.

BTK case detective and lieutenant John Garrison (WPD, retired), who was president of the Wichita Retired Police Officers Association 2003–2004, provided invaluable guidance and introductions and also served as editor of "The ReTired Copper," their association's newsletter, and he used that forum to help tell this story. It was John's idea to bring BTK's letters and poems to Professor P. J. Wyatt and that led to a breakthrough. John conducted surveillance on BTK suspects and on the Finleys in the Poet case. He is now the chief investigator for the Sedgwick County Courts. His office is next to Judge Richard Ballinger's chambers.

Judge Richard Ballinger, who went to church with Nancy Fox and introduced me to Nancy Fox's family, was in the 1970s an assistant district attorney and was present at one or more of the detective's dog-and-pony shows. In 2003 he permitted use of his courtroom as my classroom. He remains Kansas' 18th Judicial District Chief Judge. Nationally, under Judge Ballinger's administrative leadership, this court district has the swiftest proceeding from case filing to conclusion of any state district court in America. Major corporations sometimes file their cases here because they will proceed quickly. In March 2004 when the BTK letter came, Judge Ballinger and I stopped discussing this case due to legal and ethical concerns, though we still cross paths and remain friends. I'm sure that we both look forward to this case concluding.

Murder victim Nancy Fox's mother, father, sister, best friend, and Nancy's many other indispensable family and friends, who do not want their names used, remain hopeful that more of the story will be explained.

Former BTK case lead detective and retired Captain of Homicide Bernie Drowatzky, once head of the "Hot Dog Squad," who participated in this investigation from its first hour, remains police administrator of Kaw City, Oklahoma. His wife Dora Ann recently survived a cancer-treatment regimen but is in poor health. One of Bernie's sons became a Wichita Police Officer.

Retired Wichita Police Detective and Lieutenant Arlyn Smith, nicknamed "Dietrich" after the fictional Detective Arthur Dietrich in *Barney Miller*, member of the "Hot Dog Squad," whose detective work located the photocopy machines that BTK used, is a computer programmer for USD 259. His daughter just joined the Air Force, his middle-school son is fascinated by UFOs, and his wife Carol, like most wives in this story, wanted this case solved.

Retired Detective George Scantlin Jr., who worked hard at locating the photocopy machines, is a dispatcher for Sedgwick County Emergency Communications.

Retired Detective Tom Allen, who for a week took the BTK photocopies to the Xerox research facilities in Rochester, New York, is now selling new and used cars.

Retired Wichita Police Chief Floyd Hannon, who invited experts from around North America to conferences in Wichita in an effort to capture the Otero family's murderer, plays golf whenever he can in

Cherokee Village, Arkansas. He is in his eighties but remains a vigorous man of strong opinions. His wonderful wife also keeps active.

Former Wichita Police Chief Rick Stone, a former national police officer of the year, is retired and lives in Florida. I recommend his police novel *Behind the Gold Star*. He insists it is entirely fiction.

Former Wichita Police Chief Richard LaMunyon is an administrator for the City of Maize, Kansas, just northwest of Wichita.

Retired Interim Wichita Police Chief Kerry Crisp is Human Resources Manager of Boeing-Wichita and is on track to become a member of their pool of vice presidents from which the company president will be drawn.

Retired Wichita Deputy Police Chief Jack Bruce wants this case solved before he goes to his reward. He remains active with his church, family, and the retired police association. He is in his eighties and has been married to his patient wife, Bobbie, for more than sixty years.

Former BTK-case lead detective Mike McKenna remains police chief of Baldwin City, Kansas. Like the other long-time investigators he remains unsettled by BTK's reappearance and contacts. McKenna was the first to tell me that he believed BTK was still alive. He said he believed BTK had never been in custody and was walking the streets of Wichita.

The widow of BTK surveillance detective Pete Dubovich (Dubovichsky-Lupeshanski), Rita, works in Wichita. Their daughter Nora married this summer and everyone is sure that Pete attended the wedding in spirit. I was friends with Pete and miss him.

Pete's former partner, Lieutenant and Detective Robert "Pat" Taylor, is now a Kingman County, Kansas, deputy sheriff. He worked undercover on the BTK case right after the Otero murders and later during the "Hot Dog Squad" investigation. Pat has written a wry book, *Observations of a Sheriff's Patrolman*, that is both detailed about the truth of police work and the truth of the family life of police officers. If published I suspect that his book will be better received than mine because it is absolutely hilarious.

Detective Bob Cocking is enjoying his retirement. We visit sometimes on Wednesday evenings at Bigs. Detective Cocking was the first to say that he thought Shirley Vian was murdered by BTK and for his correct deduction he was told to shut up. It took nearly a year before the rest of the department realized he was right. He also picked up about twenty letters from KAKE TV that proved to be from Ruth Finley but were initially thought to be from BTK.

Retired Detective Richard Vinroe worked with Arlyn Smith in tracking down the photocopy machines, worked on The Poet case, and was the first detective to arrive at the Wegerle crime scene. He is head of security for Friends University.

Retired vice Detective Bill Ammons keeps active in his retirement.

Retired vice Detective Larry Samford keeps very busy in his retirement. He is a newlywed.

In his retirement Detective Harvey May, who participated in the surveillance of BTK suspects, is working at house painting.

Former WPD patrolman Bob Bulla, who was the first officer in on the Otero case, works in Derby, Kansas. He is a member of the Board of Governors of the Kansas Peace Officers Association.

I've lost touch with my friend H.D. Williams, who took me around with him in his patrol car for an evening in 1979. The last I heard H.D. was working security.

Jim Carney, who checked many closets for BTK while an east side patrolman, retired as a WPD captain. He is now head of security for HCA Wesley in Wichita.

Former WPD patrolman Lowell Hollingshead, who found Nancy Fox's body, is retired. Typically wearing coveralls wherever he goes, when he departs he often says that he has fish to catch.

Retired Deputy Chief Bill Cornwell, who traveled to Puerto Rico and Panama in the course of investigating the murders, is enjoying his retirement.

Retired BTK-case lead detective Ray Floyd is enjoying his retirement. He walks his dog once or twice a day, stays mentally and physically fit. He was among the best and the brightest of investigators.

Homicide Lieutenant Kenny Landwehr, with Charles Liles, started the Wichita Police sponsorship of the Special Olympics. When Kenny was a youngster he and his good friend Stuart Bevis—Clyde Bevis' son—swiped Clyde's WPD car late at night and used it to joyride around town. Kenny is a "regular guy" who worked hard, played clean, has been a good police officer and detective, and has done his best to solve this case. He has rejected retirement and promotion so that he could keep close to the BTK investigation. Kenny recently said he does more administrative work than detective work these days.

The BTK case data "funnels" through homicide Detective Kelly Otis. He, too, is a regular guy who likes sports, was a good patrol officer, and has been a good detective. He fancies himself a comedian — is abysmally poor at it — but he did his best to solve this case. He had no other agenda.

Former SPIDER (Special Police Information Data Entry & Retrieval) operator Linda Breedlove Weide told me of how that system operated. In 1979 I visited the SPIDER office with H.D. Williams, saw the huge Spiderman poster that they had on the wall, and visited with Linda that night. I talked with her again in 2003. Her brother was a WPD detective.

Victim Joseph Otero's nephew Samuel Ruiz Flores Otero of Puerto Rico corresponded with me by phone several times. He still thinks it is possible that his family's murders were racist in nature.

Otero family friend and my high school classmate Kirby Ortega is the chief flight instructor for Cessna Aircraft and was national flight instructor of the year for 2002. Kirby, I pray that you can forgive me for being the clumsy, immature, and insensitive seventeen-year-old I was in 1974 when your friends were murdered.

Charlie Otero is living in New Mexico.

Steve Relford and his wife, and Steve's sister Stephanie, are living in the United States. They do not want their location disclosed.

Denise Cheryl, Denise's son, and Denise's former roommate do not want their locations disclosed, though they live in three different states.

The Fox family still lives in Kansas.

Most of Kathryn Bright's family and friends still live in the Wichita area, though Kevin Bright no longer lives in Kansas.

Members of the Wegerle family also live in different states.

Ghostbusters captain Al Stewart's widow Leyola Stewart is enjoying retirement in Colorado. Al's oldest son Roger Stewart owns and manages Wholesale Neon in Wichita. Their lives have never been the same since Al led the investigation. Their lives were disrupted again after the *Wichita Eagle*'s receipt of the March 2004 letter from BTK.

Retired Ghostbusters detective Jerry Harper works security for Wichita's federal courthouse and is an officer in a local Bass Fishing organization.

The wisdom of retired Deputy Chief and Director of Emergency Communications Ken Duckworth pervades this story, though his influence is often hidden. Without Ken's foresight and proposals in 1964 there would have been no recording of BTK's voice and no immediate identification of the murderer's location when he made the December 9, 1977, phone call. Ken was responsible for developing the top suspects only hours after the Otero murders. Ken was responsible for SPIDER. Ken was responsible for bringing the first NCIC (National Crime Information Computer) to Wichita. Throughout my research for this book I've found that Ken is as respected by his fellow officers as anyone that I interviewed. Ken is aging, his wife has been ill, and Ken is virtually wheelchair bound due to a muscular disease. Someone should write a history of America's police department emergency communications, 911 systems, and computerization, and they should start with interviewing Ken Duckworth.

Retired Wichita police captain and chief radio dispatcher Wilbur "Bill" Mohr is another officer whose influence is often hidden. Captain Mohr explained much about the history of police radio dispatch—which we now take for granted—and its importance in managing emergencies. When Bill Mohr first became chief police dispatcher he was an experienced and respected field officer, which was who the other officers wanted in control of the radio traffic in emergencies. Like an air traffic controller, Bill built the board that was used to keep track of officers before computers. He had to physically look up license plates in big books.

Captain Harold Klein was police dispatcher during the Otero calls. Among other things during his career he was a successful hostage negotiator. His calm manner and wisdom in a true crisis saved several Wichita police officers and the man who was holding a gun on them. He provided me many years of issues of "The ReTired Copper" and hours of fascinating conversation.

Retired Lieutenant Phil Bond helped me understand parts of the investigation. He is struggling with arthritis but remains as active as he can be.

Private Investigator Emery Goad remains very busy operating Kansas Investigative Services.

Former U.S. Attorney for Kansas and former Sedgwick County Deputy District Attorney Jackie Williams is teaching in the Criminal Justice Department at Wichita State University.

Former Sedgwick County lead prosecuting attorney Stephen Robison is an attorney with the Wichita law firm of Fleeson, Gooing, Coulson & Kitch. In the 1970s he prepared for a prosecution against BTK that never materialized. He remains optimistic.

Keith Sanborn, former Sedgwick County District Attorney and judge, is retired.

Vern Miller, former Sedgwick County District Attorney, Sedgwick County Sheriff, and Kansas Attorney General, maintains an active law practice.

Clark Owens was a Sedgwick County District Attorney and is currently a judge.

Wichita criminal defense attorney Richard Ney keeps a full legal practice.

Wichita criminal defense Jay Greeno has a full schedule. He remains actively opposed to the death penalty.

Investigative reporter Cathy Henkel, now an editor at the *Seattle Times*, broke the BTK story in 1974. She shared information with me but never betrayed the identity of her original source.

Dan Rouser, former Wichita police beat newspaper reporter, former Wichita police officer, and former chairman of the board of the Wichita Art Museum, works for an architectural firm.

Former KAKE-TV, *Wichita Sun*, and *Wichita Eagle* reporter Randy Brown is now a professor in the communications department at Wichita State University.

Ron Loewen, former *Wichita Sun* executive and KAKE-TV news director, who was among the first to understand the BTK story, was featured in a *Dateline NBC* program. He is now a vice president of the Liberty Corporation, a holding corporation that owns many television stations.

Former *Wichita Eagle* reporter Bill Hirschman is now at the *South Florida Sun-Sentinel*.

Former *Wichita Eagle* reporter Casey Scott is now at Kansas State University.

Former *Wichita Eagle* reporter Ken Stephens is now at the *Dallas Morning News*.

Former *Wichita Eagle* writer Shannon Littlejohn is a freelance writer and editor.

Wichita Eagle crime reporter Ron Sylvester is writing a book about the Carr brother's trial.

James P. Girard, former *Wichita Eagle* editor and author of Wichita crime novel *The Late Man*, which includes elements of the BTK case, is writing a nonfiction narrative about a case in northeastern Kansas.

Former *Wichita Eagle* reporter Susan Edgerley is now Metro editor of *The New York Times*.

Glen Horn remains KAKE-TV's news director.

Brooke Erickson, who shared BTK's May 2004 letter with me and select members of the greater Kansas chapter of the Mensa High IQ Society, has left KAKE-TV.

Former KAKE-TV cameraman and current independent producer Darrell Barton, a member of the Oklahoma Journalism Hall of Fame, is doing freelance photojournalism.

Mark Chamberlin has retired from KAKE-TV but remains active in television.

Rose Stanley works in a Wichita business but is no longer in television.

Reporter Larry Hatteberg remains at KAKE-TV.

Former KAKE-TV cameramen and broadcast technicians Scott Taylor and Todd Gearheart each provided rich history and background about KAKE-TV's operations and personnel during the 1970s-1980s BTK/Poet era.

Paul Fecteau, Washburn University of Topeka, Kansas, English professor, is writing a book about the Fager family murders and trial of Bill Butterworth.

Bill Peterson, known online as "Runes1," is still an administrator of the online Crime & Justice forum.

"Sisu 55" is the Crime & Justice website moderator and administrator.

Wichita Eagle newspaper reporter Hurst Laviana, who in March 2004 was the first to realize that BTK was still in Wichita, remains a crime reporter.

Wichita Eagle reporter Fred Mann, who was the exclusive media "inside" man on 'The Poet' investigation and wrote the best unpublished book about the episode, is primarily a sports reporter, but takes on other assignments.

Buzz Merritt, *Wichita Eagle* editor-in-chief during the 1970s BTK era and advocate of "Public Journalism," is retired.

Firearms expert Kenny Hauschild still works in the industry.

John Polson, who was cheek-swabbed and cleared, remains active in community affairs.

Jeff Garrett, who was cheek-swabbed and cleared, does a lot of work in radio commercials.

Dr. Jim Erickson, retired WSU English professor who once shared an office with P.J. Wyatt, and who was cheek-swabbed and cleared, does movie reviews for Wichita's National Public Radio station and is active on several boards, including the library board.

John Pieratt, who was cheek-swabbed and cleared, continues in his business.

Dr. Samuel Harrell, Ph.D., who in 1974 recommended a sting operation to lure BTK into revealing himself, maintains an active psychology practice in a Northeast Wichita office.

Dr. Tony Ruark, Ph.D., whom the Hot Dog Squad consulted, survived a recent aortic aneurysm and has stopped practicing for the time being.

Dr. John Allen, Ph.D., who worked as psychologist consultant for the Ghostbusters, continues an active practice.

Mathematician Dr. Stephen W. Brady, Ph.D., who worked for decades on the BTK case, mostly as an unpaid police consultant, continues teaching at WSU.

Psychologist Dr. Delores Craig-Moreland, Ph.D., who explained the psychology of felons to me, and explained her views on BTK's probable motivations, continues teaching in the Criminal Justice department at WSU.

Psychologist Dr. Jody Gyulay, Ph.D., who explained to me the clinician's and researcher's views about the grief and bereavement of the many victims in this horror story, maintains a consulting practice.

Psychologist Dr. Julie Allison, Ph.D., who has studied the behaviors of the families and friends of victims of crime, is teaching at Pittsburg State University, Pittsburg, Kansas.

Investigative criminal profiler Pat Brown remains available for consultation. She maintains the online Sexual Homicide Exchange.

Dr. Maurice Godwin, Ph.D., the geographic profiler who placed BTK on the block Dan Rouser lived, is an assistant professor in the criminal justice department at Methodist College in Fayetteville, Arkansas. He is available for consultation through his business, Investigative Process Management.

Retired FBI profiler Roy Hazelwood works for The Academy Group. He has authored or co-authored several excellent books, including *Dark Dreams*.

Retired FBI profiler John Douglas did not reply to my messages but I cited his work several times. He may be reached via his website.

Newman University librarians Joe Forte, Rita Sevart, and Steve Hamersky were of the greatest assistance.

Wichita State University special collections librarian Mary Nelson helped me with research in 2003. In 2004 she formally offered the WSU special collections library as the repository for my original notes and writings for this project, to be made available to the public only at the appropriate time, decided either by time (e.g., fifteen years) or event. My records would be safer there than in my office, so I may do that.

Friends University Behavioral Science Department Chair Dr. Donna Stuber-McEwen, Ph.D., is still teaching. Her husband, former cop Mike McEwen, also aided with research and commentary.

Dan Fahnestock, DNA analyst at the Sedgwick County Regional Forensic Science Center, provided three fascinating lectures or interviews.

Polygraph expert Doug Williams is available for consultation via his website at polygraph.com.

Drew Richardson, Ph.D. (brainwavescience.com), former FBI polygraph operator and former chief of the FBI's counterterrorism unit, provided fascinating insights.

Brenda Huntsinger Williams, who has received awards in Kansas and Nebraska as Investigative Journalist of the Year, provided ongoing inspiration and encouragement.

I acknowledge a half-dozen Mensa members, master puzzle solvers, who presently wish to remain anonymous.

I thank two-time Pulitzer Prize-winning nonfiction author Jon Franklin, whose e-mail exchanges and book *Writing for Story* helped provide guidance and inspiration for this book.

I appreciate Governor Kathleen Sebelius' patience with me. My report for her will be the next thing I write—probably.

Ghostbuster Detective Gary Fulton retired as Deputy Chief. He is an investigator for the Kansas Securities and Exchange Commission.

Ghostbuster Detective Mark Richardson is an instructor for the Kansas Law Enforcement Training Center in Hutchinson, Kansas.

Ghostbuster Detective Paul Holmes still lives in Wichita.

Ghostbuster Detective Erwin Naasz is deceased.

Police chaplain Reverend Bob Ely is deceased.

And this book would not have been published and be what it is without the intense work and feedback of a number of book world superstars, including this book's editor Dan Slater (who previously worked on the revised editions of Smith and Guillen's *The Search for the Green River Killer*), literary agent Jake Elwell, Hollywood agent Stephen Fisher, writer Michael Benson (author of *Who's Who in the JFK Assassination*), editor Martha Bushko (without whose intense work this book would not have been published), editor John Paine (who has worked uncredited on true crime books such as Michaud and Hazelwood's *The Evil That Men Do*), and attorney Robert Callagy, Esq., of Satterlee Stephens Burke & Burke, who, for much of his career, has been fighting to vindicate the First Amendment not only in words but in deeds. Thank you all.